Microprocessor Development and Development Systems

Microprocessor Development and Development Systems

Edited by
VINCENT TSENG

GRANADA
London Toronto Sydney New York

Granada Publishing Limited – Technical Books Division
Frogmore, St Albans, Herts AL2 2NF
and
36 Golden Square, London W1R 4AH
515 Madison Avenue, New York, NY 10022, USA
117 York Street, Sydney, NSW 2000, Australia
60 International Boulevard, Rexdale, Ontario R9W 6J2, Canada
61 Beach Road, Auckland, New Zealand

British Library Cataloguing in Publication Data
Microprocessor development and development systems.
1. Microprocessors—Design and construction
I. Tseng, Vincent
621.3819′5835   TK7895.M5

ISBN 0-246-11490-8

First published in Great Britain 1982 by Granada Publishing
Reprinted 1983

Typesetting by MJL Ltd, Hitchin
Printed in Great Britain by Mackays of Chatham

Granada ®
Granada Publishing ®

Contents

Contents

Preface

With the growth of microprocessor applications, the need for development tools and aids is shown by the proliferation of microprocessor development systems (MDS) on offer. However, what constitutes a development system is not often clear. In addition, the dividing line between what may be called a development system and some microcomputers can be very fine.

The objective of this book is not merely to compare one system with another, but to examine closely the work which needs to be done for a microprocessor application development, with a view to identifying the critical stages and the tools/facilities to aid these stages. The approach, then, is to clarify what needs to be done in an application development and to explain the primary differences from developments in other, allied fields (e.g. computer software development). The need for a development system is explained, as well as the features which make the systems different from any other microcomputer.

Detailed discussions of the identified important facilities are given. Due to the different approaches from different manufacturers, leading authorities contribute to give their insights to the designs and reasons for their particular method of implementation (for example on the different architectures of systems). There is also a study of working without the use of development systems, to highlight and recommend possible enhancements or additions to current facilities, or to offer an alternative using equipment which the readers may already possess.

The book has been written at two levels to ensure fuller understanding of the need for correct development tools in a project, as well as the subtleties in the implementation of, or provision for these tools. The contributions can sometimes be very detailed and technical, whereas the first part of the book is at an introductory level, to which the readers can refer for clarity.

Most of all it is hoped that this work will help readers to understand what is involved in the process of a microprocessor application development, to identify and decide what is important for themselves and to have the knowledge to select the facilities necessary for the successful implementation of their own microprocessor application project.

Vincent Tseng

Authors' Biographies

Vincent Tseng

Vincent Tseng is recognised as one of the leading authorities on the subject of microprocessors and in particular microprocessor development systems (MDS) in England. He has presented numerous papers at international and national conferences and seminars. He has also had several papers published on the subject.

Vincent is Principal Consultant for Microcomputing at ICL (Dataskil), in Reading, England, where he started the company's work in micro technology and set up and specified the development facilities and equipment for the company. He holds a Master's degree in Automatic Control from UMIST (University of Manchester Institute of Science and Technology), and an Honours degree in Physics from Imperial College, London.

W. Conings

W. Conings gained a degree in Chemistry at the University of Brussels in 1971. He spent eight years at the same University in the Department of Chemical Engineering, focussing his attention mainly on the use of mini- and microcomputers for controlling chemical reactors that are operated in non-steady state conditions. In 1979 he joined Intel as an application engineer supporting Intel's growing line of software products. In 1980 he was given the responsibility to manage the European Systems Application Group. Today he is responsible for the marketing of Intel's OEM operating systems.

Bernard Lejeune

Bernard Lejeune received his degree in Electronics in 1976 with strong emphasis on microprocessor applications. He started his career in heavy industrial environment, developing new techniques for low frequency vibration measurement and analysis. He joined Intel in 1978 as a member of the technical support centre in Brussels covering the complete range of Intel systems products. He later on specialised in the in-circuit emulation product line, actively participating in the implementation of the Intel European service centre installed in the UK. He then moved to the training department, handling at first service training then general software courses. He has been instructing PL/M, PASCAL and RMX, the Intel real time multitasking operating system software for the last two years. He is now involved in teaching the new Intel 432 Micromainframe architecture and the ADA programming language.

Jack Kister

Jack Kister was awarded a BSEE degree at the University of Nebraska. In 1974 he joined the Monsanto Chemical Company as Instrument Engineer. From there he moved to his present position as Hardware Engineering Manager at Motorola Inc. where he has been responsible for the design management of the TEH MC68000 16-bit microcomputer development system. He is the author of six publications primarily on semiconductor chips.

Sam E. Lee

Sam Lee gained BSEE and MSEE degrees from Texas Tech University. He served a term as Vice President of Tau Beta Pi, and was honoured one year as the Eta Kappa Nu outstanding member. His masters report described a feasibility study of a method for nondestructive reliability testing of metalised mylar capacitors. He joined the Colorado Springs Division of the Hewlett-Packard Company in February 1969, as a Research and Development Engineer. Early assignments included the design of custom-integrated circuits for oscilloscope products. This lead to the exciting challenge of establishing the computer based test, characterization and process monitoring tools for a new captive bipolar i.c. facility for the division, as well as establishing a Computer Aided Artwork facility. In 1977 he became the Product Manager for the HP 64000 Logic Development System which was introduced in September 1979. At present he is developing new products based on the HP 64000 system.

Geoff Bristow

Geoff Bristow is currently Manager of one of the North European business entities of Texas Instruments – the Custom Microfunction Pcc. This group is responsible for speech, telecommunications and microcomputer devices (4, 8, and 16 bit) as well as custom products. His career began with a degree course at Imperial College in Electrical and Electronic Engineering and he was awarded the Royal Society of Arts Silver Medal for his combination of academic and social activities. He then moved on to a period of research at Peterhouse, Cambridge, leading to a PhD award. The subject of his research was 'Speech Training for the Deaf using Computer Colour Graphics'. Moving to Texas Instruments in 1979, he became the Product Marketing Engineer responsible for microprocessor components, and then became Product Marketing Manager for 16-bit microprocessor products in August 1980. In June 1981 he moved to his present assignment where he has overall product marketing, engineering and financial planning responsibility for TI's high volume mask programmed devices (the TMS1000, 2000, 7000 and 9940) and various other related product ranges such as speech synthesis and telecommunications.

Dave Wollen

Dave Wollen is currently Product Marketing Manager for microprocessors and systems for Texas Instruments Northern European Semiconductor Division in Bedford. He obtained his Honours degree in Physics from Imperial College, London. Dave developed his main interest in microprocessors and computers while a design engineer at Marconi Space and Defence Systems. His increasing use of software led him to return to Imperial College, where he obtained a Masters degree in Computer Science and studied several computer languages. His research project entailed the design of interactive software for three-dimensional computer graphics using a large CDC computer. Subsequently, he joined the European Microprocessor Technology Centre at TI, where he developed software based on TI's 16-bit TMS9900 family and 4-bit TMS1000 series of microcomputers, mainly for customer applications. He was appointed Microprocessor Systems Development Manager with responsibility for the new Microprocessor Systems Centre, a customer-funded group formed to develop larger microprocessor systems based on microcomputer boards and to form a pool of technical expertise in microprocessor applications. He then became a microprocessor systems specialist within Central Marketing. Before taking up his current position Dave was concerned with the marketing of TI's latest 16-bit microprocessors, the TMS9995 and the TI 99000 series under development. He belongs to the Institute of Physics and the British Computer Society.

Peter Vinson

On gaining an honours degree in Physics at the University of Surrey in 1973, Peter Vinson stayed on at Guildford to do research work in semiconductor physics. This research used high pressure effects on the high field properties of three–five semiconductor compounds as a tool to investigate the energy band structure of those materials. Industrial experience was also gained at this time as this work was partly carried out at STL Laboratories, Harlow, Essex and RRE, Malvern, Worcestershire. After the results of the research were presented at the bi-annual 'International Conference on the Physics of Semiconductors', Rome, 1976, Peter joined what is now Plessey Research (Caswell) Ltd., Towcester, Northants to work on microwave oscillators using two-terminal devices. At the start of 1978, he joined Texas Instruments Ltd., Bedford, joining a group working on systems engineering and bread-boarding of Teletext and Viewdata integrated circuits. In the middle of 1980 he transferred to the marketing group as a Product Marketing Engineer; initially with responsibility for development systems but later also for 9900 MOS processors and peripheral devices, and military microprocessors. More recently Peter has transferred to the Custom Micro-functions group, taking responsibility for the product engineering of TMS1000 microcomputers, speech and telecommunications devices.

Mike Mihalik

Mike Mihalik is the project leader of the 16-bit emulation program for the 8500 series of microcomputer development systems at Tektronix, Inc. His responsibilities are to manage the hardware and software design of emulators for the Intel 8086/8088, the Zilog Z8001 and Z8002, and the Motorola 68000. In addition, Mihalik managed the design of the recently introduced 4-channel microprocessor analyser, the trigger trace analyser (TTA). A graduate of Clarkson College of Technology, Potsdam, New York, with a bachelor's degree in Electrical Engineering, Mihalik joined Tektronix in 1975. Initially, he served as a design engineer for TM 500 modular instruments. While in TM 500, Mihalik completed the digital hardware design, and the design and implementation of the operating system firmware for the CG 551AP.

Previously, Mihalik has written three articles for *Electronic Design* magazine, one co-authored with Bob Francis of Tektronix, and an article for *Electronics Test* magazine.

Professor J. L. Alty

Professor Alty took an Honours degree in Physics in 1961 and spent four years completing a PhD in nuclear physics research. From 1966 he spent two years in the Metallurgy Department at Liverpool as Leverhulme Research Fellow carrying out research into the Hall Effect in alloys. In 1968 he joined IBM (UK) Ltd. first as a Systems Engineer on large operating systems, and later as an Account Executive marketing medium and large systems to local authorities and Government organisations. In 1972 he was appointed Director of the University of Liverpool Computer Laboratory. In 1977 he set up one of the first Microprocessor Support Units in the U.K. and later chaired the Computer Board Working Party on Microprocessors – the recommendations of which resulted in over £2 million being given to Universities to set up microprocessor units. He was appointed Professor in 1978 and has been a member of a number of Government Committees – the

Computer Board for Universities and Research Councils, the SRC Interactive Computer Facilities Committee, and a number of inter-University bodies.

Introduction

The invention of the microprocessor opened a new era of electronics and computing. The technology of fabrication, in the ability to integrate a very large number of components onto a tiny sliver of silicon took the world by storm. Inherent in the high degree of integration was a magnitude of complexity never before encountered in a component. Add to this the fact that the microprocessor is a programmable device, and the need for tools to aid application development soon becomes clear. There must be the facility to enable the user to program the microprocessor and to test out the system under development.

The early attempts at providing these tools, under the collective name of microprocessor development systems (MDS), were, not surprisingly, from microprocessor manufacturers. The systems were sometimes very basic, being no more than a single or a collection of circuit boards based around the microprocessors to be used. Being essentially a computer configuration, these fairly crude systems allowed entry of program code and the running of the program for testing purposes. But the requirement and demand from the users for better and more powerful development tools have seen the MDS evolve into various different forms. The newer generation of MDS are sophisticated and powerful computers in their own right and there are some innovative and original aids provided in their facilities.

There are currently over a dozen different makers offering MDS in varying forms, which, of course, all claim some advantage over the others. Many development systems appear to be radically different and this can be confusing for the potential user. Are we trying to compare apples with pears? Despite their differences, development systems should all have the same objective, that is to provide the user with the tools to aid in the development of a microprocessor application.

The aim of this book is to help the readers help themselves, by discussing the criteria with which to select a development system. This is best achieved by the examination of the development cycle and highlighting the important and critical stages. The tools which aid in the critical stages can then be identified and discussed in more detail.

Because of the differing approaches from different suppliers of MDS, I have asked for contributions from manufacturers of development systems to discuss specific topics on the MDS and we are privileged to have contributions from some of the leading authorities on the subject in the world. With the benefit of this insight we can get a clearer understanding of why certain things are (or have to be) done in certain ways.

For balance a contribution was also included discussing application development without development systems. This illustrates what can be achieved by using existing equipment and may also highlight areas for future development/enhancement in development systems. This is to make the reader aware that tools are available in forms other than those which are actually called microprocessor development systems. The contributions were chosen to give a balanced representation of the different approaches taken in providing aids to a common problem. Guidelines were given to each of the contributors to discuss the insights and the reasons for taking certain approaches, as opposed to giving merely a product description. They were encouraged, however, to use their own current systems as illustrative examples. There has been only minimal editing, so that the views, philosophies and concepts presented are those straight from the contributors.

The readership is likely to be of differing levels of knowledge, and the book had to be written so as to take account of this. The editor felt it was his responsibility to ensure a common basic level of understanding. Thus of necessity the first four chapters had to be written to a lower level. However, these chapters discuss in detail the essential principles in microprocessor application development and the need for the correct tools to do the job. An understanding of these principles is vital to be able to read the contributions, some of which can be very advanced and highly technical, since they are all from persons at the forefront of MDS technology. More advanced readers may feel confident enough to skip or scan the first four chapters, only referring back to them if there is some difficulty in understanding the contributions.

There is a leaning towards software in this book. This is not because we have underestimated, or wish to belittle the task of hardware development, but due to the concensus opinion of all the contributors, and the editor, that software is the critical element in microprocessor development. The concepts of software may not be fully understood by everyone, especially professionals and engineers outside of the computer and microprocessor industries.

As an aside, it may interest the readers that your author/editor found that the principles of project management, design and structuring as discussed in the book applied well to the organisation and writing of this book! And the excellent contributions received have been a real revelation of insight and understanding in the manufacturers' thoughts and reasonings. Since all the contributions and the general chapters written by your author/editor were done in parallel, separately, over the same period it was both surprising and gratifying to find how well they come together and complement each other. There are some general principles which have had better coverage in the contributions and, rather than rewriting some of my own chapters to cover these items, I have left them as they stand; after all, if I knew everything I would have written the book on my own!

Finally I hope that you, my readers, will find this book as beneficial as I have found it in writing and organising it.

CHAPTER 1

What is a Development System?

This chapter is intended as a simple and brief introduction to the components and facilities of a typical microprocessor development system (MDS). Its aim is to achieve common terminology.

The MDS

There are many microprocessor development systems available from different suppliers. They sometimes appear to be different physically, and certainly the manufacturers may claim some unique features. However, they do have in common the basic configuration, even if some of the actual electronic components which go to make up the system may be different. Fig. 1.1 shows what is generally accepted as the recognized configuration of an MDS.

Processor

At the centre of the system is the processor unit of the MDS. The processor unit usually consists of a microprocessor connected with memory, both read only memory (ROM) and random access memory (RAM), and input and output (I/O) circuitry – this is shown in fig. 1.2. This configuration is normally implemented on several printed circuit boards (PCB) and linked together via a rack system and a backplane 'motherboard' – this is done to allow flexibility and future addition of hardware features. There are variations to this, such as all of the processor unit circuitry incorporated on a single PCB, or in some cases more than one microprocessor is used for different functions. But basically this configuration constitutes that of a computer.

Console unit

For a user to access the MDS at least one console device has to be attached to the processor. The visual display unit (VDU) is commonly used for this function, although again there are variations where other devices may be employed, such as keyboard/printing terminals. Terminology sometimes used for consoles are KSR – keyboard send and receive, or ASR – asynchronous send and receive. The function that has to be fulfilled here is the capability to allow the user to enter data into the processor (e.g. a keyboard) and some means for the processor unit to indicate messages back to the user (e.g. a display of some form).

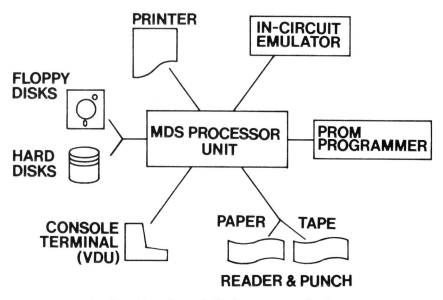

Fig. 1.1 Configuration of a typical microprocessor development system

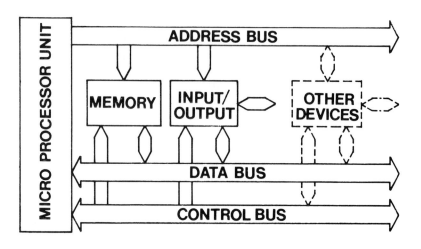

Fig. 1.2 Typical microcomputer configuration

Mass storage unit

Flexible or floppy discs are usually associated with microprocessors. This is not due to any technical affinity between microprocessors and floppy discs, but mainly because floppy disc drives are relatively inexpensive to purchase for a reasonably fast access mass storage device (in fact, floppy discs were developed for local storage on intelligent terminals for mainframe computers). Although cheaper to purchase, initially, floppy discs work out to be more expensive on a cost per bit stored than the more costly installed hard disc systems. More recently hard discs have been dropping in price with the introduction of Winchester disc technology and there will be more of these units used with MDS. Other means of mass storage more commonly used are magnetic tape/cassettes, bubble memory, charged coupled devices and even paper tape reader/punches. Quite a few suppliers offer the capability for attaching different types of mass storage devices.

The choice is dependent on the performance (speed of online data access), the amount of data to be stored and the price. There is no clear cut advantage of one device over another, at the moment (although dependency on serially accessed devices, such as tapes, should be avoided due to their slow access), but floppy discs in the 8-in diameter are the most commonly used.

The purpose served by these devices is to have some form of more permanent storage of information or data, since storage on the system memory (RAM) is only temporary, as the data is lost on switching off the power. Also to a certain extent, there can be the capability of moving information/data from one system to another by the use of the mass storage media (e.g. discs or tapes). This latter ability usually only applies to the same systems using the same mass storage devices.

Printer

Some means of obtaining a print out of information or data is more or less essential for keeping a record of development work. With the amount of information that needs printing during a microprocessor application development, a reasonably fast printing device is advisable (with a throughput of 100 characters/s or above). The most commonly used printers are line printers, which are receive-only devices attached to the processor via either a serial I/O or parallel I/O link. Variations include printing terminals used as consoles (e.g. terminals with keyboards and printers).

Many printers of more recent design are in fact microprocessor controlled, where throughput has been improved without having to significantly increase print head speeds, but by bidirectional printing and logic seeking. This means that the printer moves the print head in an optimal path, moving the head only to the line length necessary and printing the next line backwards if this would be quicker than returning the print head to the lefthand margin and printing forwards. This technical advance has also reduced the price of printers, which means that most development systems should be able to afford a reasonably fast throughput printer.

PROM programmer

In microprocessor applications, programs and data often have to be placed in ROM. Programmable ROMs (PROMs) and the ultraviolet light eraseable PROMs (EPROMs) enable the user to program their own memories. The PROM programmer is a common facility offered as an option on development systems to allow the development program and data to be programmed from the MDS into PROM or EPROM.

As there are many different types of PROM and EPROM available, the PROM programmers are designed either to program a single or limited number of types of PROMs/EPROMs or as generally is the case, a general purpose one where different 'personality' printed circuit cards (which configure the programmer for programming different PROMs and EPROMs) are accepted. The latter type of PROM programmers are often called universal PROM programmers.

Software support

Although the hardware equipment which goes to make up the development system is the most visible, and therefore more tangible, there is a very important 'component' of the MDS which may not be quite as easily discernible as the hardware, but if 'it' were missing one would soon notice the absence – this is the software support, sometimes called the system software. In fact if one really wanted to be pedantic about it, the MDS would not work without software support, and would be less than useless, since the software tools and facilities have first to be developed before any work can begin on the actual application development.

Software support on an MDS consists of programs that provide the operational access to the various devices/facilities; this collection of program routines is usually called the operating system (OS) software. There are also programs which allow the user to write programs for the target microprocessor(s); these program packages are the compilers and assemblers.

Obviously the topic of software support is a much larger issue than the very brief treatment given here. There will be more detailed discussions in chapter 4. Development Aids and in chapter 6. Software Facilities.

In-circuit emulator

Having written a program for a target microprocessor system on an MDS, one of the essential tasks is to test the program. There are many software packages that will allow the user to run and examine the program under development on the MDS. These range in sophistication from the simple monitor to full trace and debug facilities. There are also devices implemented in hardware which aid the debugging process. These are known as in-circuit emulators (although some suppliers may call them by different names). The in-circuit emulator gives the ability to link the target hardware/prototype to the MDS thus allowing the user to use the MDS to test out the development program on the actual target hardware under development.

Differences

The devices and facilities described so far are the ones which usually go to make up an MDS. Although, physically, MDS may be different in appearance, for example there are MDS which incorporate the processor and even the (floppy) disc drives into the VDU console as a single compact unit, whereas some manufacturers prefer to offer the MDS as separate units, the principle remains the same: that is the MDS is essentially a computer configuration designed to have attached to it various devices which provide the facilities to aid microprocessor application development.

The MDS as described above is made up of various components and facilities. In a discussion on how to understand and choose a microprocessor development system, it might seem obvious that all that we would have to do is merely compare the components by studying them in more detail to make a choice. But is this the right way? Although there is some validity in examining the components in more detail, any comparison and measurement with no knowledge of what is important, or the emphasis of specifications without known criteria, would give very misleading conclusions.

It is far more important to understand the aims and principles in a microprocessor application development project, to be able to identify the critical stages and to match the facilities needed to aid these stages.

Summary

An MDS is a computer system specifically designed to use various devices or peripherals to aid application development. It is more important to understand the process and objectives in a development project and identify the development aids required than to merely compare the performance or specifications of the components between systems or against some arbitrary criteria.

CHAPTER 2

The Need for Microprocessor Development Systems

This chapter discusses the necessity for microprocessor development systems (MDS) and clarifies the differences between an MDS and a microcomputer.

The microprocessor

The microprocessor is basically an electronic component, which on its own is more or less useless. Before the microprocessor can become functional, it needs to be instructed on what to do – that is it needs a program, which comprises instructions and data stored in memory. However, even in this situation, this is still not much use, since all that the microprocessor is doing is merely talking to itself. To become really useful, the system needs to be able to communicate to the outside world; to do this the configuration needs input and output (I/O) components (see fig. 1.2). This is essentially a computer configuration. There is nothing particularly revolutionary in the microprocessor application, the principles and theories are based on those of conventional computing, the differences are only the size and the lower costs in implementing a small system.

Computer development

The application of a microprocessor is in principle the application of a computer. In traditional computer application development, the computer which is eventually applied for the end use and the one used for the development work (i.e. the development system) are usually one and the same. This is since the computers used are normally supplied with development software and debugging testing packages – that is there are suitable assemblers and compilers which allow the user to write programs for the computer, plus operating and testing facilities to run and test the development programs. If the use of microprocessors is the application of a computer, why then do we need a separate development system?

Microprocessor application development

In applying microprocessors, with a few exceptions, the envisaged end system (which we will call the target system or hardware) will be one which is dedicated for a single purpose and usually required to be as inexpensive as possible (i.e. to use as few and as cheap components as possible). This usually means the target system hardware is minimal – a very bare system. For example, in the case of some controllers, the system can consist of as few as three chips that satisfy the configuration previously discussed in chapter 1.

Even when the components are connected together correctly to form the required configuration, there is still a long way from a completed working system. There is still the problem of testing and proving the circuitry and of designing and programming the software.

The microprocessor target system is usually in an isolated and naked situation. In the majority of cases there may not be means to program the target system on its own, and certainly the program development tools (i.e. the assemblers, compilers) would not exist nor be capable of being supported by the target system. Moreover, even if the programs could be written and somehow transferred onto the target system, there would be no means of testing and checking that the system is functioning properly, because full debugging and testing would be unlikely to have been incorporated.

Difference

This is essentially the difference between a microprocessor application development and development on a conventional computer system. That is most of the accepted development and testing facilities are unlikely to have been incorporated into the end target system. Indeed most applications would not want nor can afford the overhead of these development facilities on the target system. Hence the target system itself is not suitable for being its own development system. What is needed therefore is the provision of aids and facilities elsewhere to enable program development to be carried out and some means of checking and testing the behaviour of the program and target system – i.e. some form of host development system. This is what a microprocessor development system (MDS) sets out to provide.

It can be argued that it is not impossible to develop a microprocessor application without a microprocessor development system (see chapter 8. Development Without Development Systems). Many a keen hobbyist would be able to attest to this; complete systems have been built literally from scratch, from chip level. However the argument is not whether development is possible or not without MDSs. For most (professional) applications, working without appropriate and adequate tools is unacceptable. Timescales are likely to become inordinately long and the intended end result may never see the light of day. In trying to base the development tools and facilities on the target system, separate development is entailed to provide the necessary aids before the actual development project can even begin. More than that, one would be trying to use the target system as a tool and monitor for development work – and this needs to have high integrity and reliability when the target system is itself a prototype under development! Hence the need for separate microprocessor development systems.

MDS vs microcomputers

If a block diagram of the facilities of a typical development system and the configuration are examined (chapter 1. fig. 1.1 and 1.2), it would be recognised as that of a small computer system. So what is the difference between an MDS and a microcomputer?

Firstly, a microprocessor development system *is* a microcomputer; most MDS are based on the same microprocessor as the one to be used in the target hardware. The MDS, as discussed, have been specifically designed to provide the operating systems, assemblers, compilers and appropriate peripherals and devices to aid development work. There are also test and debugging packages, and, as the development system in most cases uses the same microprocessor as the target system, some indication of the development program may be obtained by running it on the MDS. All this constitutes a host coding station. Many 'matured' personal microcomputers have now evolved such that they can go some way to provide similar facilities. Some of them may possibly rival the previous advantage which the MDS enjoyed of offering these facilities in a convenient all-in-one package. Certainly, if the application is to use such a microcomputer as the end target system, then that microcomputer can adequately fulfil the role of being its own development system.

However there is one facility that sets the MDS apart from being just any microcomputer. This is the capability of monitoring and controlling the behaviour of a separate piece of microprocessor hardware (i.e. the target system) and development program in real-time. This is a very important point and a facility which distinguishes an MDS from being just a microcomputer. There will be more detailed discussions and justification of this in later chapters.

Summary

The application of microprocessors is in principle the application of a computer. In traditional computing, the computer is both the target system and its own development system. Microprocessor applications are more usually for specific dedicated purposes and the configurations for the eventual target system will not have, and cannot afford to incorporate, the extra facilities of development aids. Therefore there is the need for a host development system, the MDS. An MDS is a microcomputer, but the ability to monitor and control a separate target system sets the MDS apart.

CHAPTER 3

Microprocessor Application Development

This chapter examines the stages and principles of a microprocessor application development. The aim is to recognise and explain the important and critical stages in an application development project and to identify the tools and facilities needed to aid these stages.

Background

The microprocessor has been hailed as new technology and, as with all new technology, at the early stages of the introduction there is inevitably a scarcity of skills and expertise. Although the fabrication process to make the actual microprocessors and the related components certainly is new technology, the use of microprocessors is based on known principles of computing and electronics. It is therefore important to realise that skills do already exist, in very similar forms – in both computing (designers and programmers of small systems) and in electronic hardware (designers and engineers). What is needed is the correct utilisation and coordination of the existing skills.

The microprocessor development project

The description of an application development project in this chapter will be from a commercial basis. That is the end result – the product – will be for a commercial purpose, to be sold or to be used in an organisation's professional environment. Note the definition of product here – it is not used only for an item for sale, but also applies for an end result which may be used by only one person for a specialised purpose (i.e. a one-off special). The term product is used for an end result for which a complete working system is designed.

There are many levels of starting points in an application development. It can literally be starting from scratch – selecting and using chips and electronic components, developing software for the naked minimum system built – or using built circuit boards fulfilling some of the purposes of the product. Also some parts of required software may be purchased, although this is rare. At the other extreme complete microcomputer systems with the necessary software support could be bought. Of course a project could be a mixture of these, e.g. where some parts can be ready-built/off-the-shelf and some parts have to specifically designed and built. The choice of starting point will depend on the particular application and the commercial implications.

For the purpose of this chapter, the development project will be examined for one which is starting from scratch. That is a project where everything has to be designed and developed, both for target hardware and software; no off-the-shelf parts are used. The starting point for the target hardware will be from the chip/components level and the software will have to be developed for a naked target system. However, most of the principles discussed on the application development will be common and applicable no matter which starting point is chosen, even if some details may differ in parts for some stages.

Implications

A microprocessor application in a professional business environment means that the activity is nontrivial, even if the application may seem to be technically simple. There are many implications affecting the commercial aspects for the company or organisation using microprocessors. Eventually microprocessor usage may become commonplace, where just about every company will be applying them, so that the microprocessor will no longer be new or novel. But at the time of writing (1981) and in the near future, there will be many organisations using microprocessors for the first time, and for some it may even be the first time using anything electronic, much less microprocessors. Bearing this in mind the implications may be much wider ranging than just affecting the finances of the organisation, but livelihoods could depend on the success of the application. Therefore this activity needs to be put into the correct context. Although the scope of this book covers the technical aspects of microprocessor development, it cannot be done in isolation, and some mention has to be made of the reality and commercial aspects of it.

Project management

To undertake a microprocessor application with a reasonable chance of success and the minimum of risk, the use of microprocessors, like any other technology or business activity, needs to be put on a proper footing.

The appointment of a project manager is essential, even if the same person may have to fulfil other roles in the project. No project is too small to have a person responsible for it. The project manager will have the responsibility to ensure the success of the project by:

- identifying correct objectives
- using resources effectively, i.e. staff, equipment and finance
- monitoring agreed milestones and timescales
- being able to make contingency plans should deviations occur in the original plans

Otherwise, there will be a waste in time, resources and money, which no organisation (large or small) can afford.

Feasibility study

One of the first activities to be undertaken in a project should be a feasibility study. This need not be a lengthy process, but it is nevertheless important even if a solution may seem obvious. The feasibility study should be carried out to clearly identify the objectives and to ensure that the objectives pursued are sensible, both technically and commercially. Alternative methods should be considered, so that one is not jumping at the first solution offered.

Although it is generally acknowledged that a feasibility study will examine the technical aspects, it is not usually realised that the study should also consider the commercial viability of the project. The feasibility study can be regarded in two parts: the technical, where the merits of the technical solutions are compared and choices of components to be used are considered; and the commercial, which weighs up the benefits against the investment and risks. Sometimes the benefits are not quantifiable, but nevertheless need to be identified and clearly stated. This should indicate whether there is a real need or market for the envisaged product. It is important to realise, however, that the study is to see if the proposed project is sensible and viable both technically and financially, and not to get too carried away at this early stage in turning it into purely a design study, i.e. getting too deep into technical details and losing sight of the objectives.

The feasibility study gives us the viability and feasibility of the project (and if nothing else, it will at least confirm that what we wish to do is sensible). Far more important is that the feasibility study allows us an early decision point, to decide whether to pursue the project further, with or without modifications to the original ideas, due to its technical or commercial viability, at a stage where a relatively low amount of investment has been made. Far better to decide to stop at this point than to find out months, if not years, later, and after substantial investments, that the project was not viable right from the start!

User requirements

Having decided that the project is sensible, and with a project manager appointed, we move onto the user's requirements. This is an important stage, as here we look at how the user wants to see the end product and what are the user's needs. Too many so called products have been made, which may have been technically superb, but were not wanted or ever used because the user's requirements were neglected.

The user's requirements thus define what the user ultimately needs in the product. Consideration has to be given to the ease of use, what the end users are used to and even the acceptability of the product, in terms of the objectives of the envisaged product i.e. suitability for the purpose that the product was aimed at.

Functional requirements
The functional requirement is the definition of what the final product has to do to fulfil the user's requirements. This stage may seem to be the same as the previous stage, and in some cases the two stages may well have been combined as one activity and report, but there is a distinction between the two, and even if they are to be incorporated into a single document, the two elements should have both been taken into consideration. The distinction between the two is that the user's requirements say what the user wants and needs, whereas the functional requirements define what the product has to do to fulfil these needs.

System requirements and specifications
It may seem to be complicating the issue by mentioning a third type of requirement, the system requirements, however, fortunately, there seems to be less confusion about this part. The system requirement is a statement of the performance levels of the product necessary to fulfil the functional requirements. The systems specifications then follow to spell out these performance levels into figures and criteria which will go to define what is needed to make up the final product.

EXAMPLE
A simple example may help to illustrate the relationship of these various stages. Take an electronic calculator – a partial user's requirement may be, say, the user needs to use the product for arithmetic, to calculate shopping bills. The functional requirement which follows on from this is that the product has to be capable of doing addition, subtraction, multiplication and division, with some means for the user to enter the digits and some way of indicating the answer. The systems requirement would identify that some form of computing element has to be used (e.g. a microprocessor), with data entry by keys and display by liquid crystal display (LCD). From these the product may be specified – the systems specifications would say the calculations have to be accurate enough for chain calculations, therefore precision to eight digits, this implies that the display has to be capable of showing eight digits and at least some indication of sign. The input keys have to represent all the possible numbers, hence ten keys, coded 0 to 9 with a decimal point key and keys for the operations $+$, $-$, $\times$ and $\div$, with an $=$ key to execute the sequence.

Development

Only after having carefully considered the preceding stages should development begin. A microprocessor product is made up of hardware and software. The development, broadly speaking can be split up into these two areas.

Hardware/software tradeoffs

As the project gets into detail, the possible tradeoffs between hardware and software should be considered with the systems specifications, before the development is split up. In a microprocessor application development there will be parts which are clearly either hardware or software, but there will be other parts which may not necessarily be so clearly defined. These functions can be implemented by either hardware or software. The decision is made at this detailed stage and is dependent on both technical and commercial considerations.

In general terms, and without going beyond the scope of this book, commercially the decision for the tradeoffs is based on whether the product is going to be high or low volume, and therefore on whether it is repeatable or nonrepeatable cost sensitive. A high volume product, one which has to be duplicated many times, can spread its development cost/expenditure over many units, but the cost for the basic materials for production (as well as the production costs themselves) cannot be reduced beyond a certain base level – the repeatable cost items. With this sort of product the aim should be to keep the repeatable costs to a minimum (so that the total costs are reduced), which means that software should be used to fulfil as many functions as possible, within reason (this is a development cost, which is nonrepeatable) to reduce the hardware component count. The converse is true for a one-off or very limited number product, i.e. try to shorten the development as much as possible, by using as many ready-made or easy solutions and as much hardware, since the hardware component costs are normally insignificant compared to development costs (man-time) for one-offs or limited production. In a pure research and noncommercial environment, the decision may only depend on technical grounds of which is the easier to do, or the more elegant, or even novel solution. There are obviously many other considerations which go well beyond the scope of this book, and only a very simplified picture is given here.

Hardware development

The first step in hardware development is the writing of the hardware requirements and specifications, after the hardware and software split and tradeoffs have been decided. This is not done in isolation, but in conjunction and in parallel with the software. As more details become clear, perhaps more tradeoffs could come to light. The requirements for the hardware identify the aims and the objectives specifically for the hardware system, with reference to the features it needs to provide for software. The specifications spell out the required performance levels to fulfil these aims.

Design

From the hardware requirements and specifications, the hardware configuration may be designed. Fortunately, much of the hardware design for microprocessors has been standardised, i.e. basic configuration circuitry are known and in fact sometimes circuit diagrams for these may even be obtained from the microprocessor manufacturers. The parts which pose more difficulty and usually are more specific to the particular application, are the input and outputs and outside interfacing. Since these are specific, they may well be unique to the project. Although new ground may be broken, basic good hardware practice and experience may be used – it is worth bearing in mind that there are very few instances of completely new and original requirements. Therefore there are always similar or other applicable experiences to draw upon to help in hardware design.

Interfacing has been recognised as one of the more difficult aspects of hardware development, and it is here that more savings and tradeoffs can be made. In many real applications the signals required to be detected by the microprocessor system are very seldom, if ever, compatible (i.e. digital). In the simplest case this may be just voltage conversion to compatible 5 V TTL (transistor to transistor logic) but other instances may require the use of analogue to digital (A/D) converters. A very important consideration of the hardware design should be the operational integrity and protection of the microprocessor (digital) system from the incompatible signals. Incompatible voltages can easily corrupt the processing system and signals, and in some instances can actually damage the digital hardware. This protection may be achieved by the use of isolators and shielding against voltage spikes. Inadequately designed interfaces may prevent the total system from working properly even when the processing part (i.e. the microprocessor system) may well work on its own. Therefore it is worthwhile spending a little more time, thought and effort in the design of the interfaces if these are likely to be nonstandard.

Circuit diagrams

The hardware design results in circuit diagrams. Circuit diagrams are the realisation of the designs implemented with specific components. The logic of the system can be checked from the circuit diagrams. The selection of the actual components has to be done with regard to the operation timings, by checking against the component specifications. If done correctly, the design should have identified critical parts and the timings have to be thoroughly checked out, not only for limited or specific cases, but for the worst case operation conditions. A little more effort at this stage may save headaches later, when operational inconsistencies may occur, where a fault manifests itself intermittently, and these are usually the most difficult to trace.

Timings just out of specification only under certain circumstances are one of the typical causes under this situation. Another typical cause is the one mentioned already, that of inadequate design in decoupling, suppression or shielding which leads to signal corruption.

Prototypes

From the checked circuit diagrams, prototype circuit boards (breadboards) are constructed. Some people favour going straight to a laid-out printed circuit board (PCB), others prefer going through a breadboarding stage. Neither methods are in conflict with the principles of hardware development, the differences are only in operational convenience. A PCB is neater and provided there can be a quick turnaround for changes and modifications which may sometimes involve a total new layout, breadboarding may not be necessary. Once proven to work, the PCB may be suitable to be taken straight into production without further modification. But with a one-off special, breadboarding may be a more suitable method, and in certain circumstances the circuits may never need to be in PCB form.

Testing

The constructed prototype hardware has to be tested with equipment to see if the actual operation in real life is within the hardware specifications. Some of the testing tools are conventional such as oscilloscopes, logic probes, as can be found in most electronic laboratories. But some parts of the circuits are different from conventional fixed logic electronics. A microprocessor configuration is uncommitted logic – i.e. the behaviour is not determined until a program is executed, since the program itself can be changed, or worse, sometimes it can change during execution e.g. selfmodifying (this is not normally good practice, but certainly has been used). This means that the actual behaviour may not be invoked until certain conditions are reached.

The implication is that the testing of the hardware involves the availability of some software. This software may not necessarily have to be the actual development software. In fact initially the test software should be kept simple (so that the routine's correctness can easily be shown) as this is used merely to prove that the hardware behaviour, under controlled and known conditions, is within expectations. This is where specialist equipment is necessary. The requirement of the tools used here is the capability to monitor the signals from the microprocessor and peripheral circuits. Since there are numerous signals which require monitoring simultaneously to enable the state of the microprocessor to be known (e.g. even on an 8-bit microprocessor there are normally eight data signals and sixteen address lines to monitor simultaneously plus the various control signals), although an oscilloscope is quite capable of looking at one or even a few of the signals, it would be very impractical to keep track of all the signals necessary. There are two methods most commonly used, the logic state analyser and the in-circuit emulator.

The logic state analyser has really come into its own from the use of microprocessors, many will say that it was invented for use with microprocessors. Logic state analysers can vary from the fairly simple (and therefore inexpensive) where some indication of a single multi-signal state is needed, triggered (synchronised) by a user-selected timing signal (the indicators most commonly used are light emitting diodes (LED)), to very sophisticated ones which can store several multisignal states and display the results in various forms, even to showing the instruction mnemonics. The latter type usually have to have incorporated 'personality' circuits for the particular microprocessor being tested; different microprocessors will require the change of personality modules.

The in-circuit emulator is an advance over the logic state analyser, where the more sophisticated facilities of the logic analyser are incorporated with the ability to loan additional facilities of the MDS to the target prototype hardware. The in-circuit emulator is usually an option available on an MDS, and again can vary from being fairly simple indicating one state to ones where thousands of states may be stored 'on the fly'. This is a very important item in the MDS and will be covered in more detail in the next chapter, as well as in depth in a full chapter devoted to it.

After testing, a working prototype should result, which needs to be combined with the development software to produce a prototype system.

Documentation

This item is not placed at the end of the discussion of hardware development as an afterthought, or because it is the last thing to be done. It is placed here because of its importance and so that it can be viewed in relation to the stages already discussed.

There are basically three types of documentation:

● design and development
● maintenance and support
● users'

The design and development documentation is used to record the stages in development; this ensures that there is communication and that the correct objectives at each stage have been identified and are being pursued. This is an important item in the control of the project as the documentation should record the agreed aims and specifications, and thus any deviation from the original agreement can be identified and contingency action can be taken. The design and development documentation becomes essential when updates and/or modifications have to be made at some later date.

Documentation has to be provided for the maintenance of the hardware; this may not necessarily be covered in the development documentation. In fact the field service engineer does not need to know of design and development details to be able to maintain the hardware. The maintenance document can be viewed in two parts. The first part is the regular preventative maintenance routines, if any, e.g. cleaning out filters, calibrating potentiometers etc. The second part should deal with actions that should be taken should the system not function, ranging from simple fault eliminating diagnostics, which the user could carry out before having to call out the service engineer, to more detailed repair procedures to be used by the service engineer. However in these days of ever increasing complexity and the difficulty of tracing faults without a battery of specialised equipment, the documentation may consist of advice to isolate the fault to a circuit board and the replacement of that board in the field, and more detailed diagnosis and repair can be carried out at base.

The third type of documentation is perhaps the most important, as quite often this is the only interface to the customer or end user. Without adequate instructions the hardware built may never be used to its full potential – this is especially true of microprocessor-based products, since different levels of complexity can be built in and these are not usually self-explanatory. Commercially, inadequate user documentation could well give the product a bad reputation, even though the product may be quite adequate.

User documentation should fulfil two purposes – as instructions for the operation of the product (and this should be adequate for a first time user without any previous knowledge) and as a quick reference for users already experienced with the product to be able to look up details of the system. It should be remembered that many new users are impatient to use the product, so that simple and short operating instructions which enable the new user to get the system up and running without risk of damage would be very desirable. If these quick instructions are well thought out, they would be kept handy, used frequently and a consistent routine in operating the product would develop.

One very useful exercise is the production of the user manual in parallel with the system specification, which with consultation with the end user, can show up early any inadequacies in the user and functional requirements, rather than after a good deal of work has been done in producing a proto-type.

Software development

To many, software development means the sight of programmers at terminals entering code, or working over coding sheets. So much so that there have been several articles published in eminent journals that seem to support this impression by citing statistics of software productivity in terms of number of lines of code produced per day. Programmers are thus judged by the amount of code that they can produce. In certain cases the effort involved in software development has been grossly underestimated. Software has been regarded occasionally as an afterthought after the real hard work of developing the hardware has been done – 'programmers' are merely set at a terminal to 'knock up' some code for the hardware system.

Of course this is far from the truth, as the following section hopefully will point out. Thankfully the industry has now recognised the importance of software and has identified that the difficult part of microprocessor development is the software. As already mentioned, this activity is not done in isolation, but in parallel and in full consultation with the hardware development (part of successful project management is to ensure the liaison between hardware and software).

The requirements and specifications for the software have to be clearly defined. The requirements identify the aims in relation to the functions the software has to provide on the hardware. The specifications detail the level of performance needed. Again the software requirements and specifications will bring to light further hardware/software tradeoffs.

Design

From the requirements and specifications, the software can be designed. There are various schools of thought and methodologies in software design, such as structured design, production rules, logic schematics, flowcharting, etc. They all have their followers, but their basic objective is the same – to formalise the design phase with simplified and clear documentation to a recognised convention. The rules do not possess magical qualities but merely serve as guidelines so that the ideas for design can be made clear and within the accepted conventions. The choice of methodology may depend on familiarity or the particular suitability for the project. For example there are many who hold the opinion that flowcharts are more suitable for writing programs in assembly code.

Analysis is an important aspect, where the software can be identified as either mainly processing or data manipulation, so that the software may be designed or structured with processing routines foremost or data storage and movements as the most important requirement. The analysis should also identify the critical parts of the software, where tight timing or storage constraints are recognised and taken into account in the design.

Long monolithic programs are harder to understand and mistakes are harder to find, making testing and proving of the software more difficult, whereas short simple programs are much easier to assimilate and to debug. This simple principle can be extended to large programs by dividing it into smaller manageable parts or modules. Good design practice would structure the program into logical modules limiting each module to a single or very limited simple functions. Furthermore the modules should be designed in such a way that they are capable of being tested thoroughly independently, thus each of the modules that go to make up the overall program becomes a small and simple program on its own. Again the more careful and detailed the design, the more time will be saved in both coding and testing of the software.

Coding

Coding of the program should not begin until there is a well defined design. After all, the requirements state what it is that the program is supposed to do and the design states how this is to be achieved, without this one cannot actually implement the work. This however does not mean that work on coding cannot start until every last detail of the design has been cleared up, because if the design has modularised the program, coding of the modules can start as each part of the design is completed. This is particularly advantageous in a large project using a large number of staff.

A hotly debated area is that of programming languages. Not only are there arguments as to whether one should use high- or low-level languages, there are arguments on which is the 'best' language. For example, currently in vogue is the language PASCAL, who advocates say is an elegant and structured language, whereas the language BASIC is looked down on for 'serious' usage – but it is very easy to pick up and therefore to understand. Of course, for those really in the 'know' the up and coming language is ADA or is it C? The purists will insist on the use of assembly language with microprocessors, due to the tighter control that the programmer has over the timing, storage and behaviour of the microprocessor.

Every language has its camp of supporters (and of course its knockers), but it is important not to be carried away with these comparisons, because there is no language that shows such significant advantage as to be able to turn a bad programmer or bad design into producing a good and well-structured program. Each application will have languages more suitable for that particular case. There are also other considerations such as availability and familiarity, as not every language is available for some microprocessors and again a programmer who is familiar with a language is more likely to be able to produce good code more quickly than having to learn a new language which is deemed more suitable. It is far more important to realise that programming languages are merely tools to aid the translation of design into a program, the choice of which is not dependent on some comparative consumer report of a best buy, but on clarity of the code, ease of implementation and the suitability to the application.

Testing

The performance of the end product is very dependent on the software. The quality of the product will be judged on the performance. Debugging and testing therefore becomes a very essential activity, as no matter how careful the work, there will always be mistakes in the program, either accidental or unforeseen errors. The process of debugging and testing is to eliminate these errors, but there is a more significant purpose to testing. Testing is used to prove, in practice, the theory of the design and to ensure the quality of the end product. It is at this stage when one can see if the software is working to the specifications.

Testing is not merely 'a try it and see' activity, but should be a logical and structured process. The design and the work in programming should have picked out the critical areas where more effort needs to be concentrated. It is not enough to 'prove' a program under a single or ideal condition, there are too many programs that 'work' under normal conditions but can fail with quite catastrophic consequences when something slightly out of the ordinary occurs. Thus for the critical parts thorough testing is necessary to the extent that where possible every combination of condition should be tried to prove the behaviour of the program. Sometimes this may seem an impossibly large task if done manually, however a program or routine can be exercised automatically by using another program to set these varying combinations of conditions.

The only valid way to debug and test software for many applications is to carry it out in real-time. This is a significant point as there are very few tools or aids which will allow testing of software without interfering with the running of the program under test.

Documentation

The importance of documentation was stressed for hardware development; it can be even more critical for software. It was pointed out previously that hardware has fortunately become more well known and standardised, but the software can greatly affect the behaviour of the product. The difference, however, in software is not apparent visibly until the product is set into operation. Whereas in hardware one can get an idea of the function of a system by inspecting the actual hardware circuitry, no such means exist for software. Therefore it is doubly important to record or document the software. Despite the claims, there are very few, if any, languages which are truly self-documenting. Thus a listing of the actual program, although an absolute essential part of documentation, is not totally adequate. Software documentation should be explicitly clear in the explanations of the purpose and functions of each part of the program. One cannot assume that other people are able to deduce a particular way of thinking. Any special techniques or even tricks used have to be recorded in detail, this not only aids other people in understanding, it may remind the original programmer at some later date when the trick may have been forgotten.

Documentation is normally regarded as tedious and an imposition after all the 'real' work has been finished, but it is hoped that this short piece has stressed the critical nature of documentation. Good documentation means that it has to be adequate and usable by the persons that it is aimed at. This can only be achieved by careful disciplined working and good project standards control. As mentioned previously it can be very useful to produce draft manuals at a very early stage, before even the product has been developed, so that the draft manual may be assessed by the persons concerned, who can not only make comments on whether it is understandable, but may even help in establishing more firmly the user's requirements and specifications.

Similarity

It is worthwhile noticing that both hardware and software development followed very similar lines illustrating that software requires as much disciplined working and professionalism as hardware engineering. Many people's visualisation of software being merely sitting at a terminal and typing out code is a gross underestimate of the difficulty of implementing software.

Integration

When the two parts, hardware and software have been developed into working prototypes, the product is still a long way from being completed. Next comes the process of integrating the two parts. Although this process ideally should have been going on during the hardware and software development, there may be circumstances where the two developments had to be done separately. For clarity, the integration will be treated separately.

The degree of cooperation and amount of communication between the hardware and software developments will determine how smoothly the integration stage will be. If there has been little communication between the two developments, it will be inevitable that neither development will meet the requirements or specifications of the other, unless there is a great deal of luck involved (and in a commercial development, luck should not be the major influencing factor for eventual success).

The joining of hardware and software will give a clear picture of the performance of the final product and the main consideration should be to test the combined system in a real true-to-life environment. Testing aids discussed in both the hardware and software developments are also useful in this stage.

Final product

A successfully integrated system still requires a great deal of work to produce a finished product. Below is a list of just some of the other considerations:

- packaging – both in terms of the casing as well as the packaging for shipping purposes
- installation – the suitability of the product in the eventual place it is to be used
- introduction or launch – the publicity and advertising of the product to the end users. This is as important even for an inhouse product to introduce the new equipment to the eventual users
- manuals and literature – there have to be adequate manuals for the three areas – end user, maintenance and design and development – as well as publicity literature
- training – with new products there may be the need to train the end user and sometimes for a product which is to be sold, training of marketing and sales personnel

- production – setting up of the production facilities for products which will be produced in larger quantities
- quality assurance – a very important part of production and one which is recognised as a very expensive item. However, with the use of microprocessors and good planning organisation, the product itself can help in quality assurance to a certain degree
- support and maintenance – decisions have to be made to the amount of support and maintenance a product needs and the appropriate support organisations set up

Only when all these items have been resolved can the system be called a product.

Iterative

All the stages outlined seem to be straight forward and sequential, i.e. they follow on nicely one after the other. But in real life there will be many instances where one has to back step and modify preceding work or plans, i.e. the stages are iterative. This is inevitable and part of a successful project is dependent on good project management where contingencies can be taken when a change in plans or direction becomes necessary without losing sight of the primary objectives.

Summary

Hardware and software development are similar in their stages:

- requirements – where the objectives of the development are stated
- design – a very important stage, it establishes how the work is to be done
- implementation – in hardware the wiring up of circuits, in software coding of programs
- testing – proving in practice the theory of the design and to ensure the quality of the product
- documentation – three basic requirements, for the end user, for support and maintenance of the product and recording of the design development. A vital process which has to be carried out throughout the development

An important message in software is

Software $\neq$ Coding

The success of the project depends on good project management and planning.

CHAPTER 4

Development Aids

This chapter describes the facilities of the development system which aid in the identified critical stages of a microprocessor application development. The aim of this discussion is to help readers decide what is important to look for, and for them to have the knowledge to select the facilities necessary in choosing a microprocessor development system.

Critical stages

From the discussion in chapter 3, one can see that just as hardware engineering cannot be equated to the process of soldering, software cannot be taken as merely coding, even though these are the most visible parts in development. The more critical stages in development have been identified as the design and testing stages, with documentation being an essential activity that should run throughout the stages.

Without wishing to diminish the difficulty in developing the hardware, most people in the industry have recognised that software usually turns out to be the crucial factor. As mentioned previously, the circuits for microprocessors are mostly well known and can even be obtained from the microprocessor manufacturers in some cases. On the other hand the software, which determines the function of that product, is usually unique to that system, therefore the development has to be done from scratch.

Software design cannot and should not be done 'on the back of envelopes'. Design should be formalised and methodical, drawing on past or similar experiences. There are some design methodologies based mostly on traditional computer software development and, although some parts are not appropriate for microprocessor software, most of the principles do apply. These methodologies are not ends in themselves but they do encourage careful disciplined working and the use of consistent convention.

Debugging and testing of software and hardware is normally a difficult and arduous process if it is to be done thoroughly. Thorough testing is essential to ensure that the product does perform to specification, as is 'protecting' the product when deviation from normal usage occurs. Special aids are necessary to be able to examine the running and conditions of the system. Documentation, usually regarded as an imposition and a tedious activity, has to be standardised and carefully controlled in the project, so that it is not neglected in the mistaken impression of getting on with real work, as it is a part, an essential part, of real work.

The MDS facilities

The MDS, in theory, should provide the facilities and aids to help in the various development stages, as described in the previous chapter. The emphasis should be to support the critical stages.

An essential and crucial part of development is defining the requirements first, to state the objectives of the project. There are no aids known to the author that can help with this stage. However the procedures can be formalised in stating the requirements, by identification of important subjects. The sort of subheadings to consider within the software objectives are shown in fig. 4.1. This is by no means a complete list of the topics to be considered and each of the subheadings could, themselves, be subdivided for more detailed consideration.

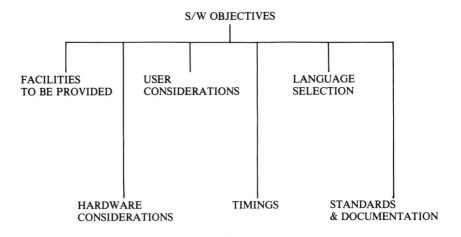

Fig. 4.1 Software objectives

Design aids

Despite this being one of the most crucial stages in a microprocessor application development, there are no known design aids or tools available on development systems at the moment. There are, however, various established design methodologies; for example the MASCOT system used in military systems. These are first and foremost design methodologies which formalise the process of design, but some have been implemented as a software system on conventional computers. The suitability of the methodology can only be judged on each application case concerned, however there is much to be gained from a standard and formalised approach to design. Hopefully, we may see some of the established schemes adapted for microprocessor development systems, in the not too distant future.

In the meantime, design has to come down to careful and disciplined work, where the temptation of skipping this stage, under the misconception of getting on with the 'real' work of implementation, should be discouraged. After all one cannot get on with doing work without first having said how you are going to do it.

Coding/implementation

The MDS gives the facility of a host environment to implement programs for the target microprocessor system, by providing the appropriate software aids such as assemblers, compilers, linkers, loaders and editors. The host environment gives a coding station, i.e. the instructions or code for the target system can be conveniently written on the MDS, whereas if the target system (normally devoid of any development facilities) had to be coded by hand without any aids, it would literally mean that the instructions for the target microprocessor had to be placed in the exact location of memory one bit at a time in binary form. This is not only tedious but very prone to error, as it is very hard to relate the very abstract binary coding to the actual instructions required. Moreover, the written program would also be extremely difficult to maintain or make any changes to, since the code is absolute or fixed so that any insertion or deletion in the code would mean hand changing of most of the address references (see fig. 4.2).

A slight improvement to the hand coding in binary is the use of hexadecimal (hex) code, which is merely the compacting of the binary code by the numerical representation to the base of sixteen. Other than being slightly more legible, all the drawbacks described for binary coding still apply however. It would not be impossible to code with either method, but neither would be acceptable for development usage for a commercial undertaking.

Assembly languages

If programming needs to be closely coupled with the hardware, where either timing or memory storage is critical, then the coding usually has to be with assembly languages. The assembly language produces code in a one-to-one relationship with the actual instruction set of the microprocessor. That is, a mnemonic name is given to each of the microprocessor instructions, so that the development program can be written in the more easily remembered and representative mnemonic code. The assembler, a program itself, turns the mnemonic codes into the executable machine binary code, i.e. the assembler performs the task of translation. However, the assembler can add a few advantages over merely giving names to the instructions.

LABELS AND SYMBOLS

A facility in an assembler is that of labels. Positions in a program can be given labels such that references to those positions can be by the labels given. This has the advantage that the programmer does not have to calculate the exact addresses and displacements (a source of likely errors). More importantly, though, with any changes, insertions, deletions to the program, the addresses and displacements do not have to be calculated or adjusted, as the assembler will automatically adjust for the changes when it translates (assembles) the changed program. Similarly, a symbol or name can be given to a variable, value or parameter in the program, so that the program can be more readable/understandable by the use of appropriate names or symbols for the values. Again any changes to the values in the program can be done by a single change of the value of the symbol, with the assembler making the corrections to all references to that symbol.

RELOCATABLE CODE

Some assemblers can produce relocatable code. This means that the code generated by the assemblers can be located anywhere in the memory space of the microprocessor system. This allows the construction of a program in smaller parts or modules without having to worry about the exact location of the addresses. Relocation also aids in modification of the program as well as allowing the writing of program modules by more than one person. The relocation is achieved by the assembler holding back the allocation of final absolute addresses by keeping relative references to a single reference point (usually the start or the end point of the program). The relative reference symbol table is used when the program is loaded and given the location point (e.g. the start address) and all the other addresses and references can thus be calculated and generated.

LINKERS AND LOADERS

Closely associated with relocatable assemblers are linkers and loaders. The linking program allows references to program routines external to the one written, for example library routines, programs written in separate modules, or programs using routines from other programs. Loaders, as the name implies, load the program and the cross-reference routines to the directed locations in memory ready for execution. Note that it is also common to find these two functions combined together as linking loaders.

High-level languages

A further step to making coding easier is the high-level language. A high-level language allows the representation of a sequence of machine instructions as a single statement (see fig. 4.2). This means that a program can be written with far fewer statements. The programmer will find it easier to keep track of the work and objectives. Also the program itself would be easier to read and understand, provided the language is a suitable one.

High-level languages are generally less compact and slower in the final machine code produced. However this is true normally for fairly short programs or short test or benchmark programs. With much longer programs when the efficiency and effectiveness of the programmer goes down due to the sheer volume of programming statements that need to be written, it becomes too easy to lose sight of the main objectives when struggling in details of coding. Using a high-level language it is easier to generate 'correct' code; quite often in large programs the actual machine code generated can be more efficient and compact since most high-level languages are designed to use and share common routines, whereas in a long program, the programmer is quite likely to duplicate code for similar functions.

However, because of their nature, high-level languages are more application-oriented, i.e. they are more suitable for certain types of programs than others. For example, it is generally recognised that COBOL is more suitable for data manipulation, FORTRAN is mathematically oriented, whereas both ALGOL and PASCAL claim to be more structural and procedural languages. At the time of writing there is no one language which is suitable for all purposes.

High Level Language	Assembly Mnemonics (Comments)		HEX	Binary
[1]C = B + A	[2]START: IN 2	; input value of B	DB ϕ2	11011011 00000010
	MOV B,A	; store value in register B	47	01000111
	IN 1	; input value of A, note:	DB ϕ1	11011011 00000001
		; the value will be in the		
		; A reg. or accumulator.		
	ADD B	; add value of B to A	8ϕ	10000000
	MOV C,A	; store result in register	4F	01001111
		; C		

Notes:
1. High level language: the range of values of the numbers used is restricted only by the range of the compiler implemented. (With most high level languages this is floating point arithmetic.)
2. The assembler mnemonics are those for the Intel 8080/8085, and for simplicity the arithmetic is limited to unsigned 8-bit integers with NO indication of overflow or carry.

Fig. 4.2 Example of different methods of programming

Compilers

The program equivalent to the assembler for high-level languages is the compiler. The compiler translates the source program written into code suitable for execution by the target microprocessor. Similar to the process of assembly languages, the relocatable code generated has to be linked and loaded before execution.

It is worth reminding the reader at this point that although time has been spent giving details of the facilities provided for coding, this stage should only be undertaken after a full detailed design stage has been carried out, and then the coding stage becomes a task of translation. Coding ≠ software (see previous chapter).

Editors

A time consuming aspect of programming is simply the task of getting the coding down, i.e. writing the computer language instructions. It is extremely important to have good facilities to aid in this task. A good and easy to use editor which makes entering code more convenient, and more importantly, which eases correction and modification of entered text or code deserves looking at. Good editing facilities encourage the more frequent use of comments in coding (a vital part of documentation) and encourage any changes and modification to development programs to be done at the source code level, as opposed to the all too frequent machine level 'patching' which tends to go unrecorded and forgotten at the end of the day. There have been many programs released where the actual code does not match the source code in the so-called documentation. A poor editing system on an MDS will definitely encourage all the bad habits which are very undesirable for any microprocessor application development, since the programmers would much rather try other methods than to have to use the tedious editor.

It is the author's opinion that many MDS and even computers can do with substantial improvements to their editors. In fact an idea worth considering by makers of MDS (and computers) is to make the direct interface for the user as a screen-based word processor type editor with links into the operating system. After all, the user is basically entering words whether they are instructing the computer what to do (an operating system), or programming (translating) or operating some other function, and every effort should be made to make this communication as easy and error free for the user as possible and make it as convenient as possible to correct any unintentional errors. For example some editors insist on using very convoluted and apparently obscure commands to reach a particular piece of text before any correction can be carried out. A typical example is shown below:

$$n\text{L} \ 1\text{T} \ m\text{C} \ \text{I} \ \text{cr}$$

meaning move down n lines, type 1 line to confirm that one is on the correct line, move to the right by m characters and go into the insertion mode (plus the entry termination by the cr – carriage return key). What a fuss when the offending part probably was already on the screen; would it not have been so much easier to merely move a pointer (a screen cursor) with cursor control keys to the desired position and either overwrite or insert as the case requires.

Debugging and testing

Many a programmer will breath a sigh of relief when a program finally manages to compile or assemble correctly without any errors, and feel that the program is now finally finished. Nothing could be further from the truth. It is true that the effort involved in reaching this state may have been immense, but this may sadly only reflect the tediousness and inadequacy of the editors, translators and even operating system in use. All that the coding stage has achieved is to type in a program and allow the computer to translate the source code into machine executable instructions, picking up any text entry errors on the way. The program written has yet to be proven to work and work correctly under all conceivable circumstances.

As already emphasised in the previous chapter, one of the most crucial stages in development is that of debugging and testing. This is proving in practice the theory of the design, to ensure the quality of the end product. Debugging and testing may take many forms (and different degrees of thoroughness), but the principal objective should be to ensure that the product's behaviour is within the required performance specifications and expectations, and also to eliminate any inadvertant or unforeseen faults.

Various facilities are fortunately available to aid in the task of debugging and testing. These facilities can roughly be divided into two general groups, disturbing and non-disturbing. These are not common terms, but they have been used to describe the two groups. Pure software facilities for debugging are normally the disturbing type, that is to say the program under test has to be disturbed or interfered with to allow testing to be carried out. For example, to facilitate a breakpoint trap by software only means that at software interrupt or restart, instructions need to be inserted/substituted in the desired position in the test program, therefore actually interfering with the code. To obtain a trace of the behaviour of the test program means that the test program needs to be interrupted or momentarily halted after the execution of each instruction. These types of disturbing or interfering methods are adequate for the initial trial of programs to eliminate any major faults which would not allow the program to run at all, but more thorough testing must be done in a real-time environment.

To enable thorough testing of programs, the state of the microprocessor needs to be known. Although one could connect to the microprocessor pins, this would be inconvenient and also probably interfere with electrical driving characteristics of the target circuitry. Therefore a special tool is needed to give the capability of monitoring and controlling the behaviour of the microprocessor on the target system. This device is now generally known as an in-circuit emulator.

In-circuit emulation

The in-circuit emulator is a part of the facilities offered on an MDS, usually as an option. However it is the author's opinion that it is the in-circuit emulator which sets the MDS apart from being just another microcomputer, and it is an essential tool for development on a separate target system. The emulator is attached to the target circuitry by replacing the target microprocessor by a multi-pinned header plug connected with multiway cable via buffering to the emulator circuitry, which is usually plugged into the main MDS housing (see fig. 4.3). The emulator actually has the microprocessor as part of the configuration, the exact positioning of which can be critical for timing (detailed discussion of this and the configuration will be covered in chapter 7). With the microprocessor as part of the circuitry of the emulator, it means that the necessary connections can be made without disturbing the target circuitry. This feature allows the possibility of full monitoring of the microprocessor's behaviour, as well as control of the processor unit's running. By using hardware controls (see chapter 7), it is possible to keep track of the running of the processor as well as to control the execution of the program in real-time and in a real environment, on the actual target system on test.

TRACE ANALYSIS

A feature commonly offered on development systems is the real-time trace analysis (sometimes called logic analysis). This is achieved by monitoring the microprocessor's signal lines in real time and in parallel, and storing this information in a separate memory (buffer) area. At the end of the particular run of the test program, this information can be analysed as a 'recording' of the behaviour. The size of this buffer area will determine the amount of information which can be stored. Although for the majority of usage, only a few hundred states need to be examined at any one time, there is the need under certain circumstances to be able to record substantially more than that (e.g. where there are several repetitive routines in the part of the program to be investigated). An additional facility offered on some MDS is that of 'windowing' and conditional analysis. This can go some way to reducing the requirement for a large trace buffer area, as the recording can be made conditional so that only certain types of instructions are recorded, or recording only takes place if a certain event takes place. Windowing can specify recording only between two address limits and gives a snap shot of events in the desired section (this is merely a special case of conditional analysis).

CONTROL

Having access to all the lines of the microprocessor means that a good degree of control may be exercised over the running behaviour of the program, even when running on a separate target system. The breakpoint or trap is a typical example. The microprocessor may be halted or put into an idle state when the emulator hardware senses a specified condition has been reached, for example, reaching a particular address (sensed on the address lines) or, say, when a particular type of instruction is fetched (sensed on the data lines). Single stepping is a debugging technique commonly used for computer software, however the in-circuit emulator will allow this capability on a remote target system, without the burden or overhead of having a debugging program on the target system (if the target system is large enough to support such a thing in the first place). This means that input and output conditions may be examined in more detail in-situ.

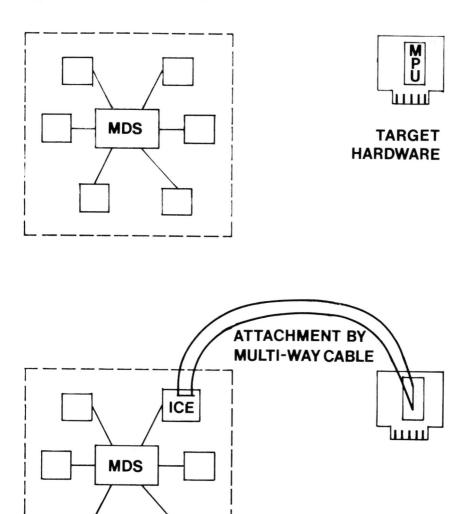

Fig. 4.3 The principle of the in-circuit emulator.
(*a*) Software development is done in the environment of the MDS, but the target system is remote from the MDS and isolated.
(*b*) The microprocessor unit of the target system is replaced by the header plug unit of the ICE, connecting the 2 systems together. This allows debugging in-situ on the target with full control from the MDS, also many of the facilities of the MDS are now available to the target hardware.

As an enhancement of the ability to examine the behaviour of remote circuitry, some more sophisticated in-circuit emulators have extra unassigned lines as part of the trace analyser which the user may attach to any desired standard 5 V TTL signal on the target system (or even off it) and the emulator system may be set up to detect any of the permutations of signal states from these extra lines or ignore them as desired by the user. Automatic monitoring and recording of I/O lines (or any other signal) can thus be achieved. With conditional analysis also, actions can be triggered by the states of the extra lines.

LOAN FACILITIES

We have seen already that the in-circuit emulator can 'lend' the separate target system facilities which the target system lacks, in terms of debugging aids. However, the emulator can also lend the target system parts of circuitry which may not exist on the target system, due to the fact that the circuitry has not yet been built or for testing out hardware/software tradeoff ideas without having to first build up the necessary circuitry. The most common use of the loan facility is that of memory substitution, especially for memory which is eventually destined to be ROM on the target system. It is infinitely more convenient to be able to test out the program in read and write memory (RAM), where modifications are easily carried out. (This brings us back to good practice where it would be much more desirable to go back to the source code to do any modifications as opposed to patching – some MDS will allow this with more convenience than others. If the MDS used is not convenient in this aspect, it is extremely important to manually document any patches or alterations, and then incorporate these changes back to the source code at the end of the day.)

The capability of the MDS to lend facilities to the target system extends further in that for most emulators just about all the MDS facilities are available to the target system. For example a most useful one is the ability to store the core/memory image or the information recorded in the trace buffer onto the more permanent mass storage devices (such as floppy or hard discs). This feature helps in documentation where it is inconvenient to get back to the source code for changes. Here, at last, one can quickly and conveniently record the changes. Similarly, one can easily load the target memory or the memory loaned to the target system from the mass storage device, such that a particular run condition may be restored or duplicated.

In memory substitution, a facility to look for is that of memory mapping. Mapping allows part of the program to run from the target memory and part from the MDS's loaned memory. It will also allow the loaned memory to appear- to have the desired address location to the target system, regardless of the actual absolute address that the memory has for the MDS itself (i.e. relocatable memory substitution). The ability to write protect memory is an advantage, not only to preserve a particular part of the program, but for emulating read only memory, which in real life obviously cannot be written to or over. The minimum block size of memory which can be substituted or relocated is also worthwhile noting; it has to be small enough to be realistic and such that any memory substitution does not infringe the desired mapping for the target system. About 1 or 2 kbyte is only just about acceptable, but 128–256 kbyte should be the size aimed for. Similar assignments can apply to input and output ports.

Taking the loaning facitity to its ultimate conclusion, there are some in-circuit emulators which can run with no user supplied target hardware at all. This may appear to be fairly useless, but in fact it is extremely useful, since this will allow the programmer to try out the development program, before any hardware is even ready, in a reasonable real environment and in real time. Also it can be used to prove hardware and software tradeoffs that may need deciding during the system design stage.

Ease of use
Throughout the previous section, the words convenient and easy have been used several times. The reason behind this has been deliberately to emphasise the fact that the facilities of the MDS have to be convenient and easy to use, otherwise they literally will not be used. For example there is no excuse at this stage in the evolvement of the MDS why one should have to tolerate the examination of the trace analysis from the in-circuit emulator in binary or hex code. After all, coding can be done by a representative language, why then when examining the recorded trace information should it not be disassembled (reverse assembly) and at least shown as assembly language mnemonics? By the storage of a symbolic table at the time of translation the same labels for addresses and names for variables may be used. This extends the use to a high-level language where each statement could be assigned a line number as an automatic label and thus the trace can be made from statement to statement. A further advance could be the cross reference to the high-level language list file so that on displaying trace information, the actual original high-level language can be shown as well as the instructions the line generated. This means it becomes easier to relate the written program to the debugging process. The use of more obscure binary or hex code would limit the use of the MDS to specialists and generate an undeserved mystique around these tools, whereas they should be shown up for what they are – ill-considered and ill-conceived collection masquerading as development aids.

Documentation – Documentation – Documentation!
Emphasised throughout this book is the importance of documentation, so what can the MDS on the market do to aid this task? Some indication of the way an MDS can help has been given above, in making facilities convenient such that users are encouraged into good practice, e.g. taking changes back to the source as opposed to leaving them in unrecorded patches.

One of the first steps is the production of a good clear listing of the developed program. Since this needs printing out to obtain a hard copy, it implies that the printer is an essential part of the MDS, and it has to have a high enough throughput, otherwise users will tend not to use it quite as often as necessary (usually a minimum print speed of around 100 to 120 characters/s should be aimed for, with higher speeds for larger application developments). What happens to the MDS when a print is in progress? Does it become unavailable for other usage? This again will discourage the use of the printer for documentation since the MDS becomes tied up during the printing process; aside from that it is very silly to use the MDS as a dedicated printer driver! So the feature to look for is the ability to do other tasks while printing, e.g. editing, compiling or assembling and so on.

Listings have to have adequate comments to be truly useful. It is very difficult to force programmers to comment on entering the source code. It has to come down to careful disciplined work and conscientiously making the effort to annotate appropriate remarks to the program. It would *not* encourage the use of copious comments if the editor is difficult to use. It appears that for many MDS (and even established computers), very little real thought has gone into the editor. The best place to store all documentation is on the MDS with the development program, so that bits and pieces do not become separated and lost. So how many MDS incorporate an easy to use and powerful word processor so that the documentation can be encouraged and kept on the MDS? This I believe is an area which can do with serious consideration. Perhaps some day we may even see simple to use graphics facilities, so that even circuit diagrams can be entered on the MDS. This is only a short step away from having the facility for automatic layout of circuits from the entered diagrams.

A useful feature is the ability of the MDS to keep a 'trail' of the operations executed on the system – this is one advantage that the old style printing terminal (e.g. teletypes) have over the now more fashionable VDUs – one merely had to roll back the paper to see what had been done. With VDUs, although paper is saved, unless care is taken, one may well forget what has been done or tried and time can be wasted in repeating ground already covered. So why not have the MDS record the commands used and store them in a file in the background? This is especially useful when testing software as it encourages a disciplined, orderly and structured approach as opposed to a try-and-see attitude.

Costs

Advanced facilities usually mean higher prices, since the MDS will have to have more memory, more mass storage and more support software. We are fortunate that with the advance in technology the prices of solid-state memory and mass storage media have been falling over the last few years. Certainly the price per bit stored has seen dramatic changes. The fall in hardware prices unfortunately cannot balance the increase in the software needed for the added facilities, hence higher prices. But as the personal and hobbyist computer market has shown, the price for (the few pieces of) good software can be lowered. This is due to the sheer economics of shipping in large quantities, and although we probably cannot expect prices as low as in the hobbyist market, lower prices are feasible by, say, standardising on an operating system and editor, with common assemblers and compilers. Although there are several manufacturers of microprocessor development systems, there is no sensible reason why they all have to invent or develop their own compiler for an accepted standard language – and make the prospective purchaser pay for the development.

Of course, each organisation will have it own justification for the amount it is willing to spend on development aids for microprocesors. But it is crucial to realise that without adequate tools, there may be a great waste in valuable man-time, so that the products intended to be developed may not be reliable, or even see the light of day. This can be far more detrimental to the organisation than the initial outlay of slightly more capital expenditure. Also it should be noted that many MDS are now available on a rental basis from equipment hire firms, which may mean that one can have the 'best available' for the duration of the project only.

How to choose

The main objective of this book is to help readers recognise the important and critical parts in microprocessor development and to have the ability to decide for themselves the useful and important features in a microprocessor development system, and not be seduced by impressive specifications, which although possibly truthful, are totally irrelevant as a guide to the performance of the system as a development tool.

The first thing to realise is that what constitutes a microprocessor development system is not limited to the offerings of the manufacturers of them. What have been discussed in these chapters are the facilities which are useful in a microprocessor application development. These facilities can be made up of existing and quite often readily available equipment. For example, almost any computer (of adequate configuration) which the organisation may already possess has a logic analyser. Crosscompilers and assemblers for microprocessors are available for the more popular and more established computers – a good source is often universities and colleges. A much fuller discussion of this is covered in chapter 8. Coordinating one's own development system from separate components does require a certain degree of understanding of system configuration, determination and a great deal of effort. For the majority, the microprocessor development system offers a convenient package which integrates the various facilities as an all-in-one deal.

Choosing the right development system involves many considerations. For example one could decide on which microprocessor to use, then let that choice determine which MDS. This seems to have been the more usual way of thinking, and it appears quite logical. But let us view this from a slightly different angle and ask the following question. Should the effort be spent on choosing a chip which costs a few pounds/dollars and let that choice dictate the purchase of a development system which costs several tens of thousands of pounds/dollars?

Of course asking such a question tends to emphasise the flaw in the logic and turns the conventional approach on its head. But there is a great deal of mileage to be gained in taking this apparent upside-down way of thinking. This is especially applicable to end productions of limited size, where development becomes the major cost item. The more powerful and useful the aids, the quicker (and thus lower cost) the development. Hence the importance in looking carefully at the tools available to work with before the choice of a microprocessor is made. The converse would seem to apply for high volume products where the repeatable costs are the sensitive area (e.g. component costs). But there is still some validity in choosing the development system first and let that make the choice of the microprocessor – since the cheapest microprocessor may turn out to lack adequate development aids, and the projected product may not be developed to time or to any reasonable standard. Cost savings can only be made if the tools to be worked with are of adequate professional standards.

From reading of the previous chapters, it should be possible to be in the position to say which are the important features in a development system. Debugging aids which enable the user to test a separate target system in real time and in-situ are an indispensable tool for true professional work. The in-circuit emulator is the facility offered by most of the manufacturers and it is this item which separates the MDS from being just another micro-computer that happens to have the right assemblers and compilers.

The editor is a very crucial item in the usability of the development system, and it is an item that appears to have been neglected by most suppliers. Even those who claim some advantages have not gone nearly far enough. Good and easy to use editors would encourage better documentation and make the programming facilities of the development system much more available. Closely linked with the ease of use of the development system is that of the operating system. With this, use common sense and do not be intimidated by jargon and specification, and do not accept that the method presented is the only way of achieving the ends. If a certain operation appears long winded and awkward, then it most probably is.

In the author's opinion, the operating system is a hangover from traditional computing, and need not be so imposing to the user. In fact a better approach would be to give the user the input interface of an easy-to-use and powerful screen-based editor/word processor which can transparently link into the operating system, translators, debugging aids, etc. Since virtually all user inputs are textual, it would make sense to make this interface as simple to use as possible. A good interface would encourage the use of the MDS as the central point for the collection of all work for development and help to instil good practice and documentation.

The program translators – assemblers and compilers – should be checked for the ability to produce relocatable code and the ability to link in from external modules or routines which may have been generated, assembled or compiled elsewhere. A very useful feature of compilers is the ability to give an optional listing incorporating the assembler mnemonics of the actual machine code generated. However the ultimate speed of assembly or compilation is not that vital, as long as they are not too slow. A quick and convenient translator, however, will encourage its more frequent use for any program changes instead of the all too common patching.

The actual capacity of the MDS again is not crucial, other than to ensure that the size will support all the envisaged facilities and that the storage is adequate for all the development work including the copious documentation. Expansion is a desirable feature so that future additions may be easily made. Similarly any underestimations made at the selection stage can be rectified by the addition of more memory or disc storage. Closely linked in with expansibility is the bus structure of the MDS, which is a good guide to the flexibility of the architecture of the system. For example there are MDS buses which can support multiprocessors, so that an in-circuit emulator can be supported on the system bus thus sharing the system memory and I/O lines. Other systems use a simple bus for the controlling processor, but incorporate a separate bus to support extra facilities. MDS from microprocessor manufacturers often have the same bus structure as the range of their ready-made microcomputer circuit cards. This can be a useful feature since if the cards are found suitable, they could be used as the target hardware, thus saving the bulk of the hardware development. By having the same bus, the cards can be used and tested out with the developed software in the MDS.

A couple of features which are not so visible are reliability and back-up support from the supplier. The MDS should be the focal point for the microprocessor application development; but this can only be so if it is reliable and 'trustworthy'. The MDS's correct functioning and reliability should be beyond question, since it is being used to test the correctness of an end product. However, the MDS is a very complex system, a computer in its own right with some very innovative and still relatively 'new' tools, so sometimes reality cannot meet the full requirements of the desired. Since there are complex designs, there have been some MDS which have had teething problems (some may never overcome them due to poorer design). The only way to find out about reliability is to ask current and past users of the system in question, not just the one or two. It is often useful to ask for reference sales from the suppliers and their distributors.

Similarly, the back-up service may tend to be overlooked due to its unquantifiable nature. But this oversight may not be so trivial when the MDS breaks down in the middle of a project with a tight deadline. The other aspect of this is the help and advice from the suppliers not only on the use of the MDS but also in the actual application development. Again, as for the aspect of reliability, the quality of the back-up service can only be obtained by users and reference sales.

Dedicated, universal and multiuser

MDS come in different shapes and forms. The first MDS, mainly from the microprocessor manufacturers, were the dedicated type, supporting only one microprocessor. However some of them evolved into supporting more than one (usually the manufacturer's range or family of microprocessors and single-chip microcomputers); this was usually achieved by using a more flexible (although more expensive) bus structure.

Universal MDS are ones which can support several different types of microprocessors; usually depending on the stage of development, some are better catered for than others. Again the capability is achieved by the bus architecture, so a careful study has to be made to ensure, for example, that the bus is capable of supporting future introductions (e.g. a bus may be very flexible for the current 8-bit microprocessors, but may find it a struggle to incorporate the 16-bit microprocessors which are now establishing themselves). The main advantage these universal MDS can claim is that one does not have to be tied to one microprocessor or range from one manufacturer.

Certainly if more than one type of microprocessor is used frequently, the economics are in favour of this type rather than several different dedicated MDS. But chopping and changing microprocessors is inadvisable as this entails new learning curves for each different microprocessor used, and there are not enough differences between microprocessors of the same word size to get sufficient advantage to justify a change. If a change of microprocessors is justified at least the universal MDS can make the learning curve less steep, as the way of operating the universal MDS would be the same. Bear in mind, though, that if more than one microprocessor is used and developments overlap, there will be contention for the use of the MDS, and the change from supporting one microprocessor to a different one on a universal MDS may not be straightforward and may involve extensive hardware changes, making sharing the MDS cumbersome and inconvenient. In this case, one may be better off with two separate MDS.

Multiuser MDS try to overcome this last disadvantage. As the name implies, this type of MDS can have more than one user on at the same time. This obviously eliminates the problem of sharing a single user MDS (as long as the configuration chosen has as many workstations as there are users). But the overhead is the cost of this type of system if only a few users are envisaged, as the software support in terms of the much more complex operating system and communications will be expensive. Multiuser systems will allow easier file sharing and encourage the use of the system as the central point for development work. There are some who would claim that multiuser systems are a retrograde step adding complexity overheads and line delays and problems, unnecessarily, to the more simple one user system. Perhaps the ideal solution is the MDS which is capable of working alone and/or linked to other similar MDS or a central resource system (e.g. larger, faster discs and a faster more expensive printer).

However, the important point to bear in mind from these discussions is the choice between dedicated, universal and multiuser systems is hinged mainly on economics, and not the more crucial characteristic of whether as a development tool it is adequate and has the right features, as previously discussed.

CHECKLIST

	DEVELOPMENT SYSTEMS				
FACILITIES					
MINIMUM USER'S EXTERNAL HARDWARE					
MEMORY SUBSTITUTION TOTAL BLOCKS MAPPED?					
I/O MAPPED?					
BREAKPOINTS					
CONDITIONALS					
TRACE RECORDED HISTORY WINDOW?					
REPRESENTATION SYMBOLIC ADDRESSING?					
OTHER CONSIDERATIONS BUS TYPE					
COMMENTS					

Fig. 4.4 Emulation checklist

Checklists

In choosing the right MDS a simple list could be drawn up of the important features to be looked for. These should be ranked in order of importance and several separate tries should be made at this task to ensure that the essential facilities are clearly identified from the desirable (but nonessential) features. The items then can be further analysed and sometimes broken down into specifications. It is very important however to have clear in one's mind what are the really important features so that emphasis is not placed on the wrong or irrelevant items, even though there may be more available specifications, facts and figures about them. An example of a checklist for in-circuit emulators is given in fig. 4.4, which should be regarded only as a guide and users should formulate their own criteria and justifications for their own checklists.

Summary

The chapter has outlined and identified such important features in an MDS as the debugging and testing aids, in particular the in-circuit emulator. The ease of use of the system was also emphasised to encourage the use of the MDS as the central focal point for development work. It was also pointed out that current MDS do not supply the need for tools to aid in the design phase of development. Also for documentation the MDS are again ill-equipped to help (e.g. having poor editors).

A choice of a development system is dependent on the criteria of the user and only the user can adequately supply this. By studying the discussions in this book the readers can agree or disagree and form an opinion. Using that as a guideline, checklists should be drawn up for the salient features, and re-examined carefully for their validity. Care should be taken to distinguish between essential and desirable features, and not to be seduced by specifications which may not be relevant or significant. Lastly, the less quantifiable aspects of reliability and supplier support should not be overlooked.

CHAPTER 5

The Approaches to the Provision of Tools

Having examined the microprocessor application development cycle and identified the facilities intended for the critical stages, this chapter discusses the approaches taken in providing the necessary tools in a microprocessor development system. The discussions have been given over to three major manufacturers who appear to have very different offerings for the same common objectives.

The contributions

The three contributions were chosen to highlight the major different development systems. Intel (Willy Conings) can claim to be the first to produce a MDS in the general form as we know it today. The Intel MDS have been through at least two generations, but have retained the same bus structure (the Multibus) which shows the foresight in the original design. They were also the inventors of the in-circuit emulator as a real-time real environment debugging tool. Certainly for many, the Intel MDS were the standards to judge by. Intel have until recently stuck to the single user dedicated type of MDS. Although classified by many as a single microprocessor support development system, the Intel MDS in fact can support all the microprocessors and single-chip microcomputers produced by them.

Motorola (Jack Kister) are, along with Intel, also major microprocessor manufacturers. For their development system which supports their latest 16-bit microprocessor, the MC68000, they have moved radically from their previous 8-bit support (6800) MDS. The EXORmacs development system is different in that it is designed as a multiuser system. It also uses two separate buses for the system processor and the development peripherals. Change from the 8-bit support system was necessitated by the more powerful nature and added complexity of the new 16-bit 68000. Motorola now offer more flexible and expansible buses than the previous simple development systems.

Hewlett-Packard (Sam Lee) are well known test instrument and computer system manufacturers. Their HP64000 MDS can be regarded as an independent MDS (although Hewlett-Packard do produce their own microprocessor but this is for their own use). The 64000 is a multi-user universal development system which achieves this by distributed processing that gives a high degree of multitasking/processing (i.e. processes can run independently and simultaneously). Hewlett-Packard's use of large capacity hard disc systems allows them to provide many facilities not as feasible on systems based only on floppy discs.

THE APPROACHES TO THE PROVISION OF TOOLS I
By W.E.S. Conings (Intel International)

Right from the beginning of the microprocessor era, Intel has acknowledged the need for specialised tools for the designers who choose to replace their hardwired applications by programmable microprocessor systems.

The traditional instrumentation builders were introducing the logic state analysers at about the same time Intel introduced the microprocessor. During the first years of this new era, microprocessors were considered as a low cost replacement for TTL hardware and designers tried to continue using the same tools as before, such as oscilloscopes and logic state analysers.

Meanwhile a few things were happening: the available hardware became more sophisticated with higher performance and designers became aware that not only was it possible to reduce the cost of their system by using this new technology but that they could tremendously boost its capabilities without adding extra cost. The software by then became an integral part of the application and grew both in size and complexity. As a result, the nature of the development environment also changed dramatically. If the first applications, done by microcomputers, were probably coded using machine language, the added complexity now called for assemblers and even high-level languages. Advances in related fields made it economically feasible to add peripherals such as printers and rotating mass storage devices to a system built around a microprocessor chip.

At this point Intel made a radical departure from the conventional design philosophy by providing a complete hardware and software development environment embodied for the first time in the 8080-based Intellec 800* microcomputer development system.

This system used the ISIS II floppy disc operating system for file handling and provided the user with editing capabilities, a macro assembler for the 8080 and PL/M-80, the high-level system-implementation language that even today remains unbeaten for its combination of flexibility and power.

The Multibus protocol and hardware interface was adopted for interconnection of the boards in the system. The Multibus standard was developed ealier for the iSBC80/10, the first of a complete line of single-board computers. Although designed for the 8-bit microprocessors of those days, all the provisions were made for supporting future 16-bit systems. Over the years, Multibus became a *de facto* standard for microcomputer hardware. (Multibus is now an IEEE proposed bus standard for 8- and 16-bit systems.) Part of its ever-growing success is probably due to the built-in possibilities for performance upgrades.

Choosing the Multibus allowed Intel to move swiftly towards more complex systems by adding standard iSBC boards like double-density disc controllers and hard disc controllers. It was easy for Intel to predict the need for more powerful development tools as they were the driving force behind many of the new microprocessor technologies.

---

*Intellec, Intel, Multibus, Credit and a combination of ICE, RMX and iSBC with a numerical suffix are trade marks of Intel Corporation.
Ethernet is a trade mark of Xerox Corporation.

The most important breakthrough, though, was the introduction of the ICE-80 in-circuit emulator, the tool that was designed to complete the development system. Throughout the years Intel remained faithful to the concept that was built into this very first stand-alone development system: to provide total solutions.

Although the development system hardware and software have gone through many changes and improvements, some of the early owners of this system are still using it for solving today's problems. This illustrates the second objective that we had in mind, right from the start: upgradability for higher performance at the lowest cost.

Development cycle

In order to understand why things were done in a certain way, throughout the text we will be looking at a typical development cycle for a microprocesor-based application. We will break the big problem down into smaller pieces and try to define the particular needs for solving each subproblem most efficiently, and then discuss the functions and utilities that were implemented in the Intel development systems that solve that particular problem. It is hoped that this approach will give the reader an idea about the reasons behind the architecture of the Intel development systems.

In order to understand why making a development system is not a trivial task, it is necessary to understand the mechanics of the development cycle for a microcomputer-based application. Fig. 5.1 illustrates this cycle. There are three distinct parts in every microprocessor-based design: writing the software, making the supporting hardware and finally integrating both into one fully functional product. Without special tools, one will typically start designing the hardware and when this is more or less functional, the software can be written. Finally both parts can be integrated.

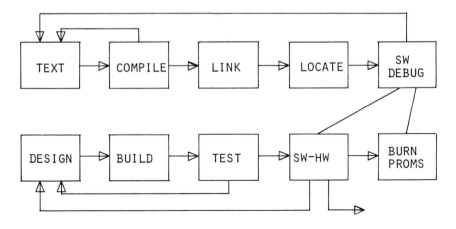

Fig. 5.1 Overview of the design cycle of a microprocessor-based application

Even using a systematic approach, one can never be sure that this integrating phase will give the correct results. Probably, many iterations will be necessary for both the hardware and the software. In today's world, the importance of the software in terms of man-hours is increasing, so that some manufacturers claim that it takes them about ten times longer writing the software than making the hardware.

If one relies upon the finished programs for testing the circuit in real working conditions, obviously the manufacturing of the hardware cannot be overlaid with the design cycle. We are convinced that it is beneficial to the user to develop and test both his hardware and his software concurrently. In order to see how this approach is built into the Intellec development system strategy, let us have a look first at the software development process.

Fig. 5.2 gives a schematic overview of how a software engineer spends his time during the process of generating the code for his application. One can see that the text input (or editing) and the debug phase are the big time consumers. If we want to make the whole process faster and more efficient, these are the two candidates for improvement.

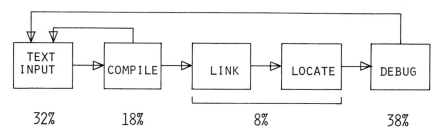

Fig. 5.2 Breakdown of time spent at the various stages of the development cycle

Editor

Credit, which is Intel's CRT-oriented text editor system, attacks (and solves!) the text input problem. It is a powerful editor package that can be used in two ways: screen mode and command mode. The command mode is basically similar to other more conventional editors, but with a macro processor added to it. This allows the user to alter text or files via the keyboard or by means of macro-commands stored on file.

A few of the possibilities are MOVEing or COPYing blocks of text, MERGE existing texts to avoid writing duplicate text, WRITE text to a line printer, READ text from files and FIND and SUBSTITUTE strings to correct errors. The importance cannot be overstressed. It can save the programmer an enormous amount of time if during debug he wants to alter parameters or expressions that occur several times in his program, especially if the programs are large.

The screen mode allows the programmer to work interactively. This mode is particularly useful for centering text or correcting single errors during program debug, because the context is fully visible and accessible via a moveable cursor and there is the possibility of unlimited scrolling up and down through the file, without ever leaving the interactive mode.

The translation, linking and relocation phases do not determine the overall speed of the development cycle if one is only looking at their raw speed. But providing the right capabilities for these utilities can dramatically decrease the total design time.

We approach this problem at three levels:

● translators
● linking
● locating

Translators

Assembly language, PL/M, FORTRAN, BASIC and PASCAL are all supported by the Intellec Series II and Series III development systems. The format of the generated object modules is the same for all our compilers. This is particularly useful if the user-application can be coded more efficiently in two or more languages instead of one. For example, a controller part is best coded in PL/M and mathematical routines can be done more easily in FORTRAN; both parts are compiled separately and the two modules linked afterwards.

This feature increases the programmer's throughput by giving him a high degree of freedom in choosing the most appropriate language with a granularity at the module level rather than at the program level.

The concept of modularity is the backbone of Intel's software strategy. It is an incentive for good programming practice, using a top-down block-structured design. It is generally accepted that this approach reduces the likelihood of error in the software development process. Modularity also supports the mechanism for coding the isolated building blocks, or tasks, in a real-time multitasking environment like RMX/80, RMX/88 or RMX/86.

Debug option

Equally important is the Debug option that is available on all Intel translators. Specifying Debug in the parameter list for the compile command, directs the compilers to create additional symbol tables that are carried along throughout the complete translate, link and locate cycle. The tables allow the user, when debugging his system, using ICE tools, to refer to program labels, symbols or line numbers in the command lines or command macros that trigger the ICE hardware. (The reader who wants to find out more about this important aspect of high-level capabilities of in-circuit emulation can refer to chapter 7 for detailed information.) This feature does considerably reduce the likelihood of error in the development process, speeds it up and provides the foundations for subsequent production testing.

Throughout the development cycle several iterations of the type compile-debug-correct are needed. This situation is not exceptional, but rather, the rule. For debugging purposes, the design engineer will probably create a sequence of command lines or command macros. This command sequence will go through the same number of iterations and become as trustworthy as the application program itself. It can be saved on a disc file and be used over and over again. This common file can then also be used in the final production environment and quality assurance testing.

For example, one can write:

GO FROM .START TILL .END EXECUTED

Here START and END are labels that were defined in the source program. There is no need for changing this command-line during the debug process, even if 50 lines of code were inserted in between. An alternative would be to use a command like:

GO FROM A00H TILL B05H

The absolute addresses used in this example need to be updated every time a change is made to the source program. Having the possibility of using symbolic references to variables and labels gives the programmer a high degree of listing independence. A given routine will probably always start at START and end at END. But the latest printout of the compiled and located routine is needed to know if it starts today at address A00H and not at AFFH as yesterday.

The synergy between the high-level symbolic debugging capabilities of the in-circuit emulator and the possibility of constructing and storing intricate command sequences allows the programmer to build a permanent test program that can be ported to the manufacturing or testing floors.

Linking and locating

To reduce the effort of managing software, modular programming is essential. Today's applications are becoming so big that the coding task for an application program must be shared between many programmers. If this is done properly, the advantages are obvious: the workload is shared between the available programmers and the program size is reduced to dimensions that are still fully understandable and manageable by the human. The linker will take care to connect all the independently written and translated modules.

For a simple explanation of linkers and loaders see chapter 4, page 26.

Modules and terminology

Let us spend some time in trying to elucidate the meaning of 'module' and 'linking' and also introduce and explain concepts like 'public' and 'external' declarations.

The most easily understandable definition of a module is: a self-contained block of language statements not nested within another block. A module can be compiled and the result from compilation can be linked with other modules, and is thus the basic building block for a program. A module also determines the scope of variables. In other words, variables are only known inside a module.

If one wishes to refer to variables or procedures not contained in the same module, some mechanism must be created to support this intermodule passing of parameters. Declaring a variable or a procedure public makes it accessible outside the containing module. In the same way, declaring a variable or procedure external, makes it possible to refer to it even if it is not contained within the module. The process that we call linking then consists of merging the code of two or more modules and above all of trying to match the external and public references.

Again, the performance of the linker is not determined solely by its processing speed, but by the numerous facilities that are included. Two main classes should be considered here. As we already mentioned, the most important one is certainly the ability of the linking program to carry through to the next stages in the development cycle the debug information and the high-level language symbol tables that were created during the translation phase. It is the linker's responsibility to check that the conventions for passing parameters from one module to the next are being respected by the programmers. Errors are detected and reported but the linking process is not automatically aborted. This gives the 'ace programmer' the possibility to override the stringent rules, if needed, for producing 'tricky code'.

Linking library routines
The next class of features provided by the linking program are those that allow the easy management of code. In today's environment one should be able to re-use, as much as possible, the software that was created previously. A library utility provided with the ISIS II operating system supports the creation and management of library files. A library file typically contains a set of translated and unlinked object modules that are logically interrelated in one way or another, e.g. a library file called MATH.LIB could contain FLOAT.ADD, FLOAT.SUB, FLOAT.MUL, FLOAT.DIV, i.e. modules that perform floating-point operations. Obviously, once developed and tested, modules like these will be used over and over again in future products.

The command format for the invocation of the linker allows the programmer to specify a library name. If a module in that particular file needs to be linked to the other modules, the linker will scan the library directory and link only the needed one to the rest of the new code. As an example, SYS.LIB is a library file that comes with ISIS II. It contains routines that access the hardware drivers of the Intellec development system.

As long as no target hardware is available for the user application, the designer can use the system routines such as CI (console input) or CO (console output) for testing the code. This is done by calling CI or CO in the program and specifying SYS.LIB during the link phase. When the target hardware becomes available the library, USER.LIB, that will now contain the CI and CO routines can be created. If these user routines were tested previously, no new errors will be introduced by the change from development system to user environment.

One can take two approaches to performing the linking process. In the first approach, all the modules are linked in one operation. This will be done if the modules are known to be correct and the interaction between modules has been tested. The new module produced by the linker has the same internal and external structure as any module produced by a translator. This is illustrated by fig. 5.3.

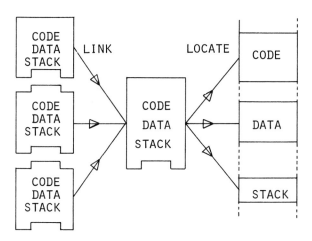

Fig. 5.3 Link and locate support modular programming

Incremental link

This characteristic of the output module brings us logically to the second way of linking: incremental linking. This means that a number of modules can be linked and the produced composite module can be treated as a simple one, i.e. it can again be processed by the linker.

This approach is particularly useful if the application is large and thus broken down in a large number of modules. Not only must each part be tested separately but the interactions between the modules must be checked as well. Experienced programmers know the value of testing one piece of code by replacing another part by dummy procedures that are simple enough to be correct beyond any doubt. This process can go through several iterations before all of the code is tested. For the attentive reader it will be clear that incremental linking implements this approach in a clean and orderly way.

An example will explain this (see fig. 5.4). Let us assume that MOD1.OBJ, MOD2.OBJ and MOD3.OBJ need to be tested and afterwards linked. MOD1.OBJ, MOD2.OBJ and MOD3.OBJ will each be linked with an appropriate dummy module for exercising their code. The next step consists of linking the tested MOD1.OBJ and MOD2.OBJ, producing a new entity MOD1.LNK. This can again be linked with a dummy module to be exercised. Linking the tested MOD1.LNK with MOD3.OBJ produces MOD2.LNK that is tested with a dummy routine. This sequence can be continued until all the modules are tested and linked together.

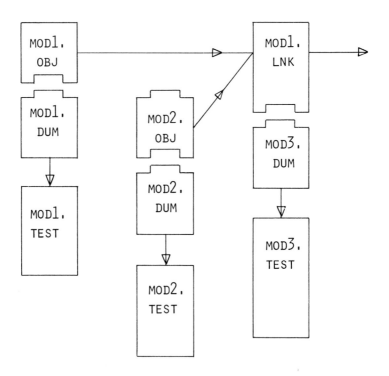

Fig. 5.4 Incremental linking supports modular testing

As has been shown earlier, specifying PUBLIC and EXTERNAL in the source code for variables, procedures and procedure calls is the mechanism that supports intermodule references. During the normal link operation the PUBLICS and EXTERNALS are resolved and the code is combined into one output module. By specifying PUBLICS, followed by a list of module names in the command line for the linker, the absolute public references are included in the output file, but the code from the specified modules is not combined. The different modules can thus be loaded separately. This mechanism supports the creation of overlay structures.

The linker produces upon request a detailed link map. The information present can be used to direct the ulterior locate phase to construct even the most intricate memory topology. To locate the linked module is the last step before the program can be run and tested. Apart from its specific function, i.e. fitting the code and data into the available memory space, it performs many of the functions that were discussed for the link utility: passing debug information to the output module for later use by the debugging tools and providing the programmer with detailed information in the locate map.

Debugging stage

As one can see from the previous discussion, our design efforts were aimed at providing flexibility and power to every part of the development system software and reducing the effort of managing large amounts of software. Though we think that every part is important in its own right, the real power becomes fully apparent at the system level where they work all together in an orderly way. All the preparative work done during translation, linking and locating was aimed at one goal: producing executable code that must be evaluated for correctness and eventually go through one or more translate-debug cycles. As has been shown previously, the debug stage is the most time consuming of all. All the effort that we put into the definition and the design of our translators, linkers and locators was aimed at optimising the debug step by making it easier and less subject to human error.

In-circuit emulation

Generally, in-circuit emulation is considered to be a hardware debugging tool. This perception of in-circuit emulation tools is certainly true but incomplete. The Intel in-circuit emulators (ICE) are capable of replacing the user's hardware. Memory, parallel I/O ports and communication channels can be borrowed from the host development system by means of the ICE hardware and firmware. In many cases a crystal for timing generation and a socket for the ICE probe is the only hardware needed. If the user hardware is very specialised, such that a direct replacement by the development system resources is not done easily, it can be simulated via software or by the ICE firmware. Again, an example will explain this best.

Taking the software simulation first, suppose that the hardware to be simulated consists of an angular encoder on a rotating shaft. This hardware can definitely not be borrowed from the development system. In the finished application program, there will certainly be a procedure that inputs the data from the encoder, converts the input data from Gray code to binary and returns this value. If modularisation is done properly, this procedure is in a separate module. During the debug phase, this can be replaced by another module with the same interface rules, issuing simulated results upon every call. The rest of the program can be a self-contained module, stored on a disc file. It will be linked with the canned angular encoder driver and the program can be exercised. When the real hardware becomes available, the real driver is written and tested with the appropriate tools and then linked to the rest of the program in the same way as discussed previously in the text on linking. Remember that the risk involved is minimal when going from one environment to the other, using the correct approach. The other possibility consists of replacing the hardware and driver by a sequence of ICE commands or ICE macros. This approach does not use all of the linking utilities as did the previous one. But by using ICE features, the completely finished program can be tested instead.

Let us try to solve the problem of the previous example again with this new approach. The code, including the driver for the missing hardware could look like this:

```
START:      statement 1
               .
               .
END1:          .
INPUT:      IN AL, BYTE__PORT
RESTART:    statement n
               .
               .
               .

END:        statement
```

The data acquisition operation at address INPUT cannot execute properly because the specialised hardware is not present yet. We will define an ICE macro that will start the execution of code at address START and stop before the input operation. We will then simulate the input by forcing a value in the AL register and resume execution from RESTART till the end. In simulating the input operation we want to pass the value of the input to the program as a parameter in the macro invocation.

```
DEF MAC TEST
GO FROM .START TILL .END1 EXECUTED
RAL = %0
GO FROM .RESTART TILL .END EXECUTED
EM
```

Once the macro is defined it can be invoked by typing simply:

```
:TEST  0AH
```

The simulated input will force the value 0AH into the input port BYTE__PORT.

After this brief overview of the software development cycle we want to go through the same exercise for the hardware design and try to understand what the Intellec Series II and Series III development systems can offer to the designer in that respect. Fig. 5.3 shows the typical hardware design cycle. We should keep in mind that the hardware that we are discussing is microprocessor-based and thus we need software in order to make it run.

The design and build phase do not differ from any other electronic design. It is really the test phase that is more difficult here. As has been already mentioned, a successful design requires concurrent development of hardware and software in order to minimise the time between the idea and the finished product. This implies that the hardware must be tested without the driving software.

In other words, the test phase needs specialised tools. We can draw a parallel here with the software design, where lacking hardware was substituted with development system resources. We can take the same approach and substitute system software for the missing application software. In-circuit emulation is once more the answer.

The approach taken here relies again very heavily on the existence of storable ICE command sequences and ICE macros. The basic mechanism is similar to the one that we discussed earlier while talking about ICE macros in the software-testing context. A detailed description of the available commands is given elsewhere in this book.

System architecture

The hardware of the development system supports a split architecture. One part is built around the Multibus and the other has dedicated hardware for managing the basic resources of the system. The advantages of this architecture will be discussed in the next section. In order to understand the 'whys', it is necessary to consider the requirements of the ideal development system: performance and upgradeability.

Performance can be understood in terms of raw processing speed, the throughput at the system level, the ability to support efficiently peripheral devices and other development tools such as in-circuit emulators.

Upgradeability is defined as the ability of the system to evolve at the same pace as the technology of the microprocessors that must be supported by the system. Factors to be considered here are memory size, speed, execution environment, peripheral devices, etc.

Due to the special nature of the development environment, having a single processor system would be highly disadvantageous. If the CPU manages system resources such as keyboard scanning, screen refresh and I/O processes while running application programs, the real-time performance would degrade considerably. These I/O processes are taken care of by an attached 8080 CPU and two 8741 universal peripheral interface slave-processors. As a result, the main CPU runs at full speed and is completely dedicated to the user application.

Throughout the complete range of development systems, some common hardware exists. It is grouped together on the IOC (input output controller) board. It supports the integral CRT, the integral disc drive and the communication channels. Starting with these foundations, the user can choose the system that is best fitted to solve the problem. As a starter the user may decide to have a Series II with an 8080-based processor and

32 kbyte of memory. From here on, several routes are open for performance upgrades:

- changing processor boards: an 8085-based system will increase the processing speed and bring the memory size up to 64 kbyte of RAM
- adding processor boards: the iAPX86-based CPU boards will increase the processing speed for 16-bit applications, provide 192 kbyte of RAM and give a resident 16-bit execution environment. This system is called the Intellec Series III. Having this large memory size presents distinct advantages such as having large symbols tables in memory when running high-level language compilers such as PASCAL-86
- adding more memory: standard iSBC memory boards or stand-alone packaged memory system, Series 90, that interfaces to the Multibus and gives the user up to 1 Mbyte of random access storage for large application programs
- adding peripheral controllers: dual density floppy disc drives and hard discs are controlled by standard iSBC boards
- adding communication controllers: this turns a stand-alone workstation into a member of the NDS-1 network development system.

Distributed processing
NDS-1 is Intel's latest addition to its high end development systems. Up to eight existing stand-alone development workstations can be connected to the network. Once logged on they become part of the distributive processing network and can share central resources such as hard discs and a central high-speed printer (see fig. 5.5).

The NDS-1 answers the need created by today's ever-growing software projects by its ability to allow users to share files that reside centrally. The problem that we have to solve here is the efficient management of large software projects. Modularity has proven to be the correct methodology to reduce the proneness to error of these programs. But even if it is applied properly, it may create a communication problem. The file sharing mechanism of the NDS-1 addresses this and implements a protection scheme at the same time. Files can be made public by their creator or they can be held private to prevent accidental or malicious modification.

In some cases the dimensions of the project may justify taking advantage of an inhouse mainframe to manage the software. The individual workstations or the members of the network can be connected to the mainframe via a mainframe link. In the context of this configuration, text entry, daily updating and file back-up can be done on the mainframe. The workstation will be used as a remote translation box and debug station for in-circuit emulation.

Basing the development system on the Multibus and industry-standard processors like the 8085 and iAPX86 has another interesting side effect. Unlike other development systems, the Series II and Series III can run user-supplied software such as compilers that can be developed inhouse for a very special application.

Futures

The future direction for development systems will be dictated by the development in microprocessor technology. Two important paths are already visible. The program size will grow as the newer processors can address memory sizes in the megabyte range and at the same time microprocessing will be used to increase the throughput and the fault tolerance of the application.

Development systems will reflect this by providing the means for supporting large programs. NDS-1 is only the beginning. It will be upgraded to NDS-2 to support the emerging local network protocol Ethernet. The number of workstations that can be logged on will also increase.

New tools will also be added to support multiple processors. Today's MultiICE tools already point to the direction that will be taken: multiple in-circuit emulators will run in parallel and more hardware functions will be added to the basic emulator.

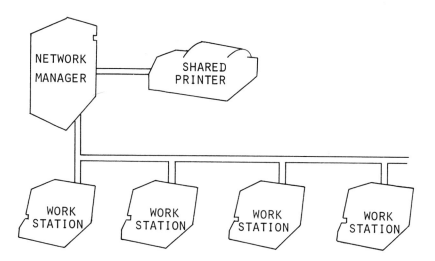

Fig. 5.5 NDS-1 – the entry in the distributed processing development arena

THE APPROACHES TO THE PROVISION OF TOOLS II
By Jack Kister (Motorola Inc.)

The EXORmacs is a state-of-the-art development system for designing and developing advanced 16-bit microprocessor based systems using Motorola families of microprocessors, microcomputers and peripheral parts. It is also ideally suited for developing applications using the VERSAmodule family of 16-bit board level application products and accessories.

Designed for flexibility and ease of use, EXORmacs takes advantage of the power and features of the MC68000 microprocessor unit (MPU). It reduces cost and development time by incorporating features which support 16-bit and future 32-bit microprocessor designs, as well as providing high-level language support through PASCAL. With additional terminals and a multiple-channel communications module, up to eight users may simultaneously develop 68000 programs.

As a family of building blocks, EXORmacs' capability ranges from the minimum requirements of single-user design up to multiuser hardware and software development system (see fig. 5.6). It will support a wide range of microprocessors from existing 8-bit processors to future advanced 32-bit processors.

EXORmacs architecture

For a development system to adequately support new generation processors, the architecture of the system must provide the insight of present microcomputers as well as microcomponents of the future. As silicon densities increase to 100 000 transistors per chip the design time from conception to working silicon will approach eighteen to twenty-four months. A support system for new silicon chips must also be developed. While this development cycle overlaps chip design six months after working silicon is usually required to complete the product. At this point earnest design by the user may begin. A typical design cycle consumes six to twelve months which means the cycle from silicon conception to user product introduction can be over three years.

Systems with an insight to future silicon can cut down this design cycle by providing hardware emulations and software simulators of future silicon. Motorola first started this advanced support philosophy in the EXORcisor by providing a hardware simulator for the 6809 microprocessor instruction set and 6805 microcomputer instruction set. In addition, software simulators were available in advance of silicon for the 6800 and 68000 microprocessors. These simulators are written in FORTRAN and are available to run on most 16- and 32-bit computers.

Motorola'a new development system, EXORmacs, was designed with a knowledge of future silicon. This knowledge has allowed EXORmacs to contain very good emulations of future NMOS chips that will be introduced by Motorola. In some chips, physical limitations would only allow a subset of the chip to be simulated. This feature of EXORmacs will provide users with the ability to examine the concepts and features of new chips before they are available. In addition, a model of the user's system may be easily built using prebuilt EXORmacs modules so that software development may commence well in advance. The advantage of predevelopment is a quicker utilisation of advanced semiconductors which gives users a price/ performance advantage over their competition.

Fig. 5.6 The EXORmacs development system

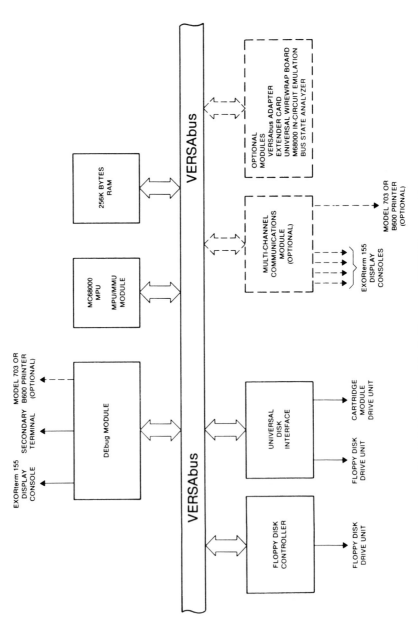

Fig. 5.7 Functional block diagram of EXORmacs system

Memory management

The central intelligence of the EXORmacs is provided by the 68000 MPU/MMU module which also contains a four segment memory management unit and diagnostic firmware. The memory management unit provides the multitasking operating system protection from user programs and helps in allocating memory to each task. The real-time multitasking operating system helps speed program development by allowing tasks to be run concurrently. An example of this advantage is an assembly which may be in progress which requires the printer, but leaves the display console free for editing other modules, or several programmers may want to develop programs at the same time.

In this environment, it is necessary to protect the operating system from the software failures which naturally occur in a development system environment. A common problem which can occur is an error in the understanding of an address, such as an array subscript being too large or too small. These kinds of problems can accidently change operating system code, device tables or actually cause a device to perform an undesired function. To prevent these kinds of problems it is important to provide protection for the operating system and other system users.

In EXORmacs, this protection is provided by the memory management unit. This unit is not used to expand the amount of memory available, like the memory management units of minicomputers, but rather to enhance the usefulness of memory and ease the creation and execution of programs. In addition to protecting the operating system from inadvertent tampering, the memory management unit also provides automatic program relocation. Through the memory management unit, memory accesses by user's programs are translated from a logical or program address to a physical or hardware address. These physical addresses may be located at a completely different place in the memory than the logical address would imply. By translating the address of user programs, the operating system and protected I/O can be removed completely from the address of the user. Any attempt to read or write to memory outside of the user's assigned address space causes the processor to abort the user's program.

Through the process of address translation, the memory management unit provides another very important function. Since the physical location in the memory of a user's program is not related to the program's internal addresses, all user programs may be placed anywhere in physical memory regardless of their program origin. This allows the operating system to use all of the memory without the need to relocate programs as they are loaded. Tasks executed under control of the operating system may be moved or placed anywhere there is space available.

Physically the EXORmacs memory management unit has four segments each of which may represent up to 65 536 pages of 256 byte each (see fig. 5.7). These segments each contain a beginning and ending address register, a physical offset register and a control register (see fig. 5.8). When a program executing in the user mode performs a memory access, the address generated by the processor is compared to the beginning and ending address of each segment. If the processor address falls between the beginning and ending address register, then the address is added to the physical offset register to obtain the two's complement result which is the physical bus address. Within the control register, segments may be designated read only or disabled. Any attempt to write to a protected segment, or if two or more segments are selected simultaneously, will result in bus error being flagged and the cycle terminated. Memory accesses performed in the supervisor mode bypass the memory management unit. Processor addresses in this mode are sent directly to the bus without translation. The supervisor mode is reserved for a small portion of the operating system which allocates memory.

MEMORY MANAGEMENT

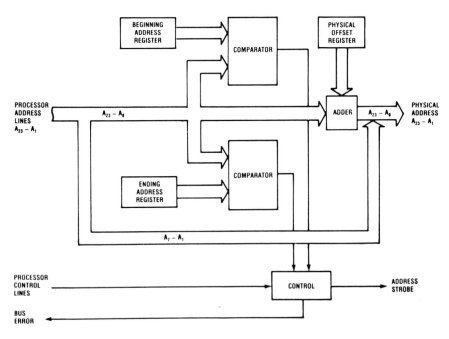

Fig. 5.8 One of the four units contained within the memory management unit (MMU) of EXORmacs

Intelligent peripheral controllers

EXORmacs enhances the processing power of the MC68000 by providing overlapped computation and I/O (see fig. 5.9). The intelligent peripheral controller (IPC) is a self-contained I/O controller which processes macro I/O commands. These macro commands are passed from the 68000 to the

IPC via 128 byte of shared memory. Once the command is issued, the IPC will manage all the I/O device mechanics. When an I/O transfer is complete, the IPC will interrupt the 68000 and pass back status information in the shared memory. An example of IPC operation in EXORmacs is the hard disc controller. To do disc I/O, the 68000 commands the disc IPC to transfer specified sectors from the disc and place them into a specified memory segment. The IPC will step the disc head to the required track and initialise the onboard DMA controller. As the data is read from the disc the IPC checks the CRC and DMAs the data into memory. If any errors occur, the IPC will retry the transfer until it is correct or determined to be invalid. When a successful transfer is complete, the status of the transfer is placed in the shared memory and an interrupt is generated.

The advantage of the IPC is that it improves system performance by providing overlapped computation and I/O operations. It also provides device independent I/O to the operating system because the IPC contains all the device dependent software. This means that the operating system can treat all types of I/O (i.e. serial communication, hard disc, floppy disc, etc.) in the same fashion. The IPC also performs diagnostic and error logging on the I/O device during power up and normal operation.

INTELLIGENT PERIPHERAL CONTROLLER

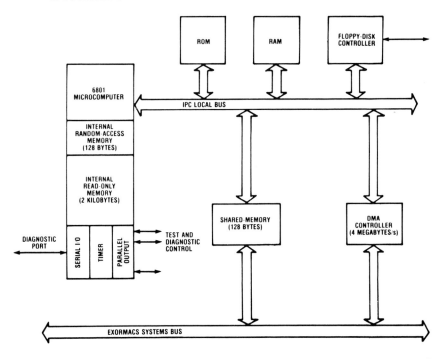

Fig. 5.9 Intelligent peripheral control which provides device-independent I/O and overlapped computation and I/O control

Multiprocessing support

A closely associated topic to peripheral processing is the development of multi-processor systems. As we go into the eighties, the understanding and use of microprocessor systems will become more common. To provide for the creation of a microprocessor system within EXORmacs, it was necessary to provide for a fast and powerful bus arbitration scheme. In designing the bus it was determined that memory transfers could be done most efficiently by block transfers. This avoids the problems of excessive overhead for arbitrating each cycle. To compliment this philosophy, a simple arbitration scheme using bus requests and chained bus grants was used, similar to that in the 68000. Arbitration is performed within the development system on a highest priority basis, unlike many schemes which use a first request algorithm. This is done by delaying the issue of a bus grant until the last cycle of the current bus master. In this way devices of the highest priority are serviced before devices of lower priority, regardless of the device that first requested the bus.

Individual devices may also dynamically increase their priority by asserting higher priority bus requests if the occasion requires, as in the case of a pending data late error on a disc drive. The arbiter also generates a signal called bus clear to indicate to devices on the bus that a higher priority device needs servicing. Because a development system is used to test unproven hardware it is sometimes necessary to interrupt the system to regain control. Even in a nondevelopment environment, certain events, such as a power failure, can require the immediate attention of the system. To provide for such necessities, a line called bus release can be asserted by a device commanding all bus masters to relinquish the bus and turn control over to the host processor. This will allow the host processor to service pending interrupts regardless of the priorities of other pending bus masters.

Looking forward to the future, one of the most difficult tasks will be to apply the knowledge we have learned from the past. It was not so long ago that we asked ourselves who would ever use up all the address space of those 8-bit microprocessors? In 1973 many designs used 1k dynamic memories. Now, 64k dynamic memories are the predominant bulk memory part. Certainly microprocessor systems of the future will grow correspondingly. Not just 64 kbyte or 128 kbyte, but Mbyte memories will be common. With 256k memories, a megabyte memory will require only forty-four memory chips with error correction on 16-bit words. In anticipation of the future with multi-megabyte memory cards, the 68000 development system has reserved eight additional address lines and 16 additional data lines for possible future expansion. This would bring the possible memory size to 4 Gbytes, which is larger than any anticipated need during the next decade.

Test and diagnostics

With such a large and sophisticated system, the ability to test and verify its operation automatically has become very important. This is especially true for a development tool where the hardware and software being developed have not been thoroughly debugged. To provide for testability, the system has been designed to perform a complete self-test. Upon power-up, the processor, bus, memory and I/O channels are functionally tested and their status displayed on the front panel. In the case of an error, a status condition is shown on the front panel and the processor is forced into a diagnostic monitor which may be used by the user or field service personnel. If the processor board or an I/O channel functionally fail the test, a lamp is lit on the faulty board, indicating the failure status.

The I/O channels, or intelligent peripheral controllers, use an onboard 6801 microcomputer for performing test and diagnostics. By using a microcomputer with complete internal ROM, RAM and I/O, the ability to diagnose faults can be retained with a minimum of parts. Besides the power-up functional test, the IPC is capable of device-level fault isolation. This function is provided through the serial and parallel I/O ports on the 6801 microcomputer. Through the serial I/O port, service personnel may attach a terminal which interfaces to a simple monitor. From the monitor, memory may be examined and changed, programs executed and breakpoints set. The monitor also provides an interface to internal signature analysis routines for device-level fault isolation. The parallel I/O ports of the processor are used for factory testing as well as in the signature analysis routines.

Software

To complement the hardware of EXORmacs, a totally new and advanced software system has been provided. This software system includes a versatile multiuser multitasking real-time operating system, a macro assembler, a PASCAL compiler and complete set of editors and debuggers. This package is supported by both disc-based software and resident firmware. The operating system and supporting software have been designed to allow expansion to a multiuser configuration using a hard surface disc.

The operating system of EXORmacs has been designed to support sophisticated multitask systems with resource sharing, intertask control and communications. Users may interface to the facilities of the operating system interactively, as batch jobs or with programs, using executive directives. The file and I/O system of EXORmacs have been designed to control through simple device-independent commands.

The macroassembler and PASCAL compilers for the 68000 provide the means to generate efficient and cost effective code for processor. The macroassembler for the 68000 includes features such as conditional assembly, complex expressions and position-independent code generation. PASCAL for the 68000 is a superset of the currently proposed standard. Calls to the executive directives, I/O routines and assembly language code have been provided to ease its use in EXORmacs. As further support to the use of high-level languages in microprocessor applications, 68000 PASCAL supports absolute addressing and interrupt handling.

The software support for EXORmacs does not end with the resident software. A set of cross software including the macroassembler, PASCAL compiler and a 68000 simulator are available on the IBM 370, PDP-11 and M6800 EXORciser. This software allows users to develop code offline and down-load programs into EXORmacs for real-time execution. EXORmacs can also be operated in a transparent mode, communicating directly to the host processor or to the EXORmacs resident firmware for online program development.

VERSAdos operating system

The heart of the EXORmacs software is the multitasking operating system. This operating system has been designed to provide support for both single or multiuser systems as well as in dedicated real-time control system environments. The operating system has been designed using a layered approach as shown in fig. 5.10. This approach allows the software to be modular and easily expansible. The software comprises a foundation or kernel which contains the basic executive, a set of executive extensions, the I/O management system and the user session management system. A complete set of user interfaces to provide for intertask communication and scheduling has been provided.

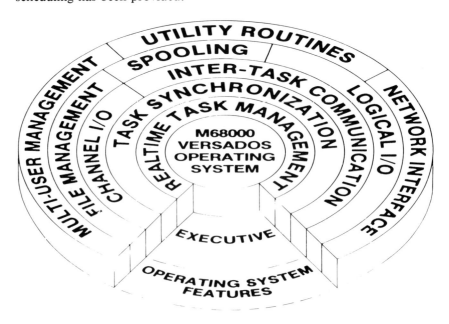

Fig. 5.10 Layers of VERSAdos

Executive
At the foundation of the operating system is the executive. The executive is the smallest unit of the operating system and has been designed to be

completely selfsufficient. Within the executive there is a task controller, an intertask communication facility, a memory management facility and an initialisation section. The executive also has the ability to load the remainder of the operating system. This feature allows the basic executive to act as a foundation for extended functions which may be added to the operating system.

Task management
The majority of the executive is called the task management system. This system is responsible for coordinating the scheduling of tasks and allocating memory. In a real-time multitasking executive, such as in EXORmacs, provisions must be made for intertask communication and dynamic task scheduling. These facilities are provided by the task management system through the use of semaphore flags, asynchronous service queues and shared memory segments. Any task within the system has the ability to affect the status of any other task through the use of executive directives. These directives can pass information, create tasks, suspend executing tasks and so on. Tasks may also be affected by interrupts, traps and scheduled events.

In addition to task management, the executive also provides the facilities to dispatch interrupts and traps. To the executive's dispatch system, users may attach their interrupts handlers; simulators, such as floating-point and string handlers; and special-service routines. To the dispatcher, the operating system's I/O management system is also attached.

I/O management
The next level above the executive and its extensions is the I/O management package. These routines execute as a system task which processes all I/O requests. When a task operating in the system wishes to perform an I/O function, the executive queues the I/O request for execution by the I/O management task. This task then verifies the request and directs the appropriate intelligent peripheral controller, or data channel, to perform the request. Upon completion of the I/O, the requesting task is resumed. The I/O management system also provides for the automatic spooling of output files. When the file has been completed, it is then despooled from the disc and printed. This allows several tasks to share the printer without delaying a task unnecessarily.

User system management
The outermost level of the executive is the user session management system. This system provides the interface between a terminal user and the operating system. Just as a task is active within the system, the user may direct and control tasks executing in the system. Through the user session management system, the user may initialise multiple concurrent batch processes and remain in an interactive mode, editing, compiling or executing user program. Each terminal may have the complete facilities normally

associated with a system console. Users may be identified as privileged or restricted according to their user identification code.

Diagnostic routines

In order to debug and maintain the EXORmacs operating system, a special set of diagnostic routines have been built in. These routines provide for on-line error detection and status indications. Errors within the executive hardware or software are detected through the extensive use of checksums and entry flags. Before the operating system enters, a routine or status indication is set on the EXORmacs front panel. If an error is detected or the processor halts due to a failure, the status can aid in diagnosing the problem.

PASCAL

PASCAL is a general-purpose user-orientated language designed to meet a wide variety of programming needs. It is a highly structured language which promotes good programming techniques and simplifies the translation of functional requirements for a microprocessor application into an operating 68000 program. PASCAL's data types express data meaningfully and its control structures permit and encourage structured thinking. The separation of data definition and algorithm expression forces logical thinking and planning. It attempts to shift the emphasis in programming development to careful design in order to reduce debugging time and achieve increased reliability.

Motorola's PASCAL includes extensions for expressing certain embedded-control type operations, an important consideration to microprocessor users. It provides a powerful software tool which can significantly reduce the time and costs associated with microprocessor software development and maintenance.

Hardware development

An example of a physically small system that requires high performance of the 68000 is a hard disc controller. Today data transferred from high speed disc drives is either transferred by DMA into memory by discrete logic or buffered into FIFOs and transferred at a slower speed by a processor. If a microprocessor is used at all, it controls handshaking, head movement, error logging and other basic functions.

However, the 68000, with the aid of an external serialiser and a minimum of external logic, is fast enough to not only control the drive but to also handle the data transfers for all but the very fastest hard disc drives.

Modelling

To develop a product of this type, a specification for the product must first be generated. Modelling of the design concept may be required to optimise the implementation method or to determine the appropriate software-hardware tradeoffs. To aid this predevelopment effort, Motorola provides a series of prebuilt development modules which contain I/O devices such as parallel interface adapters (PIA), serial communication adapters (ACIA), timers (PTM) and universal adapter modules. These modules and a VERSAbus adapter module, which contain a VERSAbus interface, may be plugged directly into EXORmacs and used. This greatly speeds the modelling time. Wire wrap space on the modules will easily allow the board to be customised.

After the modelling is complete and a system configuration has been determined, the race between hardware and software begins. Some of the software in small systems may be developed without hardware. But eventually the race ends with the software people waiting for the hardware people to complete their debug and the hardware people waiting eight to twelve weeks for PCBs to be designed and generated. Here again the use of prebuilt modules can save time by allowing program development in parallel with actual hardware development. To help make in-chassis development easier, the EXORmacs chassis is top-loading with boards inserted perpendicular to the user. This orientation provides a stable board with easy access by the user to either side for probing.

USE – User System Emulation (in-circuit emulation)

Once the user system has been created it must be connected to the development system for debug and further development. This may be done via the user system emulator, or USE module. By replacing the processor in the user's system with a plug and cable, the user's peripherals and memory are merged together (see fig. 5.11). This allows debugging of the user system by executing diagnostic software from the development system.

Resource mapping

Memory and I/O in the development system may be mapped into the target system's memory map. This allows substitution of known working I/O in the chassis for I/O not yet debugged. ROM in the target system may be emulated with RAM in EXORmacs which greatly simplifies program debugging.

EXORmacs is designed to support hardware and software development with one box. One problem which arises with this feature is that the software development hardware, such as memory and I/O, require processor address space. With 16 Mbyte of address space, it would seem that there is sufficient memory space for both the user and the system. But both the system and target programs want to control the same trap and interrupt vectors and the operating system requires protection from untried user programs and hardware. The user also wants the full capability of the processor and cannot be restricted to operating in the user mode which is required when using the memory management unit. To provide this capability, VERSAbus supports two memory maps, one for the development system (primary map) and one for the target system (secondary map).

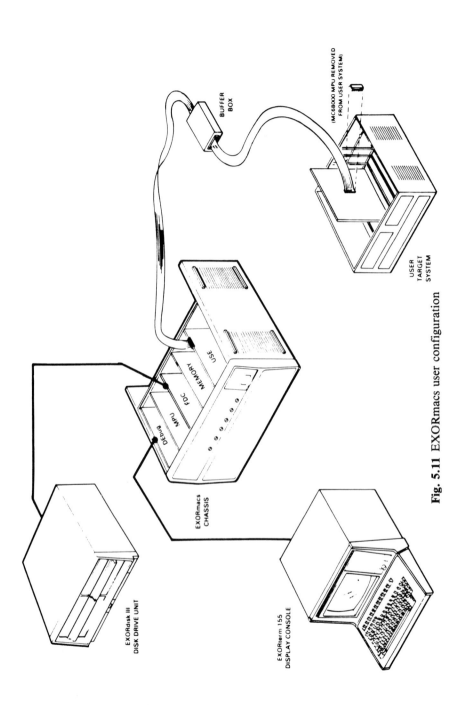

Fig. 5.11 EXORmacs user configuration

All target hardware is placed in the secondary map. When the user executes the target program EXORmacs disables the primary map hardware, enables the secondary map hardware and execution begins. Breakpoints are supported in the secondary map by substitution and illegal instruction at the breakpoint address. When this instruction is executed, the 68000 will trap to the illegal instruction vector. EXORmacs will detect this and switch the system back into the primary map for service. Tracing in the secondary map is handled in the same way but using the trace trap.

Remote hardware development

Hardware debug is typically done by making repetitive checkouts of the hardware followed by power-downs and hardware corrections. For this, EXORmacs provides a remote hardware development station. The remote station is a small box which contains an emulator, a VERSAbus and a serial connection to the EXORmacs for program loads. This allows the hardware engineer all the same capabilities found in the EXORmacs but allows the programmer to concurrently develop software.

The remote development station (RDS) is connected to the EXORmacs via a RS232 serial link. This link allows programs to be downloaded into the target system for execution and debug. The user's terminal is connected directly to the RDS for stand-alone operation. Program development on the EXORmacs can be accomplished by placing the RDS into a transparent mode. In this mode the RDS is logically connected to the EXORmacs and program development can be performed as if the terminal was directly connected to the EXORmacs.

VERSAbus EXORmacs bus system

VERSAbus is a new generation computer bus designed to serve as a comprehensive basis for microprocessor systems that are capable of supporting a wide variety of microprocessor architectures ranging from 8- to 32-bit with 5 MHz data transfer rates. It is intended to be an economical and flexible bus to serve the industrial control, communications and general-purpose business applications as well as development systems. This feature allows the development bus to be the same as the target system bus. If the two buses are the same then a lot of development time can be saved by quickly developing a system using development boards. Software may then be developed while the actual hardware is designed. When the final product is built it may be tested using the development system and bus analyser.

The VERSAbus: Just what is it?

The new bus structure is actually split between two connectors, P_1 and P_2, which contain 140 and 120 pins respectively (see fig. 5.12). The bus has been split to provide modularity in the system, since boards can come in either a full board size, which measures 9.25 in × 14.50 in or a reduced size with a 9.25 in × 8.00 in format which only uses port P_1. The basic bus breakdown, as shown in fig. 5.12, has port P_1 containing the main buses to permit a 16-bit data word, a 24-bit address range, seven levels of priority interrupt, five levels of bus arbitration, asynchronous system control, fault detection and control and the basic power buses. The secondary port, P_2, provides 50 lines for input/output interfaces, expansion for a full 32-bit bus for both data and address lines and serial communications capability.

VERSAbus

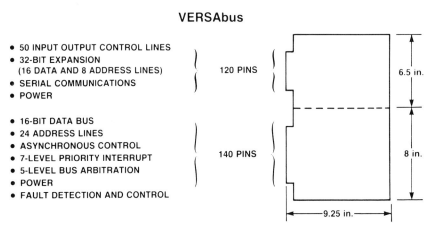

- 50 INPUT OUTPUT CONTROL LINES
- 32-BIT EXPANSION
  (16 DATA AND 8 ADDRESS LINES)
- SERIAL COMMUNICATIONS
- POWER

120 PINS

- 16-BIT DATA BUS
- 24 ADDRESS LINES
- ASYNCHRONOUS CONTROL
- 7-LEVEL PRIORITY INTERRUPT
- 5-LEVEL BUS ARBITRATION
- POWER
- FAULT DETECTION AND CONTROL

140 PINS

6.5 in.

8 in.

9.25 in.

Fig. 5.12 VERSAbus functional diagram

In addition to providing the address and data expansion capacity, connector P_2 primarily interfaces I/O signals to the backplane. There are four serial communication lines as well as the fifty I/O lines available at the connector. The I/O lines are bussed from PC card to PC card, or, can be accessed from the rear side of the backplane, each line having a corresponding ground pin. The arrangement, made possible by the physical layout of the signal pins, provides two groups of twenty-five consecutive signal pins to appear directly opposite each other on the P_2 edge connector. Each edge-connector signal pin has a corresponding ground pin mounted in the backplane on standard centres. Flat-ribbon connectors can pick up these pins on the rear of the backplane as two 25 signal-ground pairs can be used in the I/O cable without dedicating a large number of edge-connector pins to ground. One other added feature of this layout permits a similar 50-pin cable connector to interconnect all fifty I/O lines if ground lines are not used.

Both the P_1 and P_2 connectors have available supply voltages of 5, ±12 and ±15 V DC. Ground is both bussed and dispersed along the connectors to provide a low-noise interface. A separate analogue ground and a +5 V DC standby (battery backup) voltage are also available.

As mentioned earlier, parity is handled on the bus – odd parity is used in all cases with a single bit for the lower 24-bit address space and a second bit for the remaining 8-bit upper address grouping on the other connector. Byte parity is maintained for data with a total of four bits, used in the expanded 32-bit mode.

Summary

Development techniques using EXORmacs may take many forms. EXORmacs may be used in this standard form as a stand-alone hardware and software development system. The resident editor, PASCAL compiler and macroassembler allow easy program generation, while the operating system and the disc system provide convenient file storage for multiple users. The EXORterm provides programmable function keys which are tailored to the task in use. These keys provide a single-key stroke to enter software commands.

For users who own or rent time-share service, Motorola offers cross-software such as PASCAL, simulators and assemblers for the M68000 and MC68000 families. Once developed this software may be easily down loaded and executed in EXORmacs via transparent mode. EXORmacs architecture was designed with the foresight of future silicon to provide development capabilities before it existed.

THE APPROACHES TO THE PROVISION OF TOOLS III
By Sam Lee (Hewlett-Packard)

Developing microprocessor-based systems requires skills, techniques and tools which have been known to the engineering community now for decades. Even so the microprocessor development system has emerged recently as a uniquely specialised tool widely used and discussed in a way almost as passionately as oscilloscopes. In part or in whole, this is strongly influenced by the fact that the implementation of many microprocessor-based systems forces digital designers and software designers into intimate contact – a union of considerable galvanic action. Secondly the microprocessor has given system implementers the opportunity (burden) to design the computing engine along with the rest of the system logic and control, thus exposing the mass of the engineering world to design tasks which previously were only undertaken in the depths of Hewlett-Packard, DEC, ICL, IBM, etc.

Along with that opportunity comes the frightful realisation that the software designer can no longer assume that the hardware works properly (as he normally could in pure software system design) nor can the digital designer proceed with his design tradeoffs without proper consultation from the software designers. With the acceptance of microprocessors as the way to do things, came the situation that few of the system designers were currently familiar with the discipline of software development. Out of this environment has grown this unique tool we call a microprocessor development system (MDS)[1].

In order to properly address what approaches are possible to implement an MDS, a review of the pertinent components is appropriate (fig. 5.13). The software development task requires certain tools which will be discussed in chapter 6. These tools are, however, computer programs themselves which must have some computer on which to execute – that computer is commonly called the host. Special measuring tools also are part of an MDS, tools whose primary purpose is measuring the execution behaviour of the microprocessor while it is under the influence of the hardware and software of the intended system.

Each of these subdivisions of an MDS represent techniques and tools known and used for years by computer engineers. However the last category – emulation – is a concept uniquely associated with microprocessor system development. It is the inclusion of all three of these capabilities which make up a complete MDS. All three should be considered during the design of an MDS. Here the HP64000 will be used as an example of one set of design choices. The key philosophies behind the design approach will be discussed.

---

[1]Manufacturers such as Hewlett-Packard and Intel should refrain from using MDS officially since it is a registered trademark of Mohawk Data Systems. Nonetheless it is the common abbreviation known to most users.

Multiuser environment

The discussion about dedicated user systems versus central time-share systems will continue unresolved, probably forever. However certain performance benefits of each mode are presently clear. Response times of time-shared multiuser systems suffer when there are many concurrent users. In dedicated systems, information transfer from one user to another becomes physically burdensome. Many of the design choices of the HP64000 represent an effort to provide the advantages of both. Many products are designed in a team environment where access to a common data base can speed program development and software/hardware integration, while minimising file transfer mistakes. With the era of the 16-bit processor upon us, it becomes increasingly clear that the performance of the host system will affect the productivity of a team developing, say, 60 kbyte of code using a high-level language. One could say that in many design situations

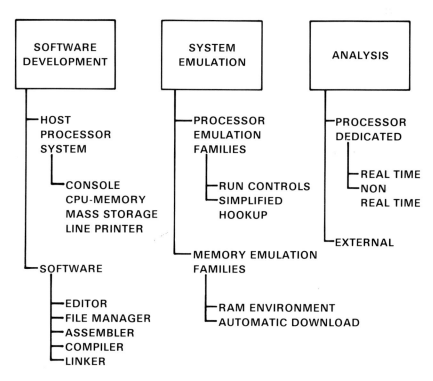

Fig. 5.13 System overview – the components of a development system

what is required is a high performance minicomputer system dedicated to each software designer.

    Examining fig. 5.14 helps identify a key consideration relating to performance. A timeshared system (such as fig. 5.14(a)) uses the disc and

CPU together to make one CPU appear like several CPUs. When one user's program has used its fair share of the CPU's time, the program is suspended and copied to the disc in its present state. Then the next user's program is brought into the main memory from the disc and given its fair share time slice of the CPU. When many users make simultaneous use of the system, then performance and response time become bogged down. The bottleneck is the high traffic rate to and from the disc. A large portion of the CPU time becomes used up waiting for swaps to become complete.

The configuration in fig. 5.14(b) obviously avoids this problem, and clearly the choice of disc, CPU and memory can be made to provide any desired level of performance. Here the difficulty is that with physically separated mass storage devices sharing of files requires some kind of physical transfer.

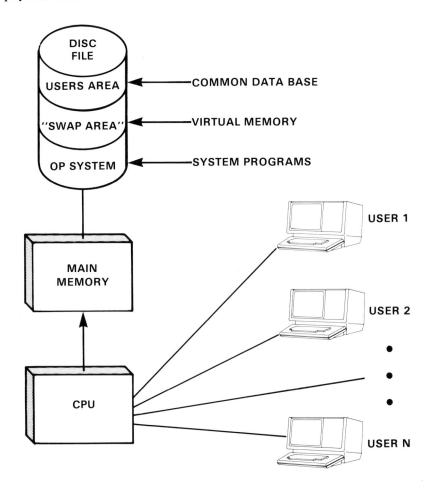

Fig. 5.14(a) Time-shared system

DEDICATED DATA BASE

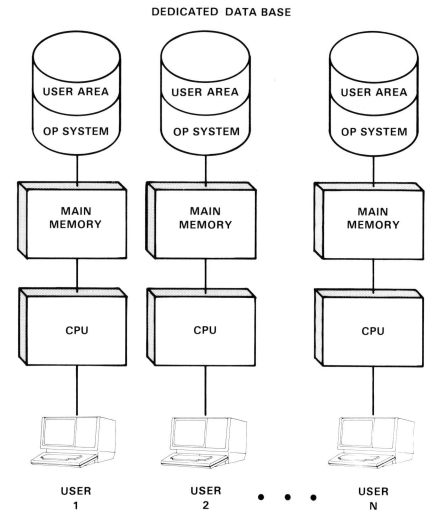

Fig. 5.14(b) Dedicated system

In the configuration of fig. 5.14(c) each user has a dedicated CPU and main memory, but all users share one disc file (mass memory). This provides a common data base for all users, but greatly reduces the data traffic to and from the disc. An example will illustrate why. Consider that three users are editing text. As each user initiates the edit session, his system monitor brings in a copy of the editor object code to his main memory. Thus each user has his own editor resident in his own system and it will remain resident until the edit session is concluded. Thus there is no 'swapping' traffic. The disc file is required only when each edit program must read or write text to the user area. Disc contention may still exist between the three users but at a much lower rate than in fig. 5.14(a). Note that if there is only one user station connected to the disc, the network simplifies to a dedicated system.

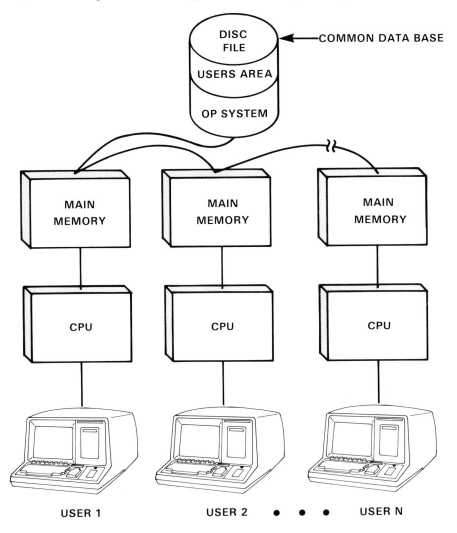

Fig. 5.14(c) Distributed system

Clearly providing a common data base to several users was a very important consideration in choosing the architecture of fig. 5.14(c) for the HP64000. I won't attempt a formal justification of that importance other than to observe that all the leading MDS manufacturers have responded to user requests and are now offering some kind of multiuser system.

Many minicomputer systems (fig. 5.14(a)) have expanded the size of main memory so that some user programs may remain resident during suspension, thereby lowering the swapping traffic to the disc. As memory becomes less expensive and memory management tasks are moved into hardware, then this approach becomes more attractive. But as CPU cost continues to erode, systems like fig. 5.14(c) have performance advantages for computer bound processes.

Work station architecture

The human interface is receiving increased attention in all computing systems. These considerations can greatly affect architectural choices. The editor function is the most highly used function on an MDS system and thus should receive due consideration. Screen mode operation for an editor is one of the most highly desirable of all possible features. By making the display controller have access to the main memory space, the highest possible screen response can be realised (fig. 5.15) making direct character overtyping possible, anywhere on the screen. This facet becomes important to the implementation of syntax tracking soft keys as well.

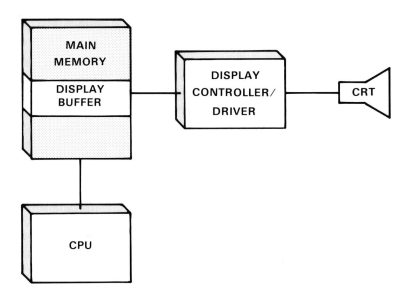

Fig. 5.15 Display controller architecture

A growth path should be provided by a universal MDS so that it may support new processors in the future. One measure of a good architectural choice will be a long lifetime through the evolution of several new micropro- cessor families. How the host controller CPU and the emulator interact is the key to whether longevity can be maintained. Fig. 5.16 shows several architectures which are represented in currently available MDS systems. Each scheme has advantages and disadvantages.

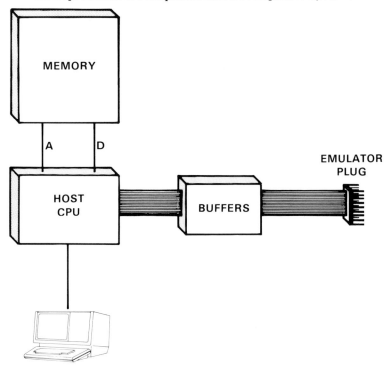

Fig. 5.16(a) Single processor host/emulator

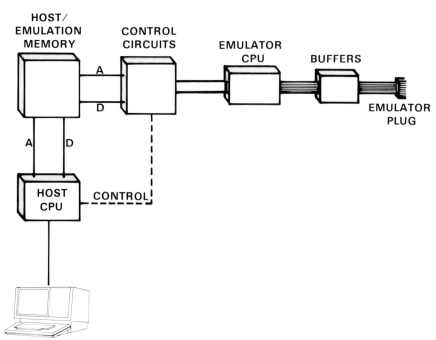

Fig. 5.16(b) Common memory host/emulator

Fig. 5.16(a) depicts the most cost effective approach to supporting one processor type (from a manufacturing cost standpoint only). In this scheme, the host CPU is chosen to be the same as the target microprocessor. This approach is obviously dedicated to that processor type.

Fig. 5.16(b) indicates that this scheme provides separate CPUs for the host and the emulator. Memory is used by both the host and the emulator, however. Hence major differences in bus schemes and memory access times of new processors from that originally considered can make it difficult for this scheme to provide real-time execution without wait states in the target system when using emulation memory.

The scheme illustrated in fig. 5.16(c) physically separates the emulation memory from the host memory. A provision is made however so that for some situations where extra host memory is helpful and the emulator function is not active, the emulation memory can be remapped for use by the host. The editor function is a typical example of a situation in which the extra memory may be used for buffer space.

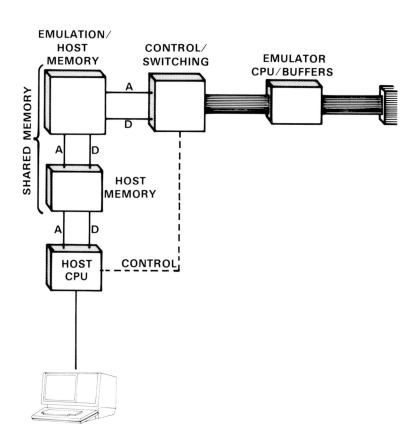

Fig. 5.16(c) Shared memory host/emulator

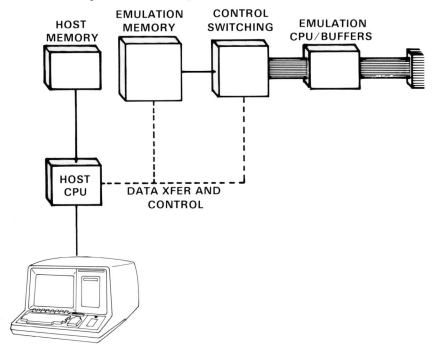

Fig. 5.16(d) Independent buses for host/emulator

The last example shown in fig. 5.16(d) is the architecture chosen by the HP64000 designers. This approach allows the emulator process, once begun, to proceed without any dependence on the host (so long as no register dumping, trace list, or other similar functions are being performed). This would allow the emulator and analyser to be set up for a given experiment, say to trace an event which happens sporadically, and only at long intervals. Having set up the emulator and analyser, the user could then leave the emulator control program and begin editing, compiling or some other function while the emulator/analyser continues its search and operation. This architectural choice also makes inventing support for new processors, whose features are as yet unknown, much less likely to be blocked by some overlooked problem. If the current emulation memory must be replaced with a faster memory in the future, then that is entirely possible.

From its earliest days the HP64000 system was viewed as a system in which logic state analysis, logic timing analysis, emulators, multiple emulators, etc. would be used by digital designers. This wide range of applicability required that the host processor and the measurement functions be carefully separated. The interconnection between the two would be restricted to control function, programming and measurement/status data readback. Each measurement function (since there might be two or more resident) would have to operate independently from the host until its function became complete. For this plan to be successful the system architecture of fig. 5.16(d) was the only possible architecture for the HP64000. Since many of the functions mentioned above do not fit on one single printed circuit card, intercard bussing must be accomplished. This is purposefully not handled by the mainframe bus. Fig. 5.17 shows this arrangement.

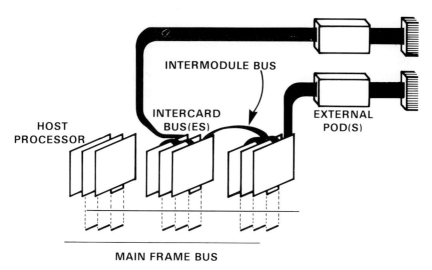

Fig. 5.17 HP64000 bus structure

An approach such as the one discussed here maximises the modularity, upgradeability and lifetime of the system definition. It also obviously has the highest initial purchase price. That is true also because the attendant power supply must be designed to carry the load of the optional modules. This represents a major cost element (roughly one third the cost of the 64000 is due to the power supply).

Mass storage

The current existence of Winchester technology hard disc drives is reshaping the thought of system designers of all value-oriented computer systems. The floppy disc will remain less costly for the foreseeable future for a minimum system, even though the cost per Mbyte for small Winchesters is eroding at a 30 per cent per year rate. The tradeoffs between systems based on floppies versus hard discs involve many factors, some of which are not so obvious. The more obvious ones are cost versus access time and cost versus Mbyte of storage. What may not be so obvious is the system personality and usability which are a product of the system's 'excess performance capacity' and the system designers' imagination for using that capacity to the benefit of the user.

The first practical computing engine invented by Babbage required Lady Ada's talent to first learn how to program it. For a long time thereafter our first concern has been to invent machines which are capable of certain tasks. Often (if not most of the time) the user is asked to conform to the eccentricities of that machine (and its operating system) with little investment made in making the machine conform to the styles and methods of humans. Each computer/operating system encountered has a distinctive 'personality', in that it is somewhat tolerant of human ambiguities in some areas but is distinctively fussy in other areas. But they are generally characterised by a cryptic secret code of magic phrases that must be memorised in order to command useful work from the beast. It is only recently that manufacturers have begun to give serious attention to the human interface problem and offer creative solutions. The HP64000 team views the syntax-tracking soft keys as a major contribution in this respect.

A census of digital designers would reveal a rapidly changing constituency. New college graduates trained in computer science and electrical engineering generally graduate with considerable hands-on experience with computer systems. Most of the experienced digital hardware designers who began using microprocessors in the place of state machines have not had much exposure to computers (note that the PDP-11 predates the 4004 by only about three years). Hence learning how to use a computer system – in addition to learning how to program – can be an overwhelming experience. Thus making the system usable to these kinds of people takes special care. If the system is too intimidating to those who are not familiar with the practice of secret codes, they will not use its power, if indeed they use it at all.

The availability of essentially unlimited mass storage in an MDS allows the system personality to be structured toward ease of use, both for the neophyte as well as the experienced user. The information needed by a user to understand what to do can be made readily available, in an intelligent presentation. One simple example is having the machine report error conditions in clearly understandable text, rather than space conserving reference numbers which point to the appendix of a manual[2]. A principal truth then must be recognised, that is, computer I/O styles can be implemented with smaller programs but human I/O styles require a lot of programming space to implement on computers. Making computers reach out to humans is hard.

A very profound reason for large fast mass storage in an MDS has to do with work efficiency and styles. Due to the nature of people, we are tempted to use short cuts. When under pressure we will use short cuts even against our better judgement. The consequences can be enormous over the long term. During the debugging of a program for a ROM-based system, it is not uncommon to see the designer make a few machine-language patches to the program using the emulator rather than reassemble or recompile the source

---

[2]In real life O'Toole's corollary to Murphy's Law is a commonplace occurrence (i.e. Murphy was an optimist). When needed, the proper reference manual is missing. If found, the list of error codes is missing. When an updated manual is received which does include an error list your error number will be missing because your software is one revision later than the manual revision.

code. Every group of designers I have interviewed have admitted to putting into production a ROM for which no source code existed. If an MDS can offer adequate turnaround time, the human can be convinced to observe good documentation discipline (i.e. make all changes in source code and keep copies of all versions of the source code).

An expansion on this point with an example will illustrate how much the disc can affect the response time for this situation. When a bug is discovered during emulation and the designer has formulated an idea of how to correct the problem, he will exit the emulation control program and invoke the editor, specifying his source file. After locating the proper lines of text and making modifications, revised text is saved. Next the assembler or compiler is invoked followed by the linker. Then the emulator may be reinitialised and object code loaded into target system memory and execution commenced. Users have learned to be sensitive to the processing rate of assemblers or compilers but program loading time can also be a major factor as well. Notice from our example the frequency of file movement:

- load editor object code into host memory
- create temporary disc work files
- load editor buffer space with text
- write modified text from buffer and work files to new file
- load assembler object code into host memory
- read source code text file
- output relocatable file to disc
- load linker object code into host memory
- read relocatable file from disc
- write absolute object file, symbol files to disc
- load emulator control software into host memory
- load object code into emulation memory

This is a simplified list of the disc transactions which is intended to illustrate how often large files are transferred from and to the disc while turning the code around. If disc access times and transfer rates are slow, even small programs take an excessive amount of time to turn the source code around. Users are then likely to make several machine language changes and will save up to five or ten patches before going back to modify source code. Then more time is required making sure the object code produced from the modified source text is identical to the patched version.

Thus to encourage users to make changes at the source code level, the total turn around time must be controlled. As high-level languages (HLL) become more widely used, this turnaround response time takes on even more importance, because modifying the object code produced by the compiler is difficult and debugging at the machine code level is counter to the very purpose of using a HLL. Manufacturers of MDS are advancing the capability of emulator-based debugging tools to allow designers to continue to operate in the language of design. Consequently, response time from source code edit to debugging the executing object code must be fast.

Program architecture is greatly affected by the size and speed of the memories available to the software system designer, and by the nature of the task being performed. The editor, for instance, can be made quite fast if the entire text file to be edited is resident in main memory. Obviously that places a limit to the size of text file that can be edited. The same comments apply for the operation of assemblers, compilers, linkers, etc. If a system designer aims at the user who works with single-chip microcomputers and writes programs of 1 kbyte or less, then a set of tools can be built which are main memory limited, but have very high performance.

However if the designer intends to adequately support today's 16-bit developments, then either multi-Mbyte of main storage are required or a mass memory scheme must be incorporated. Based on the experience of HP64000 users, each user needs about 2 Mbyte of file space, or operation becomes cramped for 16-bit development. If the system designer couples large main memory with floppy disc then program loading time again becomes significant.

The HP64000 designers concluded that a fast large mass storage device coupled with a 16-bit microprocessor was therefore key to providing reasonable operational performance to MDS users who were designers of large software systems in a multiteam member environment as well as to providing a friendly human-engineered system which a new user or hardware designer would be comfortable with.

Thoughts toward the future

At the time of writing, there were essentially three divisions emerging in MDS philosophies (not counting the MPU manufacturers versus independent universals). On the low end, there was a push toward making very low cost floppy-based single-user systems. In the middle range of the classic MDS, the performance and price continues to migrate up as multiuser and 16-bit support become standard. At the highest price range is the HP3000, VAX 11/780 type host accompanied by remote emulators. These distinctive approaches have arisen from very fundamental differences in user preferences and thus are likely to continue, just as computer systems of various types have proliferated. The user will note that the HP64000 will have a large amount of instrumentation invented into its turnkey approach. Particularly in the 16-bit arena, many of the real-time hardware/software integration problems of microprocessor multidatapath systems will require sophisticated bus measuring and analysing tools. It is clear that the HP64000 has been uniquely architectured to be able to provide a co-ordinated set of emulator/analysers and compilers to attack these special problems.

EDITOR'S CONCLUSIONS

Three approaches to the provision of tools for microprocessor application development, then. From reading the contributions, it was evident that there was a good general agreement in the types of tools and facilities to be included in a microprocessor development system. Even though the starting points for the three manufacturers were different, and their current offerings are different, there is the general trend toward multiuser systems.

Most of the facilities discussed are now quite well evolved, but there are differences in the way they have been implemented, and in selecting a MDS, the user has to identify the important features (see chapter 4) and take note of these differences. Hopefully the insight given in these contributions will help explain why the manufacturers have done certain things in certain ways. But having other opinions presented, the readers may judge which are the most sound—even better, come up with better suggestions for themselves.

Note the emphasis all three contributors have put on software development. Your editor fully concurs with this opinion, and the facilities to write programs provided by the software on MDS are discussed in much greater detail in the next chapter.

A couple of omissions by all three contributors were the lack of design aids/facilities, and much more powerful word processor-type editors. The design phase was identified as one of the most critical stages in development (again there was good agreement from the contributors), but no design packages are currently offered as part of any manufacturer's MDS. Good documentation facilities could be offered by using a powerful but very easy-to-use word processor-type editor as the prime interface to the user (see discussion in chapter 4). These two areas could do with future improvements, and perhaps more emphasis, rather than some less critical features.

CHAPTER 6

Software Facilities

This chapter discusses in detail the facilities provided to develop software on the MDS – in fact the facilities provided by software. The critical nature of software development has been emphasised by your editor and totally independently by the three previous contributors in chapter 5.

The contributions

The importance of software cannot be over emphasised (see chapters 3 and 4). Software is the one element which determines the behaviour and performance of the end product. It is difficult to visualise physically, and the principles and concepts of good practice in software development can therefore sometimes be missed or misunderstood. Despite the evolvement of the computer industry over many years, few formal methodologies for full software development exist, much less are actually practised. Software development thus tends to be regarded almost as an art form, as opposed to a problem solving discipline.

Facilities for software development on MDS are normally those which help in coding and compilation (see chapter 4, pp 25–29), and to a certain extent in documentation. The ease of use of these aids can encourage good practice in any modifications or updating of the development programs. For example, taking any changes back to the source code (with comments) rather than implementing a patch at machine code level which can easily be lost and go undocumented.

Although there appears to be an accepted 'set' of software development facilities, differing philosophies for development will put different emphasis on the facilities. Following his contribution in chapter 5, Hewlett-Packard's Sam Lee discusses the importance and difficulty of software development.

The second contribution is from a team at Texas Instruments based in

Bedford, UK: Geoff Bristow, Peter Vinson and Dave Wollen. Their discourse on the various possible facilities, clearly explains the differences and advantages of each, and they have tried to compare the reality of these against their opinion of an ideal. There are lessons to be learnt and a good deal of insight to be gained from both contributions.

SOFTWARE FACILITIES I
By Sam Lee (Hewlett-Packard)

'Software is an art.'
'Software is a science.'
'Software is an engineering discipline.'

The reader who looks to the words of this book to help him begin to grasp some perspective on the meaning and usefulness of development systems may see the three statements above as different perspectives of the same reality, perspectives which could be applied to several areas of human endeavour. I believe to do so would be as much a travesty as to believe that poker is only a game of skill in probability and memory. The practice of software is somehow different. It is an endeavour in which two people with similar training and intelligence may have productivities which differ by an order of magnitude. There are not many areas of engineering or science where this happens regularly.

Particularly in engineering there are many bright engineers who can spawn ideas by the bushel basket, but find creating a finished product ready for market difficult. And in the cold light of completing manufacturing release, the productivity of engineers faces a levelling influence. But in software, there are those who can generate a finished saleable product at a much faster rate than their peers. In its pure form, software is the product of an artist, but is a most practical art form. These sentences may seem rhetorical now, but keep them in mind as the task of guiding software projects to successful completion has bewildered many a good organisation. The best run and managed companies with years of software experience regularly miss their objectives for software projects, either in time to completion or in performance or both. It is an industry axiom that no matter what your budget the software will cost three times that amount. If you are new to the practice of software – be prepared. This stuff can be spooky.

With those words behind us (words which come from deep-rooted experience) let us cast aside the notions of software as either an art or a science and talk about the engineering tools and proven methods at our disposal for the implementation of microprocessor-based products.

Key stages in software engineering

In the context of engineering products for others use of an overview perspective of distinctively different phases in software design will be helpful in keeping the detail straight. These phases are identified around the concept that software is a language of algorithms.

(a) specify desired behaviour – specifications are part of the task but there is more. Microprocessor-based products react with things, and most often with humans. So behaviour becomes as important to document and accomplish as 'specs'.

(b) design or select algorithm(s) to accomplish the desired behaviour. With an understanding of what the objectives are come several ideas of ways to get there. These can be evaluated for desirable and undesirable side effects, projected performance, projected memory space require-ments, etc., and an approach selected.

(c) code the algorithm in a software programming language. In order to do this, an appropriate language must be selected. Often this is already determined by external factors such as language availability on the development system or current company policy. The selection of algorithms and language may be inseparable for some problems. The actual coding represents putting all the details 'on paper'.

(d) translate the code into executable form for the target system. This involves using the MDS and is a major reason for its existence. Lots of typing involved.

(e) determine whether the code actually implements the algorithm. Since there are several translation processes going on there will naturally be some translation problems.

(f) determine whether the algorithm generates the required behaviour. Is the performance adequate, is the behaviour really appropriate? If not can the algorithm or the interaction of several algorithms be modified to improve things?

(g) prepare for product release. Get the quirks out. Final documentation, etc.

It is in stages (d), (e) and (f) that the development system provides capabilities to the design team. However the capabilities of the development system must be understood while the coding phase is being accomplished because this may materially affect the architecture of the resultant code. A simple example is probably useful here to clarify terminology. If the development system does not have provision for binding relocatable modules together, then some form of link table must be used by the project team so that each program or routine may vary in length somewhat but the access location of variables is unchanged.

Editor
The user's first and most frequent contact with a development system is with the editor/file manager facilities. The text of the program which is referred to as the source code is entered through the keyboard and stored on the mass storage device. Since many changes and modifications will be made to the text over the development of the product the editor program will provide the means for readily accomplishing these changes. The file manager, which is generally considered part of the operating system, is a tool which makes possible the orderly management of many text files in which the various parts of the source code are stored, as well as the other files maintained by the system. The editor program can greatly ease the burden of creating source code as well as modifying previously entered routines if

its features are powerful. Briefly, two very important features provided by the HP64000 which illustrate this are the find and replace commands and the paragraph manipulation commands. These commands go far beyond the concept of just retyping any lines found to be in error (this is the most basic feature of an editor) and use the power of the host processor in the development system to perform automatically many changes. Some of the ways in which the hardware design of the HP64000 was structured to enhance the power and usability of the editor were discussed in chapter 5.

Directory List	User:PISCES	Disc: 0		Mon, 11 May 1981, 21:44 Page 2
NAME	TYPE	SIZE	LAST MODIFY	LAST ACCESS
ASM0A	absolute	2	7 Apr 1981, 12:56	5 May 1981, 8:17
ASM1A	absolute	3	7 Apr 1981, 13:00	5 May 1981, 8:17
ASM2A	absolute	4	7 Apr 1981, 13:02	5 May 1981, 8:17
ASM3A	absolute	4	15 Apr 1981, 7:32	5 May 1981, 8:17
ASM4A	absolute	3	9 Feb 1981, 12:20	5 May 1981, 8:17
ASMGEN	absolute	4	28 Jan 1981, 9:00	29 Apr 1981, 16:11
AZ8	absolute	2	6 May 1981, 13:11	6 May 1981, 13:13
AZ8	source	12	6 May 1981, 10:37	8 May 1981, 8:25
AZ80	source	8	31 Mar 1981, 14:36	8 May 1981, 8:08
AZ80	absolute	2	20 Apr 1981, 15:51	12 Apr 1981, 18:42
AZ8001	absolute	3	13 Apr 1981, 15:40	12 Apr 1981, 18:42
AZ8001	source	28	13 Apr 1981, 15:16	8 May 1981, 8:27
AZ8002	absolute	3	13 Apr 1981, 15:41	12 Apr 1981, 18:42
AZ8002	source	22	13 Apr 1981, 15:17	8 May 1981, 8:27
B6800	absolute	1	7 Apr 1981, 14:29	12 Apr 1981, 18:50
B6800	link_com	1	10 Feb 1981, 8:44	24 Jan 1981, 8:44
B6800	asmb_sym	1	1 May 1981, 8:59	1 May 1981, 8:59
B6800	reloc	1	1 May 1981, 8:58	1 May 1981, 8:58
B6800	source	2	10 Feb 1981, 8:44	1 May 1981, 8:57
B6800	link_sym	1	24 Jan 1981, 8:44	24 Jan 1981, 8:44
B6801	absolute	1	12 Apr 1981, 0:05	12 Apr 1981, 0:00
B8048	source	3	31 Mar 1981, 14:37	31 Mar 1981, 14:37
B8048	absolute	1	18 Mar 1981, 10:02	23 Apr 1981, 18:27
B8048	link_com	1	9 Apr 1981, 16:42	9 Apr 1981, 16:42
B8080	absolute	1	22 Sep 1980, 12:30	12 Apr 1981, 18:50
B8080	reloc	1	27 Oct 1980, 1:18	27 Oct 1980, 1:18
B8080	source	2	23 Sep 1980, 0:30	2 Dec 1980, 9:59
B8080	asmb_sym	1	27 Oct 1980, 1:18	27 Oct 1980, 1:18
B8085	source	2	23 Sep 1980, 0:34	2 Dec 1980, 9:58
B8085	absolute	1	22 Sep 1980, 12:31	12 Apr 1981, 18:50
B8085	reloc	1	27 Oct 1980, 1:19	27 Oct 1980, 1:19
B8085	asmb_sym	1	27 Oct 1980, 1:19	27 Oct 1980, 1:19
BOOTTAPA	absolute	3	3 Oct 1980, 16:52	8 May 1981, 11:26
BPG	link_com	1	27 Jun 1980, 15:20	14 Apr 1981, 13:28
BPG	link_sym	1	27 Jun 1980, 15:20	7 May 1981, 8:24
BZ80	absolute	1	22 Sep 1980, 12:51	12 Apr 1981, 18:50
Back64810	source	1	14 Nov 1980, 13:41	6 May 1981, 11:05
Boot_Z1	absolute	5	11 May 1981, 11:53	11 May 1981, 12:00
Boot_Z2	absolute	5	11 May 1981, 11:50	11 May 1981, 11:50
C1ABS	absolute	9	1 May 1981, 11:10	1 May 1981, 11:38
C68000	absolute	6	11 May 1981, 12:01	11 May 1981, 12:02
C6800A	absolute	4	17 Oct 1980, 13:35	26 Nov 1980, 15:30
C808085A	absolute	4	17 Oct 1980, 13:11	26 Nov 1980, 15:31
C8085	source	1	20 Nov 1980, 16:14	26 Nov 1980, 15:15
C8086	absolute	5	11 May 1981, 14:19	11 May 1981, 14:20
CALABS	absolute	2	26 Feb 1980, 0:08	29 Apr 1981, 16:11
CENTER	absolute	1	10 Apr 1981, 12:19	10 Apr 1981, 12:25
CHANGES	source	5	8 May 1981, 13:44	8 May 1981, 13:44
CNFG16	absolute	2	11 May 1981, 11:56	11 May 1981, 11:57
COABS	absolute	2	1 May 1981, 11:10	1 May 1981, 11:38
CONFIGA	absolute	4	20 Feb 1981, 9:19	29 Apr 1981, 16:11
CONVERT	source	1	7 Oct 1980, 7:31	13 Apr 1981, 10:24
CONVERTA	absolute	1	13 Apr 1981, 8:30	29 Apr 1981, 16:11
COPYA	absolute	4	7 Apr 1981, 13:45	5 May 1981, 8:16
CZ8001	absolute	6	11 May 1981, 11:56	11 May 1981, 11:57
CZ8002	absolute	6	11 May 1981, 11:48	11 May 1981, 11:48

Fig. 6.1 HP64000 file directory list

File manager

Since large complex programs are more successfully attacked through a modular structured approach, the team may have literally hundreds of files to keep track of. Consequently the tracking features of the file manager can aid in what otherwise can be a confusing and burdensome task. Fig. 6.1 is a reproduction of a page from a directory listing of the files stored under one user ID in the HP64000 file system. Note that the header references the date and time that the listing was created. This time stamp which is used throughout the system is one of the features which helps users keep track of complex software. Other features of the file manager which help in the same way are evident in the fig. Note that the file B6800 appears in the list six times. The type column reveals that each of these has a different type designator, however. Without direction by the user, the system accesses the proper file by the context of the operation and thus simplifies the number of file names the user must keep up with. Also listed in the directory are the last modify and last access dates. Again these tracking features allow users to unravel difficult text management problems. The user ID separates the files by user and allows duplicate file names without conflict. The dates maintained by the file manager also reduce the problem of backup since files may be saved on tape or restored using date as a qualifier. For instance the command

store all files modified after 4/5/81

issued on 11 May 1981, copies only those files which have been changed since the last backup (done for example at day's end on 4 May 1981), thereby greatly shortening the process.

The directory listing in fig. 6.2 is titled 'Recoverable Files'. These files are the 128 most recently purged files which are as yet still available. Occasionally during an edit session, a user will wish to have a copy of the file as it existed before the last changes were made. When the editor on the HP64000 updates a file it creates a new file under the same name and places the old version at the bottom of the free space of the disc. Since the file manager maintains knowledge of the free space, the file can be recovered (until the space is overwritten). Consequently recovery from a very common mistake (i.e. purging the wrong file) becomes very easy.

Modular programming

Modular programming is a notion which, among other things, means breaking a large program down into many smaller tasks, coding routines to work on each task, with special care to make each of the smaller programs or routines clear in its operation and clean in the way it communicates with other routines. Some of these modules (as they are often named) may be usable in other efforts in the future. This methodology depends on the existence of a means to bind several modules into a unified whole.

Relocation is a means for accomplishing this. As seen by the processor, the entire content of the memory is a collection of bits which are a single

program. Specifically, if one instruction commands a jump to another
location for the next instruction the processor must know the exact location
of the new instruction. Such would be the case if one of the modules passed
control to another. But the programmer would like not to be concerned
with this detail but rather concentrate on the logical flow of the program. In
our programming languages, the programmer will refer to addresses by
symbolic names and let the tools supply that detail.

```
Recoverable Files          Disc: 0        Mon, 11 May 1981, 21:46  Page  1

  NAME              TYPE      SIZE    LAST MODIFY           LAST ACCESS
---------------------------------------------------------------------------
  DIR:PISCES        listing   8     11 May 1981, 21:44    11 May 1981, 21:44
  DIR:SUPER         listing   1     11 May 1981, 21:39    11 May 1981, 21:39
  DIR:M68K          listing   1     11 May 1981, 21:30    11 May 1981, 21:30
  CHAP6_3:SLBOOK    source    1     27 Apr 1981,  0:40    27 Apr 1981,  0:40
  DIR:SLBOOK        listing   1      7 May 1981, 20:27     7 May 1981, 20:27
  LISTER:JOB        source    1      6 May 1981, 17:11     6 May 1981, 17:11
  DIR:JOB           listing   1      6 May 1981, 17:13     6 May 1981, 17:13
  TRD_DLG_4:JOB     source    1     11 May 1981, 19:51    11 May 1981, 19:51
  TRD_DLG_5:JOB     source    1     11 May 1981, 19:58    11 May 1981, 19:58
  E_DOC:GORDON      source    4     11 May 1981, 16:44    11 May 1981, 16:44
  E_DOC:GORDON      source    4     11 May 1981, 16:38    11 May 1981, 16:38
  E_STEP:EMUL16     source    3     27 Apr 1981,  2:00    27 Apr 1981,  2:00
  E_DOC:GORDON      source    1     11 May 1981, 11:45    11 May 1981, 11:45
  GOLD:JIM          source    4     11 May 1981, 16:30    11 May 1981, 16:30
  GOLD:JIM          source    4     11 May 1981, 16:30    11 May 1981, 16:30
  MON_6801:SH6801   listing   10    11 May 1981, 15:10    11 May 1981, 15:10
  S1_6801:SH6801    listing   10    11 May 1981, 15:11    11 May 1981, 15:11
  MON_6801:SH6801   listing   10    11 May 1981, 13:55    11 May 1981, 13:55
  S0_6801:SH6801    listing   10    11 May 1981, 13:56    11 May 1981, 13:56
  S1_6801:SH6801    listing   10    11 May 1981, 13:56    11 May 1981, 13:56
  S2_6801:SH6801    listing   10    11 May 1981, 13:57    11 May 1981, 13:57
  S3_6801:SH6801    listing   10    11 May 1981, 13:58    11 May 1981, 13:58
  TEMP:EM8086       listing   2     11 May 1981, 13:57    11 May 1981, 13:57
  TEMP:SUPER        listing   2     11 May 1981, 13:54    11 May 1981, 13:54
  TEMP:SUPER        listing   2     11 May 1981, 13:54    11 May 1981, 13:54
  TEMP:JHACT        listing   1     11 May 1981, 13:53    11 May 1981, 13:53
  TEMP:SUPER        listing   2     11 May 1981, 13:52    11 May 1981, 13:52
  TEMP:JHACT        listing   1     11 May 1981, 13:52    11 May 1981, 13:52
  TEMP:SUPER        listing   2     11 May 1981, 13:51    11 May 1981, 13:51
  TEMP:EC8086       listing   2     11 May 1981, 13:50    11 May 1981, 13:50
  TEMP:EM8086       listing   2     11 May 1981, 13:48    11 May 1981, 13:48
  S3_6801:SH6801    link_com  1     11 May 1981, 13:47    11 May 1981, 13:47
  S2_6801:SH6801    link_com  1     11 May 1981, 13:47    11 May 1981, 13:47
  S1_6801:SH6801    link_com  1     11 May 1981, 13:47    11 May 1981, 13:47
  S0_6801:SH6801    link_com  1     11 May 1981, 13:47    11 May 1981, 13:47
  MON_6801:SH6801   link_com  1     11 May 1981, 13:47    11 May 1981, 13:47
  SERIAL:SUPER      source    1      9 May 1981, 13:24     9 May 1981, 13:24
  INTERRUPT:SUPER   source    3      9 May 1981, 13:23     9 May 1981, 13:23
  ALL:SUPER         source    1      9 May 1981, 13:23     9 May 1981, 13:23
  INITIAL:SUPER     source    3      9 May 1981, 13:23     9 May 1981, 13:23
  MON_Z8001:PISCES  absolute  6     27 Apr 1981,  2:29    27 Apr 1981,  2:29
  CZ8001:PISCES     absolute  2     27 Apr 1981,  2:29    27 Apr 1981,  2:29
  CNFG16:PISCES     absolute  1     27 Apr 1981,  2:29    27 Apr 1981,  2:29
  Mon_Z1:PISCES     absolute  8     24 Feb 1981,  4:03    24 Feb 1981,  4:03
  S0_Z8001:PISCES   absolute  9     27 Apr 1981,  2:30    27 Apr 1981,  2:30
  E_INT:EMUL16      source    4     27 Apr 1981,  2:08    27 Apr 1981,  2:08
  DIRECT:SAVE_I     source    1     27 Apr 1981,  2:57    27 Apr 1981,  2:57
  DIRECT:SAVE_I     source    1     27 Apr 1981,  2:56    27 Apr 1981,  2:56
```

Fig. 6.2 HP64000 partial list of recoverable files

Linker

If every module were made part of one source code file and were translated
all at once, then the translator program would be able to make all address
assignments. Since this can be inconvenient and very time consuming, a
convention for allowing modules to be translated with address references

kept in a relocatable form will allow each module to be translated independently. In the HP64000, the program which binds several modules into one executable whole is called the linker.

Fig. 6.3 shows an output listing from the linking of a PASCAL program named SORTB which was stored in a file named PSORTB under user ID DAVEW. That program and several other modules have been combined into one complete program which now will occupy the address range of 0000–028D. The second part of the listing shows all the symbols which were used to communicate between the modules and the specific address assignments made to them. Several other points are worth noting as illustrations of additional features which aid the programmer in tracking down the inevitable bugs or which offer specific capabilities in architecturing the programs.

```
HP 64000 LINKER 2.0                             Tue, 12 May 1981, 20:29

FILE/PROG NAME           PROGRAM   DATA     COMMON    ABSOLUTE    DATE                   TIME    COMMENTS
-------------------------------------------------------------------------------------------------------------
PSORTB:DAVEW             0000                                     Tue, 12 May 1981, 20:29    SORTB Pascal
next address             013C


Libraries
LIB8085:HP
     Zintneq:HP          013C                                     Thu,  8 Jan 1981,    9:35
     Zintleq:HP          0148                                     Thu,  8 Jan 1981,    9:35
     Zbytegeq:HP         016B                                     Thu,  8 Jan 1981,    9:34
     CTF:HP              0184                                     Thu,  8 Jan 1981,    9:28
     Zintabs:HP          0189                                     Thu,  8 Jan 1981,    9:29
     Zerrors:HP          01A3      0800                           Thu,  8 Jan 1981,    9:29
     PARAM :HP           022A                                     Thu,  8 Jan 1981,    9:33
     Zstack:HP                     080C                           Thu,  8 Jan 1981,    9:36
next address             028E      088C

XFER address= 0000      Defined by PSORTB
No. of passes through libraries=    1
absolute & link_com file name=SRT_LNK:DAVEW
Total# of bytes loaded= 031A
```

Fig. 6.3 HP64000 linker memory map

Four possible relocation areas are mapped (this list is sometimes referred to as a memory map): Program, Data, Common and Absolute. Because microprocessor-based systems often use ROM to store the program code, the changeable data area must be separated from the unchanging code. The translator and linker work together in this respect; the translator gathering all variables into data areas and the linker allowing the programmer to assign a separate starting address from the program (an address where hopefully the system designer has provided some RAM). Since memory-mapped I/O may be the input/output scheme, certain references to absolute addresses may be necessary; these space usages are then catalogued separately. Not evident in this example is the capability to continue the linking process with a new set of starting address assignments for these memory areas.

For systems in which there is a mass storage device used for program storage, the programmer may overlay several programs into one memory area while keeping one monitor program continuously resident. Each of the overlays must be linked to the monitor and to the common area if it is used for intermodule communication. To do this requires that the address assignments of the monitor be known to the linker while that link is in progress.

LIBRARY ROUTINES

An example of a very important facility for the support of high-level languages is also illustrated in fig. 6.3. Many facilities of high-level languages are implemented in subroutines which the compiler calls if the facility is invoked. The total library needed to support every facility of the language will be enormous (the HP64000 PASCAL library for the 8085 requires 7 kbyte).

In practice most programs only refer to a small subset of these capabilities. Hence a memory space-saving feature would be to include only those routines actually used. In the example LIB8085:HP is the file name under which the entire set of support routines is stored. Only those routines which were actually used are listed and linked, however. Also evident in the fig. are several other pieces of information useful to the programmer, but of special value is the column listing date and time information. This information corresponds to the same information listed on the directory listing for each of these files. This record made at link time however can give a programmer specific clues as to the revision state of each module in a program when the behaviour of two versions of the program are being compared. Since the linking process creates so much reference information of value to the programmer, and is likely to be used many times in developing a specific program, the operating system automatically creates a command file containing the linking parameters. This file is stored under the same name the programmer specified for the absolute code, but of different type. The listed form of this information for the example is shown in fig. 6.4. Additional optional output from the linker is shown in fig. 6.5. This cross reference listing of global symbols informs the programmer of the address assignments made by the linker as well as which global symbols were referenced by what module. These definitions are also available during emulation so that they may be used for symbolic debugging.

```
                          Page #   1

    File = SRT_LNK:DAVEW:link_com    Wed, 20 May 1981, 10:04

    Record #   1     size =   56
    Linker is 18085_Z80:HP

    Object files: PSORTB
    Library files: LIB8085:HP
    PROG,DATA,COMN=0000H,0800H,0000H

    Map, xref = on   on
    End of file after record #   1
```

Fig. 6.4 HP64000 linker command file

SYMBOL	R	VALUE	DEF BY	REFERENCES		
A	P	00BA	PSORTB:DAVEW			
CASEERROR_	P	01EA	Zerrors:HP			
CFALSE_	P	0187	CTF:HP	Zbytegeq:HP	Zintleq:HP	Zintneq:HP
CTRUE	P	0184	CTF:HP	Zbytegeq:HP	Zintleq:HP	Zintneq:HP
ERR_DIVBYO	P	01A9	Zerrors:HP			
ERR_OVERFLOW	P	01A3	Zerrors:HP			
ERR_SET	P	01AC	Zerrors:HP			
ERR_UNDERFLOW	P	01A6	Zerrors:HP			
I	P	00B8	PSORTB:DAVEW			
MEMERR	P	01F1	Zerrors:HP			
PARAM_	P	022A	PARAM :HP	Zerrors:HP		
SORTB_	P	0000	PSORTB:DAVEW			
STACK	D	088C	Zstack:HP	PSORTB:DAVEW		
SWITCHED	P	00B7	PSORTB:DAVEW			
T1	P	00B5	PSORTB:DAVEW			
T2	P	00B6	PSORTB:DAVEW			
Z_END_PROGRAM	P	0205	Zerrors:HP	PSORTB:DAVEW		
Zbytegeq	P	017D	Zbytegeq:HP			
Zbytegtr	P	016B	Zbytegeq:HP	PSORTB:DAVEW		
Zint1C	P	0193	Zintabs:HP			
Zintabs	P	0189	Zintabs:HP			
Zintadd	P	019C	Zintabs:HP			
Zintleq	P	0148	Zintleq:HP	PSORTB:DAVEW		
Zintneg	P	0190	Zintabs:HP			
Zintneq	P	013C	Zintneq:HP	PSORTB:DAVEW		
Zintsub	P	019E	Zintabs:HP	PSORTB:DAVEW		

Fig. 6.5 HP64000 linker XREF listing

Programming languages

Translator tools allow the programmer to express the statements of the program in a form more attuned to human understanding and readability than machine language. Just how understandable or usable a programming language is may be quite a subjective discussion, however. The philosophy of a language may seem sound as it is being designed but may in practice prove unpopular. The actual value of the language is best proved by what it has accomplished. Also important is understanding what kind of language is best suited to the problem in hand.

ASSEMBLY LANGUAGE

Translator tools may be catalogued in various ways but for the purpose of this discussion only three variations will be examined. Assembly language is basically symbolic machine language. Addresses and instructions are represented by names (symbols and mnemonics) in the text that the programmer writes. The assembler program converts the names to the proper pattern of bits. The advantage of writing programs at this level is that a programmer has an intimate view of the processes of execution. The programmer comes to know and understand the details of that processor's resources and capabilities and thereby has insight into how to make certain things happen with cleverness and speed and/or other properties. But like other things of an intimate nature, it is fragile. And cleverness takes time to understand or figure out. It is not unusual to find that a programmer is unable to read an assembly language program one week after he has written it without considerable trouble.

HIGH-LEVEL LANGUAGES

High-level languages can make the program statements conform to the problem rather than the processor. They can increase programmer pro-ductivity by reducing the number of statements which are necessary to express a program and can lower the maintenance costs of programs by making the programs more readable to the original and subsequent programmers. In some cases they can prevent the programmer from making some kinds of errors by enforcing certain disciplines (obscure cleverness often backfires in very subtle ways in the world of software) upon the programmer. They can also make it possible for a programmer to work without knowledge of the underlying processor. And related to the processor independent programming, they may make programs portable from one computer to another.

```
 1 FILE: PSORTB:DAVEW      HP Pascal/64000[A.1]  Expanded 8085 listing
 2                                          Tue, 12 May 1981, 20:29  PAGE 1
 3
 4
 5    1 0000   1   "8085"
 6    2 0000   1   PROGRAM SORTB;
 7            0000                        NAME    "SORTB Pascal"
 8
 9    3 0000   1   $EXTENSIONS$
10    4 0000   1   $ASM FILE$
11    5 0000   1   CONST
12    6 0000   1    MAX=7FH;
13    7 0000   1   $GLOBVAR+$
14    8 0000   1    VAR T1,T2:BYTE;
15    9 0002   1        SWITCHED: BOOLEAN;
16   10 0003   1        I : INTEGER;
17   11 0005   1        A: ARRAY [0..MAX] OF BYTE;
18   12 0085   1   $GLOBVAR-$
19   13 0085   1   BEGIN
20            0000                        SORTB:
21
22   14 0000   1      { Initialize array to worst case: inverse order }
23   15 0000   1      FOR I:= 0 TO MAX DO
24            0000   31  ????        LXI   SP,STACK_
25            0003   21  7F00        LXI   H,127
26            0006   22  ????        SHLD  SORTB_D+133
27            0009   11  0000        LXI   D,0
28            000C   CD  ????        CALL  Zintleq
29            000F   CA  ????        JZ    SORTB_L1
30            0012   EB              XCHG
31            0013            SORTB_L2:
32            0013   22  ????        SHLD  SORTB_D+3
33
34   16 0016   1    BEGIN
35   17 0016   1      A[I]:= MAX-I;
36            0016   11  7F00        LXI   D,127
37            0019   CD  ????        CALL  Zintsub
38            001C   EB              XCHG
39            001D   2A  ????        LHLD  SORTB_D+3
40            0020   01  ????        LXI   B,SORTB_D+5
41            0023   09              DAD   B
42            0024   73              MOV   M,E
43
44   18 0025   1    END;
45            0025   2A  ????        LHLD  SORTB_D+3
46            0028   EB              XCHG
47            0029   2A  ????        LHLD  SORTB_D+133
48            002C   CD  ????        CALL  Zintneq
49            002F   CA  ????        JZ    SORTB_L1
50            0032   EB              XCHG
51            0033   23              INX   H
52            0034   C3  ????        JMP   SORTB_L2
//////////////////////////////////////////////////////////7/////
169                                   T2 EQU SORTB_D+1
170            013C                        EXT   Zbytegtr
171            013C                        EXT   Zintsub
172            013C                        EXT   Zintneq
173            013C                        EXT   Zintleq
174            013C                        EXT   STACK_
175            013C                        EXT   Z_END_PROGRAM
176            013C                        END   SORTB_
```

Fig. 6.6 HP64000 selected lines from a compiled PASCAL program

Fig. 6.6 is an intermixed listing of a PASCAL program, which was compiled on the HP64000 system and illustrates much of the above discussion. Each PASCAL statement is followed by the assembly language equivalent statements generated to perform that operation on an 8085 microprocessor. With a little study, it is clear that translation by rote rules leaves something to be desired (which is basically what a compiler does). Notice also the relocatable object code listed in hexadecimal form. The ???? indicates that the operand address will be assigned at link time. All other addresses in this figure are listed as if the program would eventually reside beginning at memory location 0. As an aid to debugging, the line number listed on the left of the figure and the associated address value are passed to the emulator so that statements like 'run from LINE__15:PSORTB' are possible. This particular command would cause execution to begin at the PASCAL statement 'FOR I: = 0 TO MAX DO'.

This is intended to help the programmer debug in the language rather than machine code. Two examples of the conventions followed in creating relocatable modules are illustrated in the figure. The global variables declaration near the top of the figure indicates to the linker which variables defined in this routine may be referenced by other routines. Likewise near the bottom of the figure, the external declarations are seen. This indicates to the linker which variables used by this routine are defined by another routine and which routines are called by this routine. Here the time saving power of a high-level language is again illustrated. The names 'Zbytegtr' ... 'Zintleq' refer to subroutines which are part of the HP64000 PASCAL run-time library. These subroutines supply the instructions for executing commands used by the programmer in the high-level language and greatly reduce the time that would otherwise be spent in generating these commands and calling them.

So now the process of translating source code to executable code can be represented by this flow diagram:

SOURCE	= >RELOCATABLE	= >ABSOLUTE
CODE	= >OBJECT CODE	= >OBJECT CODE
	Libraries	
TRANSLATOR		LINKER

At each of the transformation steps the translator or linker may find errors. These will be reported to the user so that corrective action can be taken. Typically this will involve editing the source code for one or more modules and retrying the transformation process. Once the link process has been completed without error, the user now possesses a syntactically correct program which is by no means necessarily free from errors. The user is now in stage five of the development process and is ready to examine the execution behaviour of the program. In the context of developing code using an MDS, this stage will be accomplished using an emulator. As execution errors are found, the source code will be modified and absolute code recreated. This process will most likely be repeated many times before the product is complete. Consequently an additional help to users is the ability to prepare a list of commands which can be stored in a file and executed very simply. The command file used for our examples of the figures is reproduced here.

File SRT__CMD:DAVEW:source

compile PSORTB listfile PSORTB options expand xref
link SRT__LNK listfile SRT__LNK
emulate SRT__EM load SRT__LNK
display memory A dynamic

The first two lines of the file command the transformation process. The second two lines initialise the emulator (using parameters stored in the emulator command file SRT__EM), cause the object code to be loaded into the target system's memory and command the content of that memory to be displayed on the MDS console beginning at the address specified by the value of the symbol A. The symbol definitions are specified by files produced by the linker which are accessed by the emulator control software. Excerpts from these two files (both global and local) are illustrated below:

Zintleq	0148H	Zintneq	013CH
ERR__UNDERFLOW	01D7H	Zbytegtr	016BH
>= A	00BAH	I	00B8H
SWITCHED	00B7H	ERR__DIVBY0	01DAH
T1	00B5H	T2	00B6H
Zintabs	0189H	Zintsub	01C3H
STACK__	034BH	PARAM__	0267H
ERR__SET	01DDH	ERR__OVERFLOW	01D4H

LINE__15	0000H Program	LINE__16	0016H Program
LINE__17	0016H Program	LINE__18	0025H Program
LINE__19	0037H Program	LINE__20	0037H Program
LINE__21	003CH Program	LINE__22	0043H Program
LINE__23	0043H Program	LINE__24	0048H Program
LINE__25	005BH Program		

INTERPRETIVE LANGUAGES

To this point, the discussion has centred around programming languages which were transformed and then executed. Another class of languages, called interpreters, approaches the problem from a different angle. In this approach a base program (called the interpreter) is first loaded into the target system's memory. Thereafter the source code is also stored directly (in cryptic form), also in memory. During execution, each statement is interpreted (translated) and executed in proper order. Note that this means that each statement is retranslated each time it is executed. This generally means a significant penalty in execution speed. But there are advantages of this approach.

Interpretive BASIC is the most widely known example of a language of this type and is famous for the interactive style in which inexperienced programmers can be helped into implementing programs. Some users have found it convenient to keep an interpretive BASIC for development and a BASIC compiler for final product release. Without dealing in detail with the aspects of language selection, it can be observed that many of the aspects of modern programming languages are not found in even the most modified and extended BASIC.

Portability

The microprocessor world has brought a particularly intense focus on an old problem, that of portability of programs from one processor type to another. Since, in the outline of the intent of the high-level language, portability was one of the features listed, then this capability would seem a natural. The problem arises that a new compiler is required for each processor supported and a new compiler is required for each language supported for each processor supported. That is $N \times M$ compilers, an overwhelming investment for the support community.

PASCAL

One creative approach to this problem has been closely associated with PASCAL (though not part of the language as defined by Jensen and Wirth). A compiler has been written which translates PASCAL source code into machine instructions for the virtual P computer. This imaginary P computer has an instruction set which is deemed 'ideal' for executing instructions translated from PASCAL. Now additional components in the form of interpreters which are written in 8085, 6800 or whatever processor language interpret the P-code into instructions for that processor. The task of writing the P-code interpreters is much less than writing a compiler. And by this approach, some of the loss of execution efficiency is recouped (one commercial firm has implemented a processor which has the P instruction set).

One very compelling reason for desiring a full compiler exists which makes the interpretive approach unattractive to many users. In many applications the product will be based on a pre-existing operating system or routines written in other languages are to be used. Using a full compiler which outputs relocatable object code in the 'native' instruction set gives the user considerable flexibility in this regard. So long as each relocatable module is compatible with the linker format, then the linker is not concerned about the source language. Specifically, this means that the user may choose to write some routines in PASCAL and others in assembler. Particularly during the performance modification phase, a user may decide to rewrite several PASCAL routines in assembler for maximum speed. The HP64000 PASCAL compiler makes an assembly language output available to aid the user in this very optimising process.

INTERMEDIATE CODE

One technique for implementing compilers reduces the difficulty of adding support for new processors. In a manner similar to the P-machine concept, an intermediate language is defined into which the first pass of the compiler translates the source code. This operation is then followed by the second pass in which the intermediate language is translated into relocatable object code for the target processor. Once the first pass has been written, only the second pass must be written for each new processor to be supported. Likewise to implement a new language only the first pass must be written to translate the new source language into the intermediate language. Since in each case the output of the compiler is relocatable object code, modules from several languages may be intermixed at link time.

This capability also suggests that if a module which was to perform some base level task has been implemented in a high-level language then it should be possible to recompile that module into another processor environment. Whether this will be successful or not depends on the context. The more 'pure' the program is, the more successful will be the move. Alternatively the more the programmer relied on some feature of the underlying processor, the more the routine will have to be revised and tuned for proper operation on the new processor.

A simple example will make this fact very clear. A program such as a bubble sort can be viewed as a pure procedure, and should yield the same results in terms of logical behaviour, independent of which processor the source code is compiled for and executed on. However surrounding the pure bubble sort program must be some facilities for inputting and outputting the data to be operated on. This implies some routines which are specific to the processor of interest. The area of input/output is one of the major areas of difficulty in moving programs from one processor to another.

A second very important area of similar difficulty is time-dependency. The time required to execute a given routine on a different processor will be different. Consequently if the high-level language program were intended to produce some output following a timer delay, then that timer program will need modification. Related to this, the execution-time performance of the same routine on two different processors will vary widely due to the efficiency with which each instruction set adapts to the problem. Obviously a 6809 which has an integer-multiply instruction will be much faster than a 6800 for programs which require multiplication.

There are other subtleties which may rise up which are dependent on how much of the data structure power of the language is used. The 8085 and 6800 have differing ways of referring to 16-bit constants. The 6800 stores high byte in the first address and low byte in the second address, while the 8085 does just the opposite. For many applications coded in HP64000 PASCAL this is no problem when a routine is moved from one processor to the other. However if the user has used pointer type variables to access the upper byte or lower byte of the quantity, then moving from the 8085 to the 6800 will clearly give erroneous results (but the program will run just fine).

The PASCAL compiler for the HP64000 was implemented with the issue of portability firmly in mind. Structured programming concepts implemented both at the programmer level and the software project management level are seen as very necessary concepts in improving software productivity. The ability to use a routine in several products is a plank in this platform. However the safest rule is to assume that some tuning will be required when routines are moved. The situation is creating new buzz words. If a routine can be moved with only a recompilation into the new processor's instruction set than the routine is deemed 'portable'. If some modification to the source code is required to accomplish successful execution then the term becomes 'transportable'.

SOFTWARE FACILITIES II
By Geoff Bristow, Peter Vinson and Dave Wollen (Texas Instruments)

The software problem

In general the most time-consuming, and therefore the most expensive, task in microprocessor project development is that of writing the software. A microprocessor is, after all, a device which has been especially designed to be general-purpose – the way it fits into any particular system is usually the same – but the software is necessarily specific to the application.

The overriding cost of software compared with hardware is particularly noticeable when the production volume of the end equipment is small. In this case, the decision will usually be made to build the product using standard microcomputer modules, which save all the chore of designing, laying out and debugging PCBs for the basic parts of the system. Very many projects can be undertaken using completely standard hardware – perhaps a CPU board, a memory expansion board and some input/output boards – but the software will always have to contain some statement of the function that the CPU is required to do. This is known as the 'application component' and is the highest level of the software in the system.

Since software requires skilled manpower to devise, its cost will always be high. Long after the cost of the standard hardware modules has diminished as a result of improved production techniques and VLSI technology, man will still be configuring them one by one into different applications with the use of software. This piece explains how software productivity can be increased drastically by the use of good software development techniques.

The ideal language

Since the application component is merely a description of how standard modules can be put to use in a particular situation, it would be most efficient to write it in an application-oriented language – that is, a language in which the structure of the application is immediately visible. For example, the following might be the application component for the controller of an automatic bowling machine for practising the very traditional English game of cricket:

```
PROGRAM AUTOMATIC_BOWLING_MACHINE;
BEGIN
INITIALISE;
WHILE BALLS_AVAILABLE DO
                        BEGIN
                        WAIT(BATSMAN_READY);
                        BOWL
                        END;
SIGNAL(NO_BALLS_LEFT)
END
```

In fact, this example has been written in the language TI Microprocessor

PASCAL which will be described later, but the concepts are shared by many similar languages. The most important point to note is that the program as shown here does not include any information at all about the hardware implementation and very little detail on the way the required algorithms are actually carried out in software – it simply states the overall purpose of the system.

The next level of software, of course, includes explanations of what is actually meant by INITIALISE and BOWL and it could be argued that these are further statements of the application. However, one could envisage a manufacturer of automatic bowling equipment who designs and builds different models of his product for different uses and markets. He would do best to configure each model from his own inhouse standard units (a bowling unit, a batsman-sensing unit, etc.), each one having its own software associated with it, such as the procedures INITIALISE and BOWL. All he would need in order to specify to the CPU what sort of control function is required in any given case would be a program similar to that shown above.

Using such software techniques (known as block structured programming in a self-documenting language) will obviously save a great deal of time, and therefore money, but that is not the only advantage – another is machine-independence. The fact that the application program above included no detail of the hardware implementation certainly meant that the application could be understood clearly without a screen of irrelevant information, but it also meant that the same summary of the purpose of the system could be made regardless of what microprocessor was actually used. If the language is suitable for implementation of detail as well – such as input/output manipulations and arithmetic – then this can be taken to the extreme and the whole top-down solution from 'application statement' down to 'device service routines' can be written in a single machine-independent language.

Several languages have been proposed for this all-embracing task on microprocessors, but few have been adopted by more than one or two manufacturers – PL/M is only an Intel language, for example. Two languages, however, have received universal acceptance in the microprocessor world: BASIC and PASCAL. Strangely enough, neither of these is inherently a system implementation language and it has been left to the manufacturers to make the necessary extensions for, for example, good input/output handling.

BASIC and PASCAL share readability, but their potential uses are quite clearly separated. BASIC is ideal as a first language – it is easy to learn and easy to modify interactively – but difficult to use for large programs. PASCAL, on the other hand, requires more discipline to start with, but is suitable even for very large systems written by several programmers. More importantly, the one which offers complete top-down problem solving and self-documentation is PASCAL. With extensions such as those in TI Microprocessor PASCAL, it can be an ideal complete system-implementation language.

Sacrifices in the name of efficiency

Why, then, would anyone choose to write software in anything other than a block-structured high-level language such as PASCAL? The reasons have been slowly disappearing since the very early days of PASCAL on microprocessors, but one will always remain: working in machine code can offer perfect optimisation in size and execution speed of the program.

Using high-level languages will always require an overhead in code. That is, even a trivial program will not compile down to a very small module of code. This is because the use of a high-level language automatically provides a structured programming environment, a framework into which simple statements can fit. (Even in a low-level language such a structured environment can be deliberately produced and would result in a similar overhead). However, in assembler (a symbolic aid to machine code programming) it is possible to write simple short programs in simple small packets of code.

The execution speed of an assembler program is generally expected to be greater than that of a compiled high-level language program simply because it can be absolutely specific – short cuts can be found. However, this also leads to difficulty in modifying the code. For example, if it is necessary to double an integer number, an assembler programmer is most likely to shift the binary number one place to the left, since the shift operation is usually much faster than the multiply. If, at a later stage, he then needs to change the multiplication factor from 2 to 2.5, the code must be changed and new errors may result.

Assembler language, then, can offer optimum program size and execution speed, but with the sacrifice of the ease of writing, reading and modifying the program that are offered by high-level languages. Estimates of increased programmer efficiency using PASCAL compared with assembler language vary between factors of three and ten times. When the size and execution speed of the code produced by some PASCAL compilers are now reaching about 80 per cent efficiency compared with good assembly code, the obligatory use of assembly code is restricted to projects where the absolute limits of the hardware are being reached, in processing time available or memory size. In addition, the power of microprocessors is growing faster than the complexity of applications to put them in, and the cost of semiconductor memory is falling faster than the cost of programmer time!

Software to write software

None of the arguments presented so far are particularly new in the world of software, although they represent comparatively recent discussion in the microprocessor world. That is to say microprocessor users are now learning the software techniques that computer users learnt perhaps 20 years earlier.

However, there is a difference. Most computer programmers write software on a mainframe or minicomputer and, having edited and computed the program, then execute it on the same machine. A mainframe user is not aware in which part of the large system his program is actually executing – the only feedback he receives will be an abstract parameter such as 'CPU time used'. A minicomputer user, on the other hand, will probably be familiar with the concept of compiling and link-editing a module of machine code for subsequent execution, but will then execute that program module on the same minicomputer that he used to produce the module.

In contrast, microprocessor programmers are generally involved in developing software for systems which have specific and sometimes rather limited capability; the system intended for execution of the software is likely not to have floppy-discs, or even a VDU, and may be most unsuitable for use in development. Accordingly, the concepts of host and target system have evolved in the industry.

The host computer is a machine dedicated to software development and the target system is the microprocessor-based end product. Writing software on the host computer for eventual execution in the target system makes available all the facilities of large memory, bulk storage and screen-based control for the task of developing the smallest and most efficient load module of code for the target.

Such an approach does, of course, require capital investment, and for a cheaper starting point in the microprocessor world it is possible to use a 'consumable development system'. This means that the host machine is actually built using standard microcomputer modules which can be used later as the target system, simply disposing of the add-on development aids. However, development software based on host systems without disc storage (with cassettes, for example) tends to be severely limited in capability, compared with floppy or hard disc systems. Disc-based systems, on the other hand, can benefit from the decades of experience of minicomputer users for the program development software, even if the additional cost of downloading the load module into an EPROM is completely new.

In the remainder of this chapter, two such systems of 'software to write software' are used as examples and examined in some depth: the advanced microprocessor prototyping language (AMPL) for assembler users, and the TI Microprocessor PASCAL system for high-level language capability. Each of these is more than just a language – it is a complete development system including full debugging facilities and control of in-circuit emulation of any of the Texas Instruments' range of 16-bit microprocessors and microcomputers.

Assemblers in detail

Assembly language is essentially a substitution of the binary representation of machine code instructions by more easily remembered mnemonics. Developing any assembly language program is usually an iterative process with many modifications being made to the program in the course of the development, as errors are discovered and corrected or as specifications are changed. In order to make this possible the Assembler program must take its input (source) from a text file or memory buffer rather than directly from the keyboard. This enables essentially the same source text to be edited and reassembled many times without the error prone tedium of retyping the whole source.

Although addressing and data values referenced can be absolute, it is more acceptable and far more convenient to use labels and symbols (see chapter 4, page 26).

Modules

On a complex Assembler project, a great deal of development time could be saved if the program was broken down into smaller blocks or modules; then when editing is done on one module, it is only necessary to reassemble that particular module rather than the whole program. This would also facilitate to some extent the concept of structured programming referred to previously, with each module's function being clearly defined at the beginning of programming. Different programmers could work on different modules, and modules written for previous projects could be reused with minimum effort.

The above scheme is inherent, for example, in TI's disc-based development systems. The output from the assembler for each module can be fully relocatable, that is can be placed anywhere in memory space and contains information to enable labels to be referenced in any other modules. To enable the resultant program to run, a linking loader (link editor) is used to assign absolute memory locations and connect the links between modules.

Assembler directives

To enable address labels to be referenced from a different module assembler directives are used. Assembler directives give vital information to the assembler but do not directly result in any machine code being generated. In the case of labels, directives are included in each module to identify labels in the module that can be referenced from outside the module and other directives define those labels that must be supplied by other modules. After the link editor has been run, a cross reference can be printed to check that all links between modules have been resolved.

Other assembler directives are used to set up tables of data or text in memory and to set the values of constants. This latter method of setting constants is useful for promoting portability of code between different but instruction set-compatible processors. The constant could be related to the clock frequency of the processor or the base address for working storage; to transfer code from one processor to another, only the constant values would need changing rather than, as in the mentioned examples, all the timing functions (both software and hardware) or references to temporary storage.

Yet more directives can assign the assembler output into distinct segments. This feature allows the fixed program storage region to be kept separate from the changing working storage region so that these can be in EPROM and RAM respectively in the final system.

On larger development systems, more facilities are available in the assembly language context. One of these is the 'macro' facility, which allows a sequence of code to be defined by a single word. At assembly time this word, which is declared as a macro, is recognised by the assembler and expanded into the sequence of code. A macro has the advantage that an often used sequence of code can be written with a single word, and this word can be chosen to be meaningful in the context of the code's use. Macros are used when a subroutine call would be inappropriate (e.g. due to tight timing constraints).

Conditional assembly

Another feature only available on larger systems is conditional assembly; one or more variables inserted into the assembly language source program can determine whether subsequent blocks of program are included in the final object code. This feature is particularly valuable in building operating systems or in manufacture of preconfigured software.

Multitasking

Finally, the larger systems support multitasking, i.e. several tasks can be running concurrently. In the assembly language environment, this means that, for example, a second module of assembly language could be edited while the first module (that had been previously edited) was being assembled. This can result in significant time-saving as tasks requiring operator intervention (e.g. editing) can be overlapped with those not requiring intervention while executing (e.g. assembly, linking and printing); this is not possible on smaller systems.

Control of in-circuit emulation

In-circuit emulation is a system of hardware and software which enables the microprocessor in a system under evaluation to be replaced by a controllable emulation of that processor with facilities for producing a record of the operation of the processor.

The in-circuit emulation hardware should simulate as closely as possible the microprocessor being emulated both with regard to electrical signal levels and timings and functional operation. These requirements can best be met by using a processor of the same type as that being emulated actually in the emulator, with buffering to overcome the extra load of the emulator-connecting cables. The emulator processor can be speed-selected to overcome the delays introduced by the emulator-cable buffers, thus ensuring real-time emulation. In addition to this, the emulator will contain logic to control the operation of the emulator processor and memory to record the execution of the program.

Emulator memory

A useful accessory to the hardware side of in-circuit emulation hardware is emulator memory; this has two main uses: to enable some testing of software to be performed before any application hardware has been built at all; and to substitute for memory regions that will be EPROM in the final system when the applications hardware has been built. In this latter case the emulator memory can be specified as write-protected from the target (application) system, while still being able to load, examine and modify from the host development system. This prevents faulty programs from over-writing themselves and necessitating a lengthy complete download of all the software for each new test. (The selective use of target and emulator memory and write-protection should, of course, be under the control of the development software.)

AMPL

The software support for the in-circuit emulation hardware should simplify the operation of the debugging aids as much as possible. After all, any extra time spent in debugging because of poor development software is time wasted. TI's emulation language, AMPL, fulfils this requirement by being a high-level block-structured language (somewhat like PASCAL or ALGOL) in its own right. However, unlike most high-level languages, AMPL is interpretively executed, rather than being compiled, allowing immediate execution after any changes, thus fitting well into the normal debug environment.

For example, once into the AMPL system, the user may type simple one line commands such as:

ADDR = >2BF0
@ADDR = 5

The first statement will create a new local variable called ADDR and set it to the hexadecimal value 2BF0, while the second will put the value 5 into the address specified by ADDR.

Another advantage of an interpretive debugging language is the inherent 'automatic display' of parameters. Any variable name or statement that is received by AMPL without being part of an assignment is evaluated and displayed as soon as the return key is pressed (no print statement is required). For example, at any time after the above example has been carried out, the programmer may simply type:

ADDR

and the system will respond with the current value of the variable.

The actual access to the emulation hardware is through predefined variable names (system symbols); however, these are in most cases not accessed directly, but rather through the use of procedures or their close relatives, functions.

Procedures are the real heart of the AMPL software as they enable new operations to be defined in terms of existing operations, and this can be repeated with more complex procedures being defined in terms of other procedures. A procedure is executed when its name – assigned at the time of definition – is encountered; a function is a procedure that returns with a value. (In fact there are many reserved keywords in AMPL that appear to be system variables but are really predefined functions.) AMPL users often build up very large libraries of their own procedures and functions and call up appropriate routines as required.

As an example of the use of procedures, let us consider a very simple target memory test routine. It may be decided that a suitable test is to check that a certain pattern of 1s and 0s can be written into memory, reading them back and alerting the operator if an error occurs. This may be achieved as follows:

```
?FUNC MEMTST (3.1) BEGIN           ..MEMORY TESTER (3 ARGUMENTS,
                                     1 WORD OF LOCAL STORAGE)
1?  LOC 1 = ARG 1                  ..SET LOCAL STORAGE WORD TO
                                     STARTING ADDRESS ARGUMENT
1?WHILE LOC 1 LOE ARG 2 DO         ..WRITE PHASE
1?  BEGIN
2?  @LOC 1 = ARG 3
2?  LOC 1 = LOC 1 + 2
2?  END
1?LOC 1 = ARG 1                    ..SET LOCAL STORAGE WORD TO
                                     STARTING ADDRESS ARGUMENT
1?WHILE LOC 1 LOE ARG 2 DO         ..READ AND COMPARE PHASE
1?  BEGIN
2?  IF @LOC 1 NE ARG 3 THEN RETURN LOC 1. .ERROR EXIT
2?  LOC 1 = LOC 1 + 2
2?  END
1?  RETURN -1                      ..NORMAL EXIT
1?  END
```

To use this procedure to test memory from address 0000 to hexadecimal address FFF0 with a pattern of alternating 1s and 0s the operator would simply type

MEMTST(>0000,>FFF0,>AAAA)

The two specified addresses are automatically passed to procedure variables ARG1 and ARG2 and the test pattern to ARG3. If the test pattern can be successfully read back from every location the -1 is displayed, otherwise the address of the first failing memory location is displayed.

Procedures can be generated and edited quickly to meet the changing needs of debug and the more generally useful ones saved on disc storage, but the majority of prewritten procedures supplied with the AMPL software system are concerned with the operation and display of data from the emulator.

These procedures perform chores such as initialising the emulator, setting the trace and breakpoint control parameters and finally displaying the captured data in an easily understood form. This latter task is achieved by using hyphens and underlining to present the data on the VDU screen in a logic analyser format, which can also be printed for future reference (see fig. 6.7).

```
? LOGIC

LOGIC ANALYZER DISPLAY:
        FIRST SAMPLE TO DISPLAY          = TTBO
        FIRST BIT TO DISPLAY             = 0
        LAST BIT TO DISPLAY              = 19
        SCALE FACTOR(POS: MARKS/SAMPLE   = 1
                     NEG: SAMPLES/MARK)

TRACE BIT     * AMPL LOGIC STATE ANALYZER *      INDEX  -254  TO  -194     EMU BIT
    0   :                                                              :
    1   :_____  _    _     _      _      _      _     _      _     _   :      IAQ
    2   :__ _____ _____ _____ _____ _____ _____ _____ _____ _____ _   :     DBIN
    3   :_   _    _    _     _     _      _     _    _     _     _    : EMU CMP
    4   :_ ___ _ ___ _ ___ _ ___ _ ___ _ ___ _ ___ _ ___ _ ___ _ ___ _:      0
    5   :_ ___ _ ___ _ ___ _ ___ _ ___ _ ___ _ ___ _ ___ _ ___ _ ___ _:      1
    6   :_  _ _  _ _  _ _  _ _  _ _  _ _  _ _  _ _  _ _  _ _  _ _  _ _ _:      2
    7   :_ ___ _ ___ _ ___ _ ___ _ ___ _ ___ _ ___ _ ___ _ ___ _ ___ _:      3
    8   :_    _    _    _    _    _    _    _    _    _    _    _    _  :      4
    9   :_____:    5
   10   :_ ___ _ ___ _ ___ _ ___ _ ___ _ ___ __ __ _ ___ _ ___ _ ___ _:      6
   11   :_  __ _  __ _  __ _  __ _  __ _  __ _  __ _  __ _  __ _  __ _:      7
   12   :_  _ __ _ __ _ __ _ __ _ __ _ __ _ __ _ __ _ __ _ __ _  __ _:      8
   13   :___ _____ _____ _____ _____ _____ _____ _____ _____ _____ __:      9
   14   :_  __ _  __ _  __ _  __ _  __ _  __ _  __ _  _  _  _  _   __ _:     10
   15   :___  ____  ____  ____  ____  ____  ____  ____  _____ _____ _:     11
   16   :_____   _    _     _    _    _     _     _    _     __:     12
   17   :_  __ __ _____ _____ __ __ __ __ _____ _____ __ __ __ __ _____:     13
   18   :_____ ____ __ _____   _  _   _   _   _   __  _____ __ __ __:     14
   19   :_____   _    _     _     _     _      _     _    _     _   :     15
```

Fig. 6.7 Typical outputs from the AMPL trace system

Automatic test equipment

Using the procedure facilities of AMPL with prewritten procedures stored on disc, a powerful automatic test equipment system suitable for prototype and limited production testing is available to users of AMPL development systems.

Once the emulator is plugged into the microprocessor socket, it has access to all of the memory and all the I/O devices normally connected to that processor. Tests can be written in AMPL to do read/write tests on RAM or verify the contents of ROMs. Often I/O devices can also be tested by driving them from the emulator and examining the resulting activity using the trace data probes; test input signals can be generated using the ability of AMPL to drive the I/O of the host development system.

Using the selfprompting facility of AMPL eliminates the need for any technical knowledge in performing the tests once they are started. As testing proceeds, information can be requested by filling the screen with a 'form' which can be simply filled in, default values being supplied where possible. Further procedures can be called from disc to replace procedures in memory that have completed their tests, and this can be conditional on the results of the tests or on inputs from the keyboard.

The following is an example of a FORM statement suitable for use with the memory test procedure given earlier:

```
?FORM MEMTST
1?':MEMORY TESTER';
1?'START ADDRESS' = ;
1?'END ADDRESS' = ;
1?'TEST VALUE' = '>FFFF';
1?END
```

To perform a memory test, the unskilled user could simply type the name of the procedure and would then be prompted for the required values. An example of the use of this form with the memory test procedure is given below:

```
?MEMTST
MEMORY TESTER
                    START ADDRESS  =  >0100
                      END ADDRESS  =  >2000
                       TEST VALUE  =  >FFFF
 −1
```

AMPL, then, is a sophisticated PASCAL-like development tool for the Assembler language user. In fact, it finds application in other worlds too – such as specific low-level language device service or interrupt handling routines in predominantly high-level-language systems and in automatic test equipment. However, let us now turn to what is available especially for the high-level language user.

PASCAL in detail

As outlined at the start of this chapter, the aim of high-level languages is to incorporate within them more of the abstract concepts for handling information which humans use, and less of the mechanical processes needed to satisfy particular machine architectures. In doing so, they also make the resulting programs more machine-independent; usually this is true more from a program design point of view than from direct transportability of code between two different machines.

Machine management

High-level languages remove from the programmer the burden of looking after the hardware resources of the machine, such as allocating registers or keeping track of machine status when performing, say, arithmetic operations. The penalty to be paid for this is larger program size compared with highly optimised hand-written assembler, and the consequent slower execution speed, but with the sophisticated compilers available today these disadvantages are now very slight, with highly optimised and efficient code being produced.

Advantage

The overwhelming advantage is, of course, the great reduction in development time, often as much as 80 per cent compared with Assembler, giving reduced costs and producing far more reliable and well-documented code. All high-level languages provide these benefits to some extent, but some are far better than others.

FORTRAN

One of the earliest high-level languages, FORTRAN (an acronym for formula translation) represented a great step forward, but nowadays it is seen to suffer from some fundamental drawbacks. Effectively, FORTRAN statements, such as $A = B + C$, provide a shorthand which can be expanded by a compiler into a series of Assembler or machine code instructions performing the required function. The control structures are basically just higher-level versions of the usual Assembler constructs, with branching, subroutines and simple decision-making, so the thought processes needed to design FORTRAN programs are still very mechanical, though less machine-oriented.

Block-structured languages

Experience has shown that this is not the correct way to go – so block-structured languages have been developed. The exact details of block-structuring are not important here, the point is that it is an attempt to break down a large problem into a series of smaller ones, and this is best done by treating it as a block, or functional module, and breaking it down into smaller blocks. Each smaller module can then be further split into finer detail in isolation from all other modules. This technique permits easier control of complexity.

In fact, techniques have been developed for doing this in languages like FORTRAN, but the onus is placed on the programmer. Over the last decade, a complete philosophy of software system design known as structured programming has been developed and block-structured languages are best for support this. PASCAL has been designed with these concepts in mind and learns from earlier languages like ALGOL 60.

PASCAL contains conceptually simple, but powerful, structures which allow the programmer to state exactly what he wants in a problem-oriented way. For example, the valid PASCAL statement:

IF FUSE-BLOWN THEN CHANGE-FUSE ELSE CHECK-WIRING

is very readable and immediately identifies what action the programmer is attempting to take. PASCAL allows these constructs to be translated easily by a compiler into efficient machine code.

It is not just control structures which make PASCAL a good language but also its powerful data structures, which permit easy and efficient manipulation of structured data like arrays, records and sets. The strong data-typing makes it hard for simple errors to creep in, like trying to assign the value 6.5 to a variable representing the day of the week; such errors can easily occur when it is left to the programmer to treat simple binary numbers as different data types.

There are hundreds of different high-level languages, but PASCAL is gaining most favour, especially for developing large programs for microprocessors and microcomputers. Microprocessor PASCAL, from Texas Instruments, was designed specifically for real-time microprocessor applications.

TI Microprocessor PASCAL

Microprocessor PASCAL provides a complete development environment for the TMS9900 family of microprocessors, the TM990 series of microcomputer modules, and the 990 minicomputers. It aids the user in his application from initial design, through program development and configuration, and then to testing and final implementation on the target system. The standard PASCAL language forms the core of the Microprocessor PASCAL language, but many significant extensions have been made based on experience of use and to support modern software design methodology.

ASSERT command
A major benefit is the sophisticated run-time checking which can be performed, particularly an ASSERT statement. This allows the user to make assertions as to the assumed state of the system at any point in a program. Optionally, code is produced to convert these ASSERTs from useful comments into run-time checks for validity. The use of such statements aids stepwise refinement and program verification.

Identifiers
It is a great help to use terminology in a program which suits the application. This is helped by allowing identifiers to be unique up to seventy-two characters and to include upper and lowercase letters and an underscore character, which is useful in multiword identifiers.

Extra constructs
Extra constructs have been added to allow ESCAPEs from within loops of structured statements and the explicit overriding of the strict data-typing by using a type-transfer operation; the latter allows integer addresses to be assigned to pointers. The use of the PASCAL CASE statement has been made safer by generalising it to include an OTHERWISE clause, and the use of subrange labels makes the CASE statement much more practical.

Example
The following examples of Microprocessor PASCAL show how some of the

extensions to the language lead to greatly increased generality and readability:

```
VAR animal: (lion, tiger, cat, dog, rhino);
CASE animal OF
    dog : pat__it__on__the__head; "this is a remark
    cat : stroke__its__back
    OTHERWISE
        IF life__isn t__worth__living THEN hang__around
        ELSE run__for__it
END;

CONST number__of__people = 50;
expected__number__of__legs = number__of__people * 2;
```

Extensions

Other extensions include support for 32-bit integer arithmetic, random files and the implementation of common variables, though these require explicit access to them in any module.

The 9900 family employs a serial I/O system, the CRU, which uses the address bus to select particular I/O ports which can send or receive any number of bits up to 16. This facility has been added to the language and permits efficient I/O bit manipulation. Also, a very powerful logic I/O system is supported and is interfaced to very simply by the use of READ and WRITE statements. The major extension is to incorporate concurrency naturally into the language itself. This provides many benefits for the user designing for real-time microprocessor applications.

Concurrency and its benefits

Concurrency (also known as multitasking or multiprogramming) means the ability to support the execution of several sequential programs at the same time. Obviously, with only one processor only one task can actually be active at any particular instant, but over a period of, say, seconds, many programs appear to progress at their own rate, and a snapshot of the system would show them all at some point in their execution path. The CPU actually executes these tasks in an interleaved fashion, swapping from one to another as required.

Parallelism

This gives many advantages in systems containing a high degree of parallelism, e.g. industrial control systems. The major advantage is the further modularity, which is a consequence of being able to associate with each physical process in a system a corresponding software process. It also makes for efficient use of resources, not only CPU time, but also memory.

Process

Microprocessor PASCAL knows this process concept, and treats a process as an independent entity competing with other such entities. Each process represents a combination of code, data and run-time support and the user can declare and concurrently start any instance of the process. For example, one terminal handler could be written and one instance created for each terminal in a system; the I/O address and terminal name would be included in the START statement as parameters.

Processes may contain other nested processes which follow normal PASCAL scope rules for procedures and functions. Up to 256 processes may exist in the system at any one time. The executing process will be the most urgent one which is ready to go, with urgency ranging from 1 (most urgent) to 32 766 (least urgent). The active process will continue to run until it can no longer do so, or until it is pre-empted by a more urgent one. Communication between processes can be effected by using shared data, or semaphore-protected message buffers, but a much higher-level, and therefore safer, method is provided by the interprocess file system. This allows processes to READ or WRITE to files connected between processes, or between processes and devices. The advantages of this method are the simple, but powerful, logical I/O interface which is presented to modules and the ease with which devices can be incorporated into it. During the checkout phase these I/O interfaces can be driven by other devices or files for testing purposes.

Microprocessor PASCAL has two special process constructs called SYSTEM and PROGRAM. The former is the single bootstrap process in which the system starts at power-up; the PROGRAM, of which there may be several, has data and nested processes which are independent of all other PROGRAMs, allowing it to be easily mapped out of memory in large systems.

Fig. 6.8 illustrates the structure of the software written for a digital voltmeter application. Each major physical process has a corresponding soft-

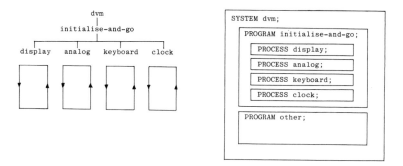

Fig. 6.8 Digital voltmeter application

ware process and they are synchronised by an interrupt-driven clock process. The code for this is shown below:

```
PROCESS clock;
CONST clock__mode = 0;          enable__clock__interrupt = 3;
        timer__on__9901 = # 100; period__for__refresh = # 65D;
        not__the__end__of__the__world = true;
BEGIN {clock}
        { # stacksize = 50; heapsize = 0; priority = interrupt__level}
        {This process synchronises all others. It initialises the 9901 clock
        register and waits for each level 3 interrupt, after which it signals
        to other processes that they can resume}

        crubase(timer__on__9901);
        ldcr(15,period__for__refresh);
        WHILE not__the__end__of__the__world DO BEGIN
          sbz(clock__mode);
          sbo(enable__clock__interrupt);
          wait(time);
          signal(time__to__strobe__display);
          signal(time__for__a__d__count);
          signal(time__to__strobe__keyboard)
          END
END;    {clock}
```

Executives and component software

It may appear that the software concepts and techniques described complicate the development of a user's software – indeed a great deal of time, effort and money must be expended to provide these sophisticated facilities if done by the user himself. Microprocessor PASCAL includes them as a natural part of the system and supports them with two powerful executives which allow the user to concentrate on just his own application software. Both executives provide similar capabilities; one, MPIX, is an interpretive executive while the other, MPX, is built upon the TI real-time executive, which offers stand-alone multitasking support for use with assembler programs.

The Microprocessor PASCAL executive (MPX) provides interface software which maps PASCAL on to the real-time executive environment and shields the user from any of the implementation features needed for concurrency, interprocess communication, interrupt processing and memory management.

General-purpose packages
The amount of software needed for large, complex systems can take years to develop, even with high-level languages. The trend is now to provide

major functional packages in a highly structured format which conforms to the system conventions set up within the language, but which is arranged so that the user can delete or modify modules, or add his own to an already developed framework. These general-purpose packages, which can be customised, can be used as major components in a complete system, and are thus called component software. Texas Instruments has already developed packages for complex file management and HDLC and EIA communications, with many more to be added. Since source code, as well as object, is provided, most of which is in PASCAL, the user can customise or rewrite modules, or use the packages 'as is'. The development effort which can be saved by using these packages can run into man-years.

The complete software development cycle

Using high-level languages leads to the need for creation, manipulation, storage, translation, testing and documentation of large amounts of textual information, requiring suites of development utilities, of which the language compiler is just one. All of these need to be integrated into one consistent user-friendly development environment which should be fast and efficient to use.

As well as providing the extended PASCAL implementation, the Microprocessor PASCAL system offers sophisticated software tools, amongst which are an intelligent syntax-checking editor, an efficient compiler and optimising 9900 code-generator as well as debugging aids for use on both the 990 minicomputer host system and the target system. Various utilities allow reverse assembly of the final object code, manipulation of host system files and devices and execution of user-written utility programs in PASCAL.

Overview of development cycle
In order to illustrate the features needed to efficiently support high-level languages, an overview of the Microprocessor PASCAL development system will now be given, with reference to fig. 6.9. Some of the features which make this system unique are described in more detail. The first phase of the development cycle is carried out on the host as shown in fig. 6.9.

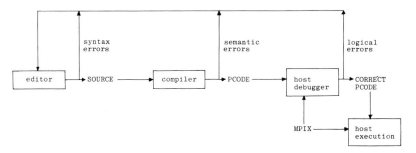

Fig. 6.9 Host development phase

Editor

The intelligent interactive screen-based editor permits efficient creation and modification of source files. It operates as a subsystem within Microprocessor PASCAL and has its own suite of commands which can be displayed at any time. The editor contains numerous features which aid the logical layout and documentation of the source and helps indentation of structured statements by automatic cursor positioning at the current indentation level.

Full use is made of function keys to make the editor easy and fast to use and special facilities are provided to manipulate whole blocks of text. The major feature of the editor is the syntax-checking option which will detect syntactic errors in the source by positioning the cursor over the error and describing it. Further syntax checking cannot be done until the fault has been corrected. This facility results in a major time saving.

Compiler

The compiler generates interpretive P-code for a hypothetical stack computer and supports separate compilation of individual routines. As well as detecting semantic errors, extensive run-time checking options are allowed; these cause code to be inserted to check for invalid subranges, array indices, set elements and pointers at run-time. Optionally, extra debug information may be inserted for testing purposes. The compiler executes very quickly because it only needs to generate the intermediate code.

Debugger

The interactive host debugger is an extremely powerful tool for detecting logical errors in the system, and is capable of debugging a full concurrent system. It, too, runs as a subsystem and has a suite of commands to provide powerful control. The complete debug session is logged automatically on a specified file or device to provide a diary of events. The session can also be driven automatically from a list of commands held on a disc file, which permits the user to quickly resume a previous debug session.

The development cycle is speeded up further by the dynamic linking of modules within the debugger, the system prompting for the files containing any required modules. The CRU I/O facility and interrupts can be simulated from the terminal; the CRU operates in three modes – OFF (i.e. does nothing), DEBUG (input from the keyboard, output to the screen) or EXECUTE (direct execution on host). At any time a detailed system status and process history is available to the user.

BREAKPOINTS

Breakpoints can be set by PASCAL routine name and statement number and tracing may be performed at statement, routine entry/exit or process-activation level. Single-stepping through the statements of any routine is allowed. The variables of any routine may be displayed and modified at any time. Variable and statement references are obtained from the listing produced during compilation. Having generated and debugged the P-code, the development cycle now moves into the system integration phase, as shown in fig. 6.10.

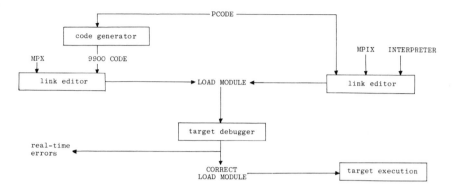

Fig. 6.10 System integration phase

Two approaches to code generation
There are two choices available in order to configure the system – the interpretive route or the native code route. This ensures maximum flexibility and the capability of trading off memory size against execution speed. In general, interpretive code is only half the size of native 9900 code, so for large systems, once the overhead of the interpreter itself has been reached, significant memory problems may be avoided using this route.

NATIVE CODE
Native code executes approximately five times as fast as interpretive. Extra flexibility is provided by easy interfacing to Assembler procedures or direct Assembler interrupt handling using either route, thus a system can be configured to meet most requirements.

If the user opts for a native code solution, then the code generator must be used to translate the P-code to 9900 code. The resulting code is very efficient due to optimisation at this stage and can be examined by use of the reverse assembler.

All that now remains to produce a load module is to link the application code with the appropriate executive and runtime support, and the interpreter if required. The option to use a full system or a kernel system is exercised at this time. A kernel system has particular features removed, e.g. error-exception handling, and results in smaller size. In either case only the modules required by the application are included.

The resulting load module optionally contains the extra debug code inserted by the compiler, which means that the PASCAL environment can be retained as we move into the system integration phase. The most powerful and effective method of testing the integrated appplication is using the in-circuit emulation capability provided by the AMPL system. This allows debugging to be undertaken in real-time on the final target hardware.

Interpretive approach

The system is controlled through the interactive interpretive AMPL language, which invokes procedures when commands are typed at the keyboard. The Microprocessor PASCAL system provides a suite of procedures written in AMPL; these allow both native and interpretive code systems to be debugged on the target system in a straightforward and consistent manner. This target debugger provides similar capabilities to the host debugger except that it runs at full speed and can also monitor the operation of the hardware.

Real-time tracing and breakpointing is supported, as are full display of process and routine information and display and modification of routine data. All this is done at PASCAL statement and routine name level, i.e. using the compiler listing once again. Although no particular knowledge of AMPL is required to run this subsystem as a PASCAL debugging session, the full AMPL capabilities are available, literally at the touch of a button.

After eliminating any real-time errors and verifying correct system operation, it only remains to remove the debug information and transfer the final object code to PROM. If memory space is not at a premium, this debugging information may be retained to provide useful back-up for field testing and maintenance.

Summary

It has been seen that high-level languages offer many advantages when developing complex real-time microprocessor software, but to use them effectively, the traditional development system must be provided with powerful software facilities. Verification and debug are important at all stages of the cycle. The Microprocessor PASCAL system provides four major levels of error-checking:

- syntactive – using the editor
- semantic – using the compiler
- logical – using the host debugger
- real-time – using the target debugger

The system designer can approach the integration phase of a project while retaining the same tools and problem-oriented approach used during the development and design phases. The same system can then be used to automatically test the final system, or even production runs.

We have also seen that under certain circumstances, programmers are forced to work in low-level languages, for subsections of a complete system, or for the whole system if the limits of microprocessor power are being reached. In such situations, powerful development tools are equally necessary, and we have seen how PASCAL – like debugging languages such as AMPL – can increase programmer efficiency.

Finally we have introduced the concept of configurable and modifiable software libraries such as TI's component software. These stop programmers starting from scratch in every situation and give packaged solutions to the known problems that programmers have already faced many times before.

In short, it is clear that as hardware becomes cheaper, software becomes the major cost of any project – it is therefore essential for all programmers to be equipped with the best software development tools.

EDITOR'S CONCLUSIONS

Two view points. Texas Instruments represent the view of a microprocessor manufacturer while Hewlett-Packard are regarded as an independent manufacturer of MDS. Very surprisingly there was a good deal of agreement from the two contributions, even in some of the details.

PASCAL appears to be the language encouraged, in one form or other. Transportability of software, directly or indirectly, is a feature which found agreement, and both contributions stressed the importance and arduous task of developing software.

Sam Lee's emphasis on the editor is important. The editor is a facility often overlooked, yet it is the interface the user most often comes into contact with during program coding. Its lack of ease of use could well be one of the main causes of the epidemic of unrecorded patches in programs.

Texas Instruments' team gave a good account of the generally accepted facilities for software programming. Their description of PASCAL is an indication of the 'readability' of a structured high level language (although it still falls short of true self-documentation). The concept of operating the MDS by programming in a command language (in computing terms this is known as JCL – job command language) is interesting, and AMPL, the Texas language, gives enough flexibility for the user to customise the systems operating procedures, with enough high level facilities for the general user.

Software design aids would be extremely useful on a MDS, but since there are no such things at the moment, the users will have to discipline themselves to methodical and orderly design and specification of software before using the powerful aids and facilities for coding the programs.

CHAPTER 7

In-circuit Emulation

The in-circuit emulator has already been identified as one of the most important features of the MDS, and in fact the editor would go as far as to say that it is the in-circuit emulator which sets the MDS apart from being any other computer. This chapter discusses this facility in great detail, where the concept of in situ debugging and the way in which the in-circuit emulator has to be implemented are examined.

The contributions

Intel could justifiably claim to be the inventors of the in-circut emulator, and, despite being the manufacturers of a dedicated MDS, have probably produced more different in-circuit emulators than any other manufacturer. Bernard Lejeune discusses Intel's concept of the in-circuit emulator, with descriptions of no less than eight in-circuit emulators for the Intel MDS series.

Tektronix, another well-known test instrument manufacturer, are independent producers of MDS of the universal type. Mike Mihalik gives a very good discussion of the implementation of an in-circuit emulator. He gives a good deal of insight into the difficulties and considerations in providing emulation facilities, especially for single-chip microcomputers. This is a very useful starting point for studying the implementation of in-circuit emulators.

The concept and principles in the in-circuit emulator are outlined in chapter 4, and readers are advised to refer to that discussion as well as to fig. 4.3 before reading this section.

IN-CIRCUIT EMULATION I
By Bernard Lejeune (Intel International)

In 1975, to meet the challenge of supplying design engineers with total development support, Intel introduced in-circuit emulation, a new concept in design aid. The increasing success of microprocessor-based solutions suddenly emphasised the need for design tools allowing easy and efficient software and hardware integration.

The new philosophy of using the same general-purpose microprocessor for many different applications made this phase of integration appear to be the most critical one. Software and hardware had never been so intimately bound together and the new microprocessor users were facing this problem with inappropriate tools and the feeling that they were reinventing the wheel for every new design.

The introduction of single-chip microcomputers reinforced the need for more sophisticated tools. In-circuit emulation brought to both hardware and software people the key features necessary for fast and efficient implementation.

Throughout this chapter, you will see how Intel has improved emulation performance to meet the requirements of more and more powerful processors. It is assumed that the reader of this chapter is already familiar with microcomputer terminology and has a good knowledge of basic principles of in-circuit emulation.

Review of development cycles

Any development can be divided into two major phases, the design phase and the implementation phase. The design phase consists of the identification and specification of the development goals by looking at the possible solution in respect to resources such as time, cost, manpower and available tools. The resulting solution has then to be developed in detail, so that the implementation phase can take place in an organised way. At this stage, software and hardware developments proceed simultaneously. The implementation phase is the execution of the specification established during the design phase. During this process, hardware and software engineers are working separately and only at the end of the implementation phase are both results integrated into the final product. Even when using strict specifications, there is a danger of incompatibilities in results. Fig. 7.1 shows the ICE* development cycle.

The ideal development tool

Both hardware and software engineers require more sophisticated tools.

*Intel, ICE and the combination of ICE with a numerical suffix are trademarks of Intel Corporation, a California, U.S.A. Corporation.

With the availability of new complex programmable LSI packages, the hardware designer's task has changed immensely. The only way that he can test his prototype is by running special test software that he would probably write himself. For systems including more than one processor, it can become extremely difficult and time consuming to debug software supporting their communication protocol and synchronisation.

The basic requirement of software engineers is to control and observe the program flow. This includes interrogation of program-defined variable and input/output ports. Ideally, programs should run in an environment as close as possible to the real one. We will see in the next section how emulation satisfies all these requirements.

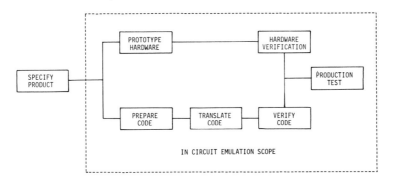

Fig. 7.1 Development cycle using in-circuit emulation module

Basic features of an emulator

The first problem a design engineer will encounter when he wants to test his software is the creation of an execution environment. All Intel ICE units provide this, by offering in-circuit emulation in real time if a prototype is available, and mapping resources if not.

A complete control of program flow is provided by a powerful breakpoint mechanism built with large hardware comparator registers. Observation of program flow is supported by single stepping and hardware tracing, relying on fast static buffer memories. Queries on program variables and program status information can be done by displaying memory locations and I/O ports.

Other interesting features that are actually becoming more and more important with the evolution of microprocessors are symbolic debugging, the interpretation of trace and memory information and the ability to allow programmers to remain at a high level of abstraction during the debugging of programs written in high-level languages. The evolution of the ICE itself, which supports a large number of commands, dictates the use of a high-level command language. Fig. 7.2 summarises the basic designer requirements and shows the corresponding ICE features.

```
Designer Requirements          Emulator Features



Implement environment        -  In-circuit emulation
                             -  Real time execution
                             -  Mapping resources

Control program flow         -  Hardware breakpoints

Observe program flow         -  Hardware tracing
                             -  Single step

Query on results             -  Display memory locations
                             -  Display uP registers
                             -  Display I/O ports

Remain at high level         -  Symbolic debug
of abstraction               -  Memory interpretation

Easy to use tool             -  Powerful command
                             -  Interpreter supporting
                                macro and compound
```

Fig. 7.2 Designer's requirements set against emulator features

Basic components of an emulator

An emulator can be seen as an integration of three main components, hardware, firmware and software. The detailed attributes of these components vary greatly from one ICE to another. This forces us to remain general enough in this section to cover all units. For each of these components, we will describe the main functions, discuss implementation issues and expose options that Intel has chosen.

In order to evaluate the number of choices and options that were available in the design of debugging tools, we need to take ourselves back to 1975, when decisions were about to be made. First software simulation was discarded since it did not meet the basic design requirements of real-time and real environment execution. This choice justifies the presence of hardware support. Two different implementations can now be investigated: hardware simulation or in-circuit emulation.

The hardware simulator offers real-time execution of a program but its use is restricted to software that is not intimately bound to hardware. The philosophy behind this concept is still characterised by the creation of a different piece of hardware that will execute the software during the development cycle. This particular hardware will only approximate the actual prototype. The approach is most feasible when the target processor is the same as that in the development system, then the development system's processor simulates the target machine.

The in-circuit emulation approach is entirely different, for, instead of simulating, you actually borrow a piece of hardware that can belong to either the user hardware prototype or to the development system. Choosing the in-circuit approach places Intel in the most general category of emulation, since all Intel emulators support a stand alone mode, if the user prototype hardware is not available.

This in-circuit choice imposes the presence of a specific element, the buffer box which allows the connection of the emulator to user hardware. Originally, the function of this first component was to electrically buffer all signals flowing on its reasonably long connection. Another important economy is gained by development system-resident emulators which can share the peripherals (terminals, disc and printer) of their development system. This solution offers the advantage of having access to a virtually unlimited range of devices from the paper tape reader to the high capacity hard disc unit.

The next problem to solve is the communication between emulator and development system. Two different approaches are possible. The emulator can be implemented in a separate chassis and talk to the development system through an I/O port as classical peripherals, or be directly plugged into the system bus. From the beginning, Intel opted for the second solution as it presents the advantage of faster communication and the sharing of bus accessible memory.

The level of debugging aid that Intel was targeting for made necessary a two-board hardware implementation. Emulators themselves are microprocessor based products. At any time, the emulator can be in one of two different modes, the emulation or the interrogation mode. The emulation mode is that particular time during which user's code is executed. All other time is spent in the interrogation mode. The firmware is the ROM-resident code that is executed on the processor board during interrogation mode. The purpose of the firmware is to implement a set of very basic commands that the hardware can execute. We say basic because each of these commands initiates only one specific and elementary hardware action.

For instance, the firmware could understand the command 'load parameter block address' or 'write byte to user memory'. The first command would cause the emulator to record the position in system memory where it can find information necessary for execution of further commands. The second command would cause a byte of data to be transferred to user memory. To do so, the emulator would then read in the system memory parameter block, the content of that byte and the position in user memory where it has to be loaded.

The software driver is the RAM-resident code executed by the development system processor. It runs under the control of the Intel software implementation supervisor (ISIS II) supporting disc operating system calls. This software package has two main functions. The first one is to interpret and translate the English-like user command into primary commands that the ICE firmware can understand. Secondly, it conveys to the operator the raw information such as trace data, error code and breakpoint data, coming from the firmware. The communication between these two elements happens without actual data transmission. As the emulator is connected to the system bus and has access to system memory, the software driver and the firmware communicate by building and modifying areas of memory formatted into parameter blocks.

To illustrate what we mean by high-level command language interpretation, we can examine the following example. The high-level command 'go from 200H until 300H executed then continue while memory 3000H = FFH' is processed by the software driver and will generate a series of elementary commands for the firmware. In this particular case, we might have the sequence:

- load parameter block address
- load breakpoint registers
- run emulation

The ICE will then enter the emulation mode and as soon as the breakpoint is hit, the sequence will continue with:

- load parameter block address
- read byte from user memory

The software driver will then compare the value of this byte with the value FF hexadecimal and stop the process if the comparison is positive or restart the complete command if the comparison is negative.

Not all the high-level commands activate hardware and firmware. Certain utility commands like 'BASE = ASCII' setting the ICE display format in ASCII mode, are entirely software supported.

Review of Intel emulators

This section is based on an historical scheme showing continuous progression of emulator performance for both general purpose microprocessor and single-chip microcomputers.

We will successively investigate ICE-80, ICE-85, ICE-86, ICE-88 for the microprocessors and ICE-48/49, ICE-22, ICE-41A, ICE—51 for the microcomputers.

ICE-30
Although ICE-30 was dedicated to emulation of a bit-slice processor, it is typical enough to be mentioned here. It is indeed the in-circuit emulator in which the original concept was developed. More than anywhere else, the software and hardware integration phase is the major difficulty during the development cycle of a bit-slice-based project. Applications using bit-slice processors are characterised by the need for a very fast response to external events. They generally use a short algorithm with a limited number of nodes. So writing the program and testing its logical functionality is one

thing, having it running in the real environment is another. This problem acted as the main motivation to produce a tool that would solve entirely the real-time and real environment simulation.

Intel brought the solution with their 3001 emulator, ICE-30 and a ROM simulator. The name emulator comes from the fact that ICE-30 circuitry does not simulate the 3001 with discrete logic but more efficiently uses a 3001 controlled in a special way.

ICE-80

With ICE-80, Intel was the first to introduce the in-circuit emulation concept to the 8-bit microprocessor world. We will now examine, in greater detail, each main part: hardware, firmware and software, and discuss their particular implementations. ICE-80 hardware is built on system-resident boards, a cable box and an umbilical cable; the classical elements that we will encounter when examining Intel emulators. The cable box provides electrical buffering of the processor signals going to and from the user prototype. The different functions have been partitioned on two boards, the processor and the trace board. We have already mentioned the emulation and interrogation modes in which an emulator can run. The ICE-80 processor board relies on a single 8080 processor to execute both functions of control and emulation of user code.

RESOURCE MAPPING

The resource mapping of ICE-80 allows the user to map the 64k address space of the 8080 in 4 kbyte increments. The user will then see these 64 kbyte as 16 blocks. He can choose which of these blocks are guarded (meaning nonexistent) and where each physically resides, either in user-prototype hardware or in the development system. Attempts to access a nonexistent block will generate a breakpoint that stops emulation. Blocks mapped into user hardware are accessed in the normal way, just as if the processor was executing on its own. When accessing a block mapped into development system, the processor will actually access the system bus memory. This capability, to map blocks of the user processor memory into the development system, is essential in answering the customer requirements concerning the creation of an execution environment. This feature allows the in-circuit emulator to be used in a stand-alone mode without any prototype hardware, so that it does not necessarily have to be in circuit.

Using the development system memory resources for mapping makes the most efficient use of the system memory. Not all of the total 64k of system memory is available for mapping resources. The system, running the software driver, uses the six lower blocks. Upper memory addresses are occupied by the ROM-based system monitor and the symbol table. The purpose of this symbol table will be explained later. As the system does not necessarily contain 64 kbyte of memory, the amount of memory available for resource mapping is expressed by the difference: [total amount available in the system − (24k + symbol table space)]. For a 64k system, the available memory is about 44 kbyte. To solve the problem of a user wanting to have his code running in the lower memory locations, the ICE-80 mapping mechanism supports the displacement concept which locates each user block into any available system block. This displacement appears more clearly on fig. 7.3.

The solution of borrowing development system memory combined with the concept of memory displacement introduced in ICE-80, and kept in further ICE products, offers maximum flexibility and maximises the efficient use of memory resources. Compared to other implementations where the emulator circuitry has its own mapping memory, the Intel solution offers the advantages of being economical, because it does not duplicate memory hardware, and flexible, because it can run in multiple system configurations.

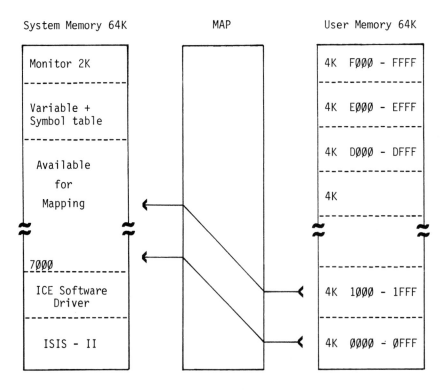

Fig. 7.3 Mapping displacement

REAL-TIME EMULATION

A large percentage of microprocessor applications are still in the real-time field, where the system has to react to external stimuli within a specified amount of time. Both software and hardware are involved in meeting these specifications. In other words, the number of instructions executed, the processor clock frequency, and the presence of wait-states generated through the processor-ready line, will directly define the response-time performance of a particular software routine. In the last phase of the development cycle, the designer wants to test his software in a situation as close as possible to the real-time. If the principle itself of in-circuit emulation offers a real execution environment, it does not necessarily support real-time operation. When starting the final test, the hardware prototype must be available anyway.

The Intel solution offers 100 per cent real-time execution when mapped in the user hardware prototype. It indeed looks logical to offer real-time when executing in the real environment. During the switching between interrogation mode and emulation mode or vice versa, all the CPU registers are saved. As this process doesn't need any user memory space, it is completely transparent to the user. Another interesting feature of ICE products is the emulation time-out. A breakpoint is automatically generated if the CPU remains inactive for more than one half of a second in emulation mode. However, it is possible to disable this time-out by an appropriate command.

TRACE

The main functions implemented by the trace board are the tracing and monitoring of the three processor busses: address, data and control. The ICE-80 trace stores the state of the three busses for a maximum of forty-four processor instruction cycles, corresponding to a program flow of ten to forty-four instructions. The trace starts recording as soon as the emulator enters the emulation mode and automatically stops when breaking the emulation and re-entering the interrogation mode.

BREAKPOINTS

The breakpoint mechanism using the same information stops emulation when a particular condition is reached. It uses a hardware comparator built with fast static memories. Two breakpoints can be set up, to break on any two 16-bit addresses on which the processor does the specific operation of execution, read, write, stack, unstack, input or output.

The 1k firmware is executed during the command mode. In this mode, the ICE-80 recognises fifteen basic commands. The RAM that records trace information in the emulation mode, can be accessed in command mode in order to transfer this information to the development system memory, for the interpretation by the software driver.

The software driver answers to the 'easy to use tool' user requirement. It extends the fifteen basic commands into a wide range of possibilities. We mentioned earlier that the only way to communicate with the ICE hardware was by exchanging parameter blocks. The software driver formats these parameter blocks, places them in system memory and tells the emulator where they are. In command mode, the ICE firmware accesses these blocks under DMA and executes the appropriate functions.

ICE-85

ICE-80, the first 8-bit in-circuit emulator, definitely established the principles of in-circuit emulation. The next Intel emulator, ICE-85, can be considered as the first of the new current ICE generation.

The 8085 processor is a superset of the 8080. ICE-85, as a matter of fact, is also a superset of ICE-80, built using the engineering experience acquired from the preceding ICE products. The major areas of improvement are related to both the software driver and the hardware capability.

The hardware offers the same basic features, but is far more powerful due to the use of new LSI devices. Although the language syntax of ICE products is quite straightforward, with the multiplication of possibilities and features, the learning of the software driver syntax is indeed the first difficulty that the user will encounter. At the time ICE-85 was put on the market, a standardisation in language syntax was defined so that all future Intel products using an operating command language would use the same syntax. The user can jump from an 8085-based project to an 8086 or 8049 without any difficulty. The investment in learning the syntax has thus to be only made once. In the same line of thought, a particular effort was made to give better intelligibility to the information that the ICE communicates back to the user.

The cornerstone of the new architecture, applied to ICE-85, is the standardisation of the firmware/hardware communication protocol and the hardware supporting it. ICE-85 is a product based on two microprocessors. We still find the two fundamental modes, interrogation and emulation, but a processor is dedicated to each of them. An 8080 is used as control processor and the emulation processor is, of course, an 8085. The 8085 processor is exclusively used for emulation purposes, acting as a slave to the control processor that is constantly executing the firmware code. The reason for choosing this architecture is the advantage of a more modular hardware that can recognise a larger number of commands. Taking the complete development station as an entity executing three types of code: software driver code, firmware code and user code, it seems logical to have three processors.

MAPPING RESOURCES

For a simple explanation of memory mapping see chapter 4, page 32.

The physical layout of the ICE-85 is very similar to the ICE-80: two boards and a buffer box. The processor board contains all the classical elements of a microprocessor-based product; more precisely 8 kbyte of firmware ROM and 1 kbyte of dedicated scratchpad RAM. Availability of larger fast static memories allowed a granularity of mapping twice as fine as that for the ICE-80 to be implemented. The 64 kbyte space addressability of the 8085 is then divided into thirty-two blocks. The new concept of shared and unshared memory has been introduced in the ICE-85 mapping. This new feature allows the user either to share the development system memory in the same way as ICE-80 or to use an extra memory area plugged into the system bus and addressed from 64 kbyte up to 128 kbyte. This makes it possible to map the full 64 kbyte address space of the 8085 into the development system. It is logical to install this feature on the processor board as it is the only board accessing the bus.

However, as the 8085 is running faster than the 8080, the real-time execution problem becomes more critical. For the reasons mentioned earlier, Intel is targeting a real-time emulation when using the actual prototype memory. Obviously the processor profits by being physically as close as possible to the user prototype. Two solutions are possible, install it in the buffer box or on the plug of an umbilical cable. The second solution was adopted because it solved the clock input problem in a very nice way. The 8085 has its clock generator integrated on the chip and the user only supplies a crystal. This remains true when using the ICE-85.

REAL-TIME EXECUTION

Having all the mapping mechanism far from the processor means that the 8085 has to access this map at each memory cycle (fetch, read, write). We can understand that this might slow down the execution time by inserting extra wait states. This drawback would be emphasised if the map mechanism was installed on the processor board. The information (address, data and control) would have to go back and forth through the buffer box cable even in the case of mapping in the user-prototype memory. To overcome this problem, a better solution has been chosen. The hardware making the decision to execute a memory cycle in user prototype memory or in development memory has been implemented in the buffer box, as close as possible to the processor. This precaution allows and guarantees a real emulation of 10 MHz parts when mapped into user prototype memory.

When using development system memory, ICE-85 supports an execution that comes close to being real-time, as the 8085 on the umbilical plug has direct memory access to system bus memory through a separate Multibus interface. The access time, in this case, will then be the summation of the system bus access time and the system memory access time. Bus access time can increase rapidly if several master boards are sharing the same bus and are requesting access to it. To overcome this problem, ICE-85 will be the only board accessing the bus during emulation and the development CPU will be maintained in halt. Another way to improve bus access time is to use the bus-lock mechanism to eliminate the arbiter logic response time.

MULTI-ICE

A completely new feature, on the processor board, is the hardware supporting the Multi-ICE operation through the use of device code and device port selection. The standardisation of this hardware makes it possible to control simultaneously two emulators plugged into the same system.

TRACE

The trace board serves two functions. The first one is to collect trace information on a 32-channel logic recorder. This recorder is built with 1k × 1 fast static memories whose addresses are automatically incremented in synchronism with the processor. This trace buffer has enough space to collect 1024 frames of processor execution. We recall that the frame is the most elementary unit of bus activity. Two 8085 frames make one cycle and one to six cycles make an instruction.

The same information is compared in real time by two hardware breakpoint registers that can break program flow on an extremely large variety of conditions. The trace board also accepts a new 18-channel buffer box tracing and breaking on general hardware signals. This gives a total width of fifty lines to the ICE-85 trace and breakpoint channels.

We have already mentioned that the buffer box contains all the buffering circuits to make the connection between the 8085 processor on the user plug and the ICE unit. We explained why a part of the mapping logic was put into the buffer box. Actually, the 8085 manipulation, allowing access to internal processor registers (A, B, C, D, E, H, L, PC, SP) is also done in the buffer box to allow faster operation. Three cables connect the buffer box to the ICE boards. One is used for control signals, the second for the DMA communication between the 8085 and the development system memory and the third for the trace information. A functional block diagram in fig. 7.4 summarises the preceding ICE-85 architecture discussion.

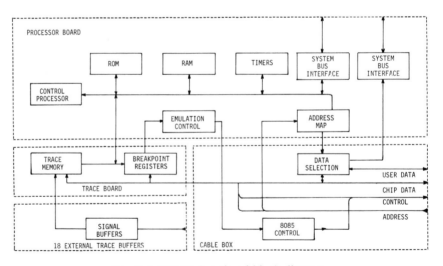

Fig. 7.4 ICE-85 functional block diagram

USER CONFIDENCE

The increase in capacity and complexity of the ICE-85 raises the question of how much confidence the user can put in his emulator. When he observes a malfunctioning of his design, the user wants to be confident that this is not due to a hardware ICE failure. The diagnostic contained in firmware can easily solve this problem. When the software driver is loaded, an automatic selftest sequence is initiated, indicating any malfunctioning or missing hardware elements. The increase in firmware size is mainly due to the Multi-ICE communication protocol implementation and to the larger number of basic commands recognised.

It would be hard to manipulate the ICE-85 hardware without the complete package of features offered by the ICE-85 software. The ICE-85 software driver resides in development system memory and runs under ISIS II. It recognises 120 keywords, about fifty commands and many more combinations of these commands. In comparison with the ICE-80, the language is more explicit and easier to use. We already mentioned that the same standardisation observed in hardware has been applied to the software driver. Conventions in command language have been established so that all further products will use the same syntax. The trace interpretation has been improved and offers three display modes; frame, cycle and instruction. The frame mode is the more basic and the closest to the hardware. It is actually the raw information from the trace RAM, arranged as a table that fits on the development system console display. A more compact display can be obtained with the cycle mode, as the two frames cycle of the 8085 is reconstructed. The third mode is the most readable one as it disassembles the trace into assembler mnemonics. A set of special commands selectively displays its contents by moving a pointer in the trace buffer.

SYMBOLIC DEBUGGING

ICE-85 supports symbolic debugging. Already provided by ICE-80, this feature tends to be emphasised by the growing popularity of high-level languages. Symbolic debugging refers to the ability to choose arbitrary but selfdocumenting alphanumeric names to designate a particular memory or I/O port address. If one knew that one's design I/O port E8H corresponds to a display device, one can tie the ASCII name DATA__PORT__DISP to the port physical address and later, refer to the port by its name. The definition of this name can be done, during the emulation session, by an appropriate command. This feature is quite interesting but we still need to enter the names manually. However, the ICE-85 software driver supports the automatic loading of the symbol tables created by the assemblers and compilers. This symbol table is a summary of all variable names declared in the source program and their corresponding addresses. The list for each software module is carried along through the link and locate processes.

On top of this, the address of each line of source code can be passed in the same way. This is particularly interesting for debugging programs written in a high-level language as you refer to source code line number without necessarily having to know where a particular micro instruction is located in memory.

ICE-86

ICE-86 offers virtually everything an engineer can require! The 1 Mbyte addressability of the 8086 requires more sophisticated breakpoint and trace control. The 8086 hardware peculiarities make its emulation more difficult. The instruction queue, in particular, was the major problem in observing and reporting the processor activity to the user. The 8086 processor maintains a queue of up to six prefetched instructions such that the processor activity does not necessarily match the bus activity. An instruction can be fetched and never executed if the processor flushes its queue, due to the execution of a jump instruction.

ICE-86 solves these problems. The internal queue mechanism is simulated outside the processor so that it can be used to supply information to the trace and breakpoint circuitry. The 8086 processor also supports two different modes of execution that can be selected by the strapping of an input pin. Using the minimum mode, the 8086 directly generates its bus control signals. In the maximum mode, the processor reconfigures its pin-out and presents a status information on three lines that need to be decoded by the 8228 bus controller.

All these new elements make a three-board implementation necessary. The trace and the processor board, now called firmware controller, contain approximately the same level of functionality as the ICE-85, but a new 86 controller board implements the features specific to the 8086 such as the queue simulation and the selection of the breakpoint level. The firmware controller gets its name from its functionality. Again it is the only board accessing the system bus. The firmware now occupies 12 kbyte of ROM and uses 3 kbyte of scratchpad RAM.

TRACE

The trace board has the same capacity as the ICE-85 trace. However, its control has been improved. The user can define trace turn-on and turn-off points so that he only records 'areas of interest' during an emulation run. These on/off points will start and stop the trace as many times as they are encountered during emulation and can be specified in the same way as normal breakpoints. The trace fully reports the processor activity: the twenty 8086 multiplexed address data lines, the five status lines, two flags indicating the presence of data or addresses, a marker indicating discontinuity in trace information, plus three lines supplied by the queue simulator indicating the number of bytes contained in the 8086 queue. As for the ICE-85, three trace display modes can be selected.

A NEW BREAKPOINT CONCEPT

Earlier, we used the terminology 'normal' breakpoints because a new notion of breakpoint range has been introduced in ICE-86. It is now possible to specify, in each breakpoint register, a break condition not only on a particular address but on a range of addresses and on multiple ranges.

If multiple ranges are used, they must all lie within a 1 kbyte boundary, starting at an even address. The most efficient use of breakpoint registers would then offer the impressive number of 1000 breakpoints.

On top of this, the ICE-86 makes the distinction between execution breakpoints and fetch breakpoints. The user can then specify a break on an instruction, either when it is fetched or when it is executed. This solves the problem of instructions being fetched by the 8086 but never executed. All these functions are hardware supported and ensure real-time operation.

The 86 controller implements three main functions: queue simulation, mapping and 8086 manipulation. The queue simulation hardware continually computes the number of bytes loaded in the queue using the queue status information supplied by the processor. The 8086 only supplies that information to the external world in maximum mode. That is the reason why the 8086 used on the ICE-86 is always running in this mode. This information is sent to the trace and used to implement the execution breakpoints.

MAPPING

The mapping granularity has been increased to 1 kbyte. The full 1 Mbyte is then divided into 1000 blocks of 1k that can be mapped guarded (meaning nonexistent), into the user prototype, into the development system memory, into the emulator or into a system disc file. This new possibility to map into a disc file offers the advantage of decreasing the memory investment cost of a 1 Mbyte 8086 design. However, if the system has enough memory, up to 960 kbyte can be mapped into it.

The 2 kbyte of ICE memory on the 86 controller can emulate time-critical portions of code in real time if the prototype does not yet provide any memory. The 8086 manipulation section of the 86 controller does the 'jam and dump' of the processor registers, using a small dual port memory for faster operation. As you can see, even if the implementation is different, the mapping philosophy of the ICE-86 remains quite the same. When no real-time execution is required, the user has the possibility to save much memory by using disc or system mapping. When real-time becomes necessary, the user gets it by using his own prototype memory or by using the 2 kbyte of ICE memory on the 86 controller.

BUFFER BOX

The ICE-86 buffer box plays an important role in implementing the two 8086 hardware modes. We mentioned that the 8086 processor used on the ICE circuitry is always strapped into maximum mode. ICE-86 however supports both modes of execution. A hold/hold acknowledge simulation, coupled to a timing generator and a bus multiplexer, provides all the signals that the 8086 generates in the min mode. Concerning the mapping mechanism, it should be noted that, due to its independent bus interface unit, the memory speed requirement for the 8086 is less critical than for other processors. This is also true for the ICE-86 itself, which explains why the mapping mechanism design was less critical with respect to speed.

The ICE-86's 12 kbyte ROM-based firmware performs three major functions. During cold start, it runs a series of hardware diagnostics to verify proper operation of all important functions and puts the emulator in interrogation mode, awaiting commands from the software driver. As soon as a command arrives, the firmware decodes it and initiates the proper hardware activity. If the command is a request to enter the emulation mode, the 8080 control processor generates the proper sequence of 8086 manipulations, puts the ICE-86 into emulation and continues, as long as this mode is maintained, to support the user program activities that require use of disc or system memory mapped, acting during this time as a slave of the 8086.

NEW FEATURES

In comparison with the ICE-85, the ICE-86 software driver supports the same package of features plus three totally new features. An online disassembler helps the operator to patch code in assembly language. The concept of macro and compound commands has been added. Until now, software drivers were able to deal with multiple command sequences, but their number was limited. You could give to the emulator a command of the type 'do this till this condition then do this then do this . . . then do this while this condition is true'. The major inconvenience of this method is that one ends up with very long commands requiring a lot of keystrokes free of typing mistakes. The possibility of using supervisor (ISIS II) submit files might solve this problem but in general the user wants to constantly remain online with his system.

The ICE-86 software driver completely solves this problem by offering a large variety of sequential operations based on three constructs, REPEAT, COUNT and IF THEN ELSE. These constructs support nesting and can be combined with the UNTIL and WHILE condition. As these commands can become fairly complex, they are entered using a step-by-step process. For instance, to enter a sequence of repetitive emulation sessions, the operator first enters the keyword REPEAT. The software driver then prompts the user for more commands until an END statement is entered. The compound command is then processed as soon as the end statement is entered. It is also possible to define compound commands that execute only when invoked.

ICE-86 literature refers to those commands as macro commands. This macro command concept offers all the advantages of both online and offline operation. When the macro is defined, the user specifies a unique identifying name and up to ten formal input parameters that will be replaced automatically by the actual parameters at invocation time. Once a macro has been defined, it can be invoked and saved on a disc file. The ICE-86 software driver maintains a directory of all the macros defined since the system start-up. Macros that were saved on file during a previous session can be recalled by a special INCLUDE MACRO command.

MACRO COMMANDS

The concept of macro commands is so powerful that there is no longer a need for a multistep command which can be built using a macro. Combined with symbolic debugging, macros allow the modification of program flow independent of the language in which the source code has been written. The following example illustrates the patching of code into a PASCAL source program. In order to have this program working we need to insert a statement that increments the index variable *j*. The operator can create a macro that temporarily corrects the program and can investigate and test the remaining part of the program without recompilation. He can create a macro called PATCH1 as follows:

DEF MAC PATCH1

  GO FROM .START TILL # 28 FETCHED
  !j = !j + 1   ;insert missing statement
  GO FROM # 28

END MAC

To run the corrected program, the operator would merely have to invoke the macro by its name preceded by a semi colon.

  :PATCH1

STMT	LINE	NESTING		SOURCE TEXT: :F1:SORT.PAS
1	1	0	0	PROGRAM sort (input, output);
2	2	0	0	CONST
				MaxArraySize = 5000;
.	.	.	.	
.	.	.	.	
.	.	.	.	
19	28	0	3	
				{Now sort numbers – use a bubble sort.}
				j : = ArraySize – 1;
20	31	0	3	
				REPEAT
20	33	0	4	Exchange : = FALSE; {No Exchange yet this}
21	34	0	4	
				FOR i : = 1 to j DO
22	36	0	4	IF NumberArray[i] > NumberArray[i + 1] THEN
23	37	0	4	BEGIN
23	38	0	5	Temp : = NumberArray[i];
24	39	0	5	NumberArray[i] : = NumberArray[i + 1];
25	40	0	5	NumberArray[i + 1] : = Temp;
26	41	0	5	
				Exchange : = TRUE; {Exchange – loop again}
27	43	0	5	END; {THEN and FOR}
				{missing statement}
28	45	0	4	UNTIL (NOT Exchange) OR (j<1);
28	46	0	3	......

ICE-88

Today's 8-bit Intel microprocessor is, without contest, the 8088. The 8088 processor may be considered as the 8-bit image of the 16-bit 8086. It has the same architecture and address space, and executes the same instruction set.

By doing this, Intel brought the 8086 performance to the 8-bit world. Its in-circuit emulator, ICE-88, reflects this similarity. Anything that has been said for the ICE-86 applies directly to the ICE-88.

ICE for single-chip microcomputers

The present chapter would have been incomplete without talking about single-chip microcomputer in-circuit emulation. Let us first recall that single-chip microcomputers distinguish themselves from microprocessors by the fact that they have their memory – ROM and RAM – and their input/output integrated on the chip itself. More than anywhere else in the microcomputer field, the need for real-time and real-environment emulation has been demonstrated.

Once again, being the leader in single-chip microcomputers, Intel felt the need for supplying customers with an impressive collection of in-circuit emulators tailored to the various processor architecture requirements, going from ICE-49 supporting 8048, 8049, 8035, 8748, 8749, 8021 to ICE-22 supporting 8022, to the ICE-41A supporting 8741A, 8041A, to the recent ICE-51 supporting 8051.

Even if microcomputers generally offer a hardware single-step capability, it remains difficult to develop single-chip microcomputer-based applications without the help of in-circuit emulation. It can be done but not efficiently. As the address space of single-chip microcomputers is smaller, their emulators are offering built-in memory mapping resources. All Intel single-chip microcomputer emulators provide real-time emulation and are supported by a software driver having the same range of performance as the ICE-85 software driver.

The same standardisation applies to their hardware and firmware so that they all support the Multi-ICE drivers. This is particularly important for microcomputers as they will frequently be used as slaves to microprocessors. Intel Multi-ICE software drivers consist of a software package that allows an operator to control the operation of two ICE units plugged into the same system. These drivers obey the same language syntax convention as any other ICE driver. Three Multi-ICE drivers are now available, 85-85, 85-49, 85-41. They also support the concept of macro and compound commands and might, possibly, for this reason, be used to drive a single in-circuit emulator.

Conclusion

In the beginning of this chapter, the need for in-circuit emulation during the integration phase was extensively demonstrated. Today, everybody agrees that the cost of the majority of designs resides in software development. It was therefore natural that the ICE concept would evolve in the direction of more support for software. This review allows us to observe the Intel in-circuit emulator evolution. We realise that ICE can now be considered as a true interactive software development tool.

The ICE solution is now becoming necessary to support both the implementation and the integration phase. The new features adopted allow the software engineer to stay at a high level of abstraction during his debugging session. The hardware engineer can still verify that the software runs correctly on his prototype. Both have the opportunity to use the efficiency of a common tool.

IN-CIRCUIT EMULATION II
By Mike Mihalik (Tektronix Inc.)

The basic principles and the importance of in-circuit emulation have been outlined in previous chapters. This chapter describes the components that make up an emulation system and the capabilities provided by this system.

To understand the utility of emulation, it is necessary also to include a description of a typical emulator, how it works and how to use it in the development of microprocessor-based products. By knowing the capabilities and limitations of an emulator, it is possible to speed the development process, unhindered by its idiosyncracies.

Examples of emulation provided in this chapter are based on principles used by Tektronix Inc. in emulators provided for its 8001, 8002 and 8550 microprocessor development labs.

What is emulation?

Emulation is the replacement of a microprocessor in a prototype by a piece of test equipment intended to provide all the functionality of that microprocessor, along with capabilities to assist in the integration of the hardware and software components of this prototype.

The emulator provides the means for the software engineers and hardware engineers to communicate with the prototype under development without the necessity of including test fixturing and test software in the design of the prototype. This becomes especially important when considering the design of price-sensitive products. With the emulator, the engineers and technicians gain the capability of controlling the microprocessor in the prototype as the software or hardware go awry, interrogating the prototype for clues to the source of this failure and the facility of altering the software to correct for these errors. All is within the capabilities of the emulator, provided the emulator and its development system are easy to use, and its limitations are known.

What makes up an emulator?

An emulator is usually considered to be the hardware and software necessary to replace the microprocessor in a given prototype. An emulator by itself will not aid an engineer without the requirement of an environment to operate within.

An emulator is usually the prime component of a microprocessor development system. This system provides capabilities for developing software in either high-level or assembly language, mass storage facilities for saving program source and object modules and an emulator environment. This emulator environment consists of the emulator, debugging resources, memory for the replacement of prototype RAM and ROM and possibly a logic analyser function characterised to the target microprocessor.

The development system is controlled by the user through an operating system that manages the resources of the development system and communicates the needs of the user. Especially important is a user interface to the emulator; this is the window between the user and the microprocessor executing the prototype software. The user language must be simple to understand, without limiting the power that an emulator can provide.

The emulator is the interface between the development system resources and the microprocessor. The emulator communicates with the operating system during overhead functions (transfer of control) and with the prototype when executing the prototype software program. A probe assembly is the part of an emulator that provides the physical connection of the prototype to the development system. It is a component which connects to the prototype in the same manner as the microprocessor it replaces – via a socket in the user prototype.

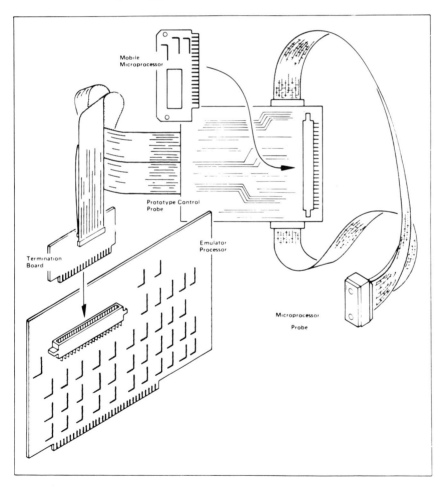

Fig. 7.5 Major components that make up a development system emulator

Fig. 7.5 shows the major components of a typical emulator as might be used in a development system. The three major components are the emulator processor, the emulator control probe and the microprocessor probe, which is inserted into the prototype's microprocessor socket. For applications that do not require integration of software into a prototype, some development systems allow operation of the emulator without the latter emulator control probe and microprocessor probe. Such operation allows software development and testing without the need for prototype hardware.

The emulator processor module forms the interface between the development system bus and the microprocessor bus, allowing emulator use of development system resources such as memory and debugging aids. This module contains the circuitry used to control the operation of the emulator. Its primary functions are starting the execution of the prototype program, stopping the execution, interrogating the status of internal microprocessor registers, changing the status of those registers and converting the address, data and control signals of the emulator's microprocessor to a form compatible with the development system bus.

The emulator processor module resides in the development system mainframe, but this does not provide a convenient means for connecting to the prototype hardware. Therefore, a prototype control probe is used to connect the emulator processor module to the microprocessor probe. The prototype control probe is connected to the development system by a length of flat cable that is a compromise of user convenience and minimising the propagation delays that the length of cable introduces. This cable must have several conflicting characteristics:

- flexible yet durable
- good electrical characteristics to minimise cross talk and ensure signal fidelity
- long enough to reach the user's prototype

The prototype control probe contains the circuitry that drives and receives signals transmitted on the interconnecting flat cable, the microprocessor used to emulate the target microprocessor of the emulator and control circuitry that switches the microprocessor signals between the prototype and the development system. The microprocessor is located in the prototype control probe and is electrically as close to the processor as current technology allows, in order to minimise propagation delays and skewing of key microprocessor signals. Faster processors means these delays have to be minimised or emulation would not be possible.

Final connection to the prototype is provided by the microprocessor probe. The probe may contain circuitry to buffer key signals to and from the prototype, such as clock and interrupt lines for example. These buffers are necessary because the clock source in the prototype may be a crystal or RC network intended to tie directly to the replaced microprocessor pins. The interconnecting cable of the microprocessor probe may add capacitance or inductance which could prevent oscillation, although still connected to the intended microprocessor pins.

Ideally, the microprocessor probe should have the same electrical characteristics as the microprocessor it replaces. Although possible with present technology, it has not been demonstrated by any emulators to date, due to costs involved in the development of special integrated circuits (ICs) and hybrids necessary to duplicate the electrical interface of the microprocessor. Some vendors of emulators place the microprocessor at the microprocessor probe end, putting it at less than an inch away from the intended prototype. While minimising skews and propagation delays, there is some disadvantage, since the microprocessor's MOS drive levels were not designed to drive both the prototype circuitry and the cables back to the prototype control probe.

The method of emulation described in this chapter does not allow the attachment to the prototype by clipping over the microprocessor while it remains in the circuit. As will be explained later, it is necessary to break certain connections between the microprocessor and the prototype circuitry to perform the emulator control functions. Merely clipping over the target microprocessor would not offer this isolation, unless measures were taken within the prototype to do this control function.

As mentioned before, it is possible for some emulators to operate without a prototype control probe. Here, the microprocessor module would be removed from the prototype control probe and connect directly to the emulator processor module in the development system. This modularity of design also introduces the concept of altering the function of an emulator by changing a personality module in the emulator. Microprocessor vendors have produced families of microprocessors that have similar characteristics. It is possible to design an emulator that can accommodate different members of the microprocessor family by changing the personality module, the emulator's controlling software and, if the pin-out or physical characteristics are different, the microprocessor probe.

What does an emulator provide?

An emulator lends itself to a number of applications. For the software engineer, it provides a target processor to execute software well in advance of a working prototype. For the hardware engineer, the emulator can be considered as the only device whose operating characteristics are known, allowing the testing of prototype circuitry surrounding the microprocessor.

In the early stages of the design of a product, it is important that the selection of a microprocessor is investigated as thoroughly as the specifications of the desired product. It is beyond the scope of this chapter to go into this, but it can be said that the emulator could be used for this selection process by allowing the execution of benchmark or qualification programs. An important characteristic of an emulator is the ability to operate without a target prototype. For the hardware designer, the emulator can be used to read signals coming from peripheral circuitry in the prototype, or force certain logic levels on control lines without writing special test software.

Before the debugging capabilities of an emulator can be discussed, it is necessary to investigate the basic architecture of an emulator. The technique described is one of many in use today, but is typical of most first- and second-generation emulators; first-generation is typified by the location of the emulated microprocessor being within the development system, while second-generation designs place the microprocessor electrically and physically closer to the prototype, in the prototype control probe.

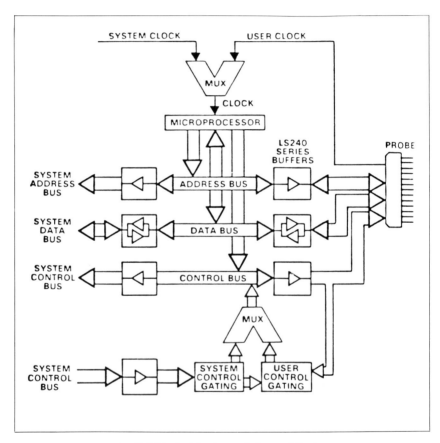

Fig. 7.6 Typical basic emulator architecture

Processor switching

Fig. 7.6 typifies the basic architecture of an emulator. When a stop in the prototype program is encountered, control is switched from the prototype microprocessor to that in the development system. This break or stop may have occurred due to one of the following reasons: a matched breakpoint condition, a service call to the operating system, a manual stop initiated from the user, or a detected fault condition. This switching function is achieved by multiplexing the processors' signals.

The user may select one of two clock options: one for use without a prototype and one for use with a prototype. The microprocessor clock, address, data and control lines are buffered and sent to both the microprocessor probe and the development system bus. The latter allows the development system to monitor the activities of the various lines driven and received by the microprocessor. The status of these lines can be used to trigger events within and external to the development system.

Sharing circuitry

In emulator systems using this architecture, the debugging capabilities of emulators can be shared. Within the development system is a module that provides control of switching the microprocessor between the prototype and the system bus. Also this module contains circuitry to monitor the status of the microprocessor address, data and control busses to provide triggers to be used in the generation of breakpoints or triggering external devices such as oscilloscopes or logic analysers. Certain conditions may be detected to alert the operating system that a special request is necessary (service request or SVC). This is used to simulate I/O operations of the target microprocessor.

Providing this circuitry on a common module simplifies the vendor's design of an emulator, since common circuitry need not be duplicated for each emulator needed. Users of more than one emulator will appreciate the lower costs involved.

Debugging capabilities

The preliminary use of an emulator is centred on its debugging capabilities. These can be divided into four areas:

- triggers and breakpoints
- logic analysis
- tracing instruction execution
- memory examination/modification

If all designers were perfect, there would be no need for these capabilities, provided the parts used were perfect. However, since this is not the case, designers have come to depend on these debugging features to integrate their hardware and software efforts into a working product.

Triggers and breakpoints

Triggers, or breakpoints, are defined to be some combination of the microprocessor address, data and control lines used to identify a particular event in the prototype program. There are many mechanisms, both hardware and software, to generate one of these breakpoints.

SOFTWARE BREAKPOINTS

In software debuggers, reliance is made on a processor's software interrupt instruction to signify a trigger condition. To set a breakpoint at a particular point in a program, an instruction in the prototype program is replaced by the particular software interrupt instruction. When this instruction is executed, program flow is transferred to the software debugging program, which may display current status information to the user.

There are several problems with the software triggering mechanism. First, to use this method there must be memory space available in which the software debugger can reside. This also precludes the prototype from using the particular software interrupt instruction, making it difficult to debug a software debugging program. Also, the instruction in the prototype program must be replaced by the special instruction, another difficult task when the program may be located in ROM. Finally, the breakpoint is only triggered when the instruction is executed; it would be impossible to trigger the breakpoint if a memory reference is the desired condition.

HARDWARE BREAKPOINTS

In light of the deficiencies outlined for software breakpoints, most emulators rely on hardware to generate breakpoint conditions. The simplest implementation is monitoring address lines from the microprocessor with 'equal to ' comparators, which generate a signal when the address bus is equal to a desired condition. This trigger is then used to stop prototype program execution, transferring control to the development system's operating system to display current status conditions. The trigger will be generated for both instructions executed at that address, or memory references.

CONDITIONAL TRIGGERS

If control lines are also monitored, specific bus transactions can be used to define triggers. The following bus conditions can be used to further define triggers:

- instruction fetches
- memory reads
- memory writes
- I/O reads
- I/O writes
- any I/O operation
- any memory operation

Any combination of the above may also be specified. The utility of this can be demonstrated with the following example:

A particular I/O port in the prototype is being reset when the program is executing. The port is only supposed to be reset when the prototype is first powered up. Of course software is suspected, so to identify the program section that is resetting this I/O port, a breakpoint can be used, thus:

- set the address comparator to the address of the I/O port
- set the bus control line comparator to trigger on I/O writes
- set a breakpoint so that the prototype program will stop executing when the condition defined·by the address and bus control line comparators is met

The emulator is started, and the prototype is reset to simulate a power-on condition. Each time the particular I/O port is written to, a break condition is generated. In Tektronix emulators, a trace line is displayed to the user by the operating system each time a breakpoint is encountered (fig. 7.7). This trace line contains the following information:

- the current contents of the microprocessor's registers
- the instruction just executed
- the location of the instruction just executed
- the reason the trace line was displayed

If the I/O port in question is written to many times by the prototype program, the program may have to be restarted several times, continuing from where execution was stopped, until the data pattern that clears the I/O port is seen by the user.

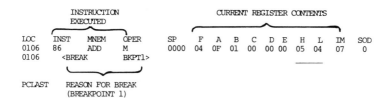

Fig. 7.7 Trace line information for 8085 emulator

A refinement can be included to the breakpoint comparators, by also providing comparators that monitor the data lines of the microprocessor. The data comparators can then be programmed to the particular pattern to reset the I/O port and a trace line will only be displayed when that pattern is written to the I/O port. By examining the trace line for the location of the instruction just executed, the user may then identify the program module that is performing the undesired write operation to the I/O port.

Logic analysis

Logic analysis capabilities can be defined as the ability to acquire a sequence of bus activity as the microprocessor executes the prototype program. In most emulators, there is a logic analyser built into the emulator or development system that acquires address, data and control line information during each bus cycle of the microprocessor. When the development system has stopped the program execution, the acquired information may be examined sequentially right up to the point where the prototype program was stopped. This information will show the individual bus cycles for each instruction executed, and the data read or written by each memory of I/O reference.

The value of this information can be gleaned by going back to the example just given for the resetting of a particular I/O port. It was stated that the trace line would show the location of the instruction which reset the I/O port. Investigation of the program showed that the software module identified was a general subroutine used to communicate with the I/O port, called by various parts of the overall program. The calling sequence passed a variable to the subroutine, which in turn wrote that value to the I/O port.

To identify what part of the program was calling the subroutine and resetting the I/O port, the logic analysis capability just described can be used. By examining the address, data and control line information acquired from bus cycles leading to the breakpoint condition, the instruction sequence executed can be examined. Just prior to the starting address of the subroutine should be the instruction used to invoke the subroutine, along with its location (see fig. 7.8).

ADDR	DATA	MNEMONIC		EXTERNAL	BUS		
0207	36	MVI	M	00000000	M	R	F
0208	00			00000000	M	R	
0251	00			00000000	M	W	
0200	F3	DI		00000000	M	R	F
0201	11	LXI	D	00000000	M	R	F
0202	75			00000000	M	R	
0203	02			00000000	M	R	
0204	21	LXI	H	00000000	M	R	F
0205	50			00000000	M	R	
0206	02			00000000	M	R	
0207	CD	CALL		00000000	M	R	F
0208	00			00000000	M	R	
0209	03			00000000	M	R	
F012	02			00000000	M	W	
F011	0A			00000000	M	W	
0300	3F	CMC		00000000	M	R	F

Fig. 7.8 Display of bus transactions

CONDITIONAL ANALYSIS AND 'WINDOWING'

The simple logic analysis capability just described may be sufficient for most problems. What would happen if the display of previous bus cycles did not contain enough cycles to identify the problem, or a snapshot of bus cycles at a particular time is desired? A solution provided by some development systems and emulators is to add trigger comparators to the logic analyser function to control the acquisition of bus information.

Much like stand-alone instruments, the logic analysers incorporated into development systems have flexible triggering mechanisms for qualifying acquired data. As mentioned previously, the simplest form is the acquisition of all bus cycles up to the breakpoint. Usually 128 or 256 bus cycles can be saved in the logic analyser buffer. This is commonly called post-triggering. Another way of acquiring bus transactions is to define a start and end trigger condition, thereby defining a window. Bus cycles would be stored in the logic analyser buffer after the start trigger until the end trigger ends the acquisition. The end trigger may also define a breakpoint to stop program execution so that the acquired data may be examined. Alternately, another trigger may be defined as a breakpoint, producing a 'snapshot' of the bus cycles.

ANALYSIS BY TYPE

Just as triggers may be used to define when information is to be stored in the logic analyser buffer, triggers may also be defined to specify what kind of bus cycles are acquired. Because of the limited size of the buffer, bus cycles can be qualified as to type before being saved in the buffer. For example, by defining that only instruction fetches be stored, only instruction OP code cycles will be acquired. Instruction fetches are defined to be the memory reference occurring as the first byte or word of an instruction sequence, usually sufficient to describe the nature of the subsequent bus cycles. The address information stored with the instruction identifies where in the program the instruction resides. Other combinations of bus cycles may be used for qualification, as described in the breakpoint trigger discussion.

Including the logic analysis function with the emulator allows tailoring the specification of trigger information and the display of acquired data in a format closely associated with the microprocessor being emulated. Also, there is no need to keep track of connections to the microprocessor as in a conventional logic analyser, because the emulator probe provides the connection and translation of address, data and control lines.

Memory access

Another debugging capability is the examination of memory used to store the prototype program and its data. Commands from the user to the development system are used to read or alter memory in different formats. The simplest way to examine memory would be to direct the emulator to read memory from a starting address to an ending address. The display is usually in hexadecimal, although binary, octal or decimal is also possible. Another display format is to translate byte data into the corresponding ASCII-equivalent character. These methods of displaying memory are primarily for examination of program data (fig. 7.9).

Memory may also be read corresponding to the instructions of the prototype program. The development system instructs the emulator to read the memory and then translates the information back into mnemonic form;

a reverse assembler or disassembler (fig. 7.10). The resulting display closely resembles an assembly language source listing, minus the comments.

Provisions for altering memory are also provided by the emulator. Again several formats may be allowed, permitting memory to be changed by specifying an address and hexadecimal, binary, octal, ASCII, etc. data. The development system translates the command and data, then instructs the emulator microprocessor to write the data to the designated address. The exact methods used will be discussed later.

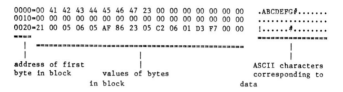

Fig. 7.9 Memory display

```
LOC   INST     MNEM OPER
0100  210005   LXI  H,0500
0103  0605     MVI  B,05
0105  AF       XRA  A
0106  86       ADD  M
0107  23       INX  H
0108  05       DCR  B
0109  C20601   JNZ  0106
```

Fig. 7.10 Example of development system instructions to the emulator

Instruction trace
The last debugging capability to be described is tracing instruction execution. Unlike the logic analyser capability, this is a method used to display microprocessor status information instruction by instruction by single-stepping the microprocessor. The logic analyser can only monitor the address, data, and control line information available external to the microprocessor. Also changing as the prototype program executes, are the internal processor status and data registers. Recall that when a breakpoint was triggered in the emulator, a trace line was displayed which indicated the last instruction executed, its location and the contents of the microprocessor's registers.

Single-stepping the microprocessor is essentially setting a breakpoint automatically on each instruction as it executes, displaying a trace line after each. This allows the user to monitor program flow and register contents as the prototype program executes.

Total control of the prototype is provided by the emulator and development system, allowing the user to exercise all the address, data and control lines of the microprocessor provided by the connection of the microprocessor probe and the commands directed to the emulator by the user. As long as the prototype provides a microprocessor clock, the design of the emulator allows the user to manipulate the signals of the microprocessor as a special test program may have done.

Memory in the prototype may be verified by reading and writing to it using the debugging commands mentioned previously. The I/O ports may be manipulated in a similar manner, simulating the operation of the application program, before complete software is available. Prototype-program execution can be started, stopped and restarted as easily as using any of the debugging capabilities described.

Memory mapping

Another debug aid is the simulation of RAM or ROM in the development system, rather than providing it with memory from the prototype. This allows execution of the prototype program on the microprocessor in the emulator without requiring PROMs or memory in the prototype during early stages of integrating the hardware and software.

Memory is available in the development system for use by the emulator. This memory should be fast enough, i.e. sufficient access time, such that the program can run at the same speed as it would if the prototype were supplying the memory. Most development systems rely on the use of fast static memory to perform this function, eliminating the need for the emulator to insert wait states when accessing the memory.

The user allocates memory in the development system where it is required for the prototype program in blocks of a given number of bytes; for processors that access up to 64 kbyte of memory, the resolution or block size is usually 128 byte. Larger address-space microprocessors place a burden on the emulator if the same block size were allowed, settling for 2k or 4k block sizes for processors that have greater than 1 Mbyte of addressing range. This function of using development system memory in lieu of prototype memory is referred to as mapping.

Memory mapped to the development system should take on the characteristics of the memory as it would exist in the prototype. The emulator has circuitry which monitors access to this memory and can identify these accesses as ROM or RAM accesses. When the user specifies the mapping of memory where the firmware would reside, the emulator would characterise this as ROM-type memory with write-protect circuitry. This circuitry interrupts, or stops prototype program execution if the program attempts to write to this area, informing the user of the undesired instruction sequence.

The emulator has both read and write access to this memory during operating system execution so the prototype program can be loaded into the memory. During the debugging phase, it is important that the user not alter his program inadvertantly while it is executing; the write-protect capabilities of the emulator make sure the program does not get altered.

If the concept of mapping and RAM/ROM provisions is expanded further, the development system and the emulator provide the user with a memory management function. Some microprocessors can distinguish normal accesses or privileged accesses to its program, data or stack spaces. The triggering mechanism described for breakpoints can be used to specify when those accesses are valid for different parts of the prototype program, and then cause a break when a memory violation occurs. This would signal the user that something is wrong with the program and that corrections should be made.

Emulation without prototype

Going back to the statement made concerning using an emulator without a prototype, this capability is provided by the emulator and special communications to the operating system. As the software engineer develops the prototype program, there comes a time when testing of the software modules is necessary, but the prototype may be unavailable at that time. Testing of the program involves executing the instructions on the emulator, stopping execution at an appropriate time and examining memory or processor register information for the desired result.

Service requests (SVC)

Provisions are included in the operating system of the emulator to display information on the development systems terminal, read from its keyboard and read or write information to its mass storage or other peripheral devices. The user of the emulator also has these resources available and may use them in testing the prototype program. The resources of the development system are used in lieu of the prototype. The software engineer is provided with a means to perform simulated I/O through the use of service requests (SVCs) to the operating system. While developing software, SVCs are used to transfer data between the prototype program and the development system peripherals. The SVCs permit the program to accept and display data in a format other than that provided by the processor's registers, or memory contents.

As the development of the prototype hardware progresses and testing of the program indicates correct functioning, the SVCs are replaced by the I/O instructions or routines in the microprocessor's assembly language. The software is then tested in the prototype environment.

SVCs are activated by the prototype program using a special instruction sequence in the microprocessor program. Executing the instruction triggers a special break to the operating system, instructing it to perform a sequence other than a trace line. The microprocessor in the emulator is paused, waiting for the development system to complete the function requested.

The operating system program reads data from memory set up by the prototype program, instructing it to perform a function with the data also provided. Typical parameters of a service request are a function identifier, a channel to designate destination or source of data, status information for error conditions, actual data, amount of data and sometimes the location of an I/O buffer used for large transfers of data. The resources of the development system are then used to present data to the user in a more easily understood format, or to substitute for the prototype peripherals.

How does an emulator work?

Previous sections have described what an emulator is and what were its capabilities. This section will describe how the combination of the electronics and software in the development system work together and provide the user with an emulator.

The key component

The most important part of any emulator is the device that will execute the prototype program exactly as the microprocessor would and in the same length of time. Another constraint is that the address, data and control lines of the microprocessor probe must appear as the pins of the microprocessor would when also executing the program. The complexity of microprocessors emulated to date dictates the use of the same type of microprocessor in the emulator, or in some cases one in the same family. The central component of emulators discussed here will assume this fact.

Therefore the microprocessor is the key component of the emulator, with the peripheral circuitry functioning as directors of the address, data and control lines to either the development system or the user's prototype. The fine art of emulation is revealed in the discussion of this peripheral circuitry, and the description of the software which orchestrates the transactions.

Operation of an emulator

The following sequence describes the operation of an emulator during a typical debugging session:

1 the microprocessor registers are set to desired values
2 the microprocessor starts executing the prototype program
3 some time passes until a break in execution is desired
4 the microprocessor stops executing the prototype program
5 the emulator is interrogated for the contents of the microprocessor registers
6 the status information is displayed to the user for analysis
7 some change may be made to the program, the prototype, or the values of the registers
8 go to step one, repeating until all is well

This, of course, is a simplistic view of emulation, but the sequence is one that every emulator and its user performs. Definition of terminology relating to this sequence is necessary to understand the discussions which follow.

STEP 1 (SET REGISTERS)

The user may specify the initial values for the microprocessor registers that will be used when starting prototype program execution. This operation is called 'restoring the registers'. The development system operating system software reserves space to save copies of the registers for user status displays. The user can then use commands to alter the contents of this memory, corresponding to values desired for the registers. Just prior to the starting of the prototype program, the operating system instructs the emulator to read this memory and load the values into the corresponding registers inside the microprocessor. The microprocessor actually is executing a special program sequence, accessing the development system's memory rather than the prototype system's memory.

The 'restore' program must have certain special characteristics, and the emulator must provide circuitry to switch the microprocessor so that the development system reserved space is used during this short sequence. The program will be loading the normal registers and the condition code registers, and the execution of the program must not alter the registers in the process of setting the desired values; this involves some ingenuity on the emulator designer's part. The special program must also read the register data from a reserved space of the operating system memory; this is not mapped memory as described before, since the user's prototype program may respond to the same address. The emulator switches these accesses to an address outside of the normal addressing range of the microprocessor.

Once the registers have been set to the desired values, the emulator control circuitry leaves the processor in a state in preparation of starting the execution of the prototype program, not allowing the registers to change from the preset values.

STEP 2 (START EXECUTION)

The microprocessor is instructed to start executing the prototype program. There are three possible starting points:

- from a power up, or reset state
- at a user specified starting address
- start from where the emulator was last stopped

The last two are implemented in the same way on an emulator, by treating the starting address as a settable register as far as the user is concerned. Most microprocessors do not have an instruction accessible register for the starting address; this is called the program counter (PC).

Starting execution from a power-up, or reset state is done by momentarily resetting the microprocessor on the emulator and allowing it to go through its normal reset sequence. Most microprocessors will vector to a predefined address and start executing the program. The emulator's involvement in this sequence is minimal, since it must only isolate the RESET line from the prototype for a short time while asserting the reset state. The connection to the prototype of the RESET line must be isolated during this sequence since the nature of the prototype circuitry driving this line is unknown to the emulator. The emulator may damage the prototype by arbitrarily asserting this line since it is not expected that a microprocessor may assert its own reset line. There are some microprocessors that can do this, e.g. Motorola's MC68000.

The behaviour of the RESET line in the prototype must be considered when using an emulator and the reset command in the development system. Other hardware in the prototype may also need initialisation by the RESET line.

Another obvious approach is to keep the prototype powered off when starting the emulator. Once the emulator is started, power is then applied to the prototype, providing a true power-up situation. Unfortunately the microprocessor probe cannot be powered-down to simulate a switched-off microprocessor. The emulator has circuitry to detect lack of microprocessor clocks and prototype power to protect emulator circuitry and to identify user faults. The development system and emulator must remain powered-up to maintain the integrity of controlling software and the emulator control circuitry.

To simulate the prototype reset condition, the user must provide access to the system RESET line via a switch or special jumper arrangement, or configure the prototype so that the assertion of RESET by the microprocessor probe will not cause any damage to the prototype.

The other approaches of starting prototype program execution by the emulator involve forcing the microprocessor to leave the emulator-idle state and vector to a specific address where instruction execution will continue. Again special switching is performed by the emulator control circuitry, whereby the microprocessor executes an instruction sequence to direct the next instruction fetch from the desired prototype program starting address. This function must again have the characteristics of not altering the previously set register values.

Two methods are used to set the starting address. One is a 'forced-jump' sequence and the other is a 'faked' return from subroutine or interrupt. The architecture of the microprocessor dictates the method used for a given emulator.

In the forced-jump sequence, the emulator's microprocessor is removed from its idle state and the data pattern for a jump instruction and its operand are placed on the microprocessor's data bus, regardless of the address put out on its address lines. The data link to memory is broken for the duration of this forced instruction. Once the microprocessor completes this instruction, it will then start fetching instructions starting at the location specified by the operand of the jump instruction. The operand is usually loaded into a special control register on the emulator by the operating system and a user command.

In order for this method to work, the emulator circuitry must be able to determine when the microprocessor is fetching instruction bytes and operands, so the switching of the jump instruction and its operand occur at the right time. Not all processors indicate this status information, so the emulator designer may design what is called a 'fetch predicter' to decode when instruction fetches are occurring from the signature that a microprocessor leaves as it executes instructions.

Instruction synchronisation

Digressing for a moment, how does a fetch predicter work? A state machine is started from the reset state of the microprocessor. The reset sequence for all microprocessors is well defined, so an algorithm can be formulated detecting this sequence. By counting processor cycles, it can be determined when the first instruction data is being read from memory. The value of this data determines what instruction is about to be executed. The state machine determines from this data the length of the instruction, its operands and the number of bus cycles. Counters are then programmed by the state machine to countdown the length and bus cycle information. Terminal count of the counters then indicates when the next instruction will be read from memory, and the sequence is repeated.

The terminal count of the counters thus indicates instruction fetches used to control other operations in the emulator. The state machine must be fast enough to account for the shortest and most complicated of instructions. Some processors may not have a so well defined sequence, or the look-up tables in the state machine for some instruction sets may overwhelm the other circuitry of the emulator. In this case, the presence of instruction fetch information must be precluded and other methods used.

The second method of using a return from subroutine or interrupt instruction sequence is used when synchronisation to instruction fetches is not feasible or possible. In most microprocessor instruction sets, a return from subroutine or interrupt routine will read data from the stack and use that data as an address to indicate where program execution should return or continue. Additional information may also be read from the stack during this sequence in the form of processor status information and register contents; so all or part of Step 1 may be done in this sequence.

This method works in a manner similar to the first described. As will be seen in a later step, the microprocessor in the emulator was left in an idle, or halted, state just prior to it executing a return from interrupt instruction in the emulator's special control routines. When the processor is brought out of this idle state, it will read from memory its stack, data to be used as return addresses and, in some cases, register data. As in the forced-jump sequence above, alternate data is forced on the microprocessor's data bus, indicating the user specified starting address for the return address.

In this method, it is only necessary for the emulator control circuitry to be aware of when this return is pending and when memory read bus cycles are occurring. The data presented to the processor data bus is read from a section of reserved memory in the operating system or within the emulator. The emulator control circuitry monitors the bus cycles of the return instruction, switching the microprocessor between the reserved memory and the prototype program memory space.

STEP 3 (EMULATION RUN)
During this phase, the emulator is operating as the user would expect the microprocessor to perform if it were directly controlling the prototype. The emulator circuitry and the development system's debug capabilities monitor the address, data and control lines, waiting for some trigger condition, or perhaps some breakpoint or fault. Most of the control circuitry on the emulator is disabled at this step, except for circuitry which will stop the current prototype program execution. It is waiting for the fault or trigger condition to start Step 4 of the emulation sequence.

STEP 4 (STOP EMULATION)
On the emulator is circuitry to stop execution of the prototype program. There are a number of sources which will harm this circuitry and cause a break condition. Breakpoints, prototype clock or power-fail, illegal instruction execution, memory protection violations, SVCs, or simply a user request may each trigger the stop sequence. SVCs require special action and will be covered separately. The remaining will be referred to as a break condition.

Break condition
Once started, the break condition will start a sequence which determines the current processor state. This information is as follows:

● the instruction just executed
● the instruction's location
● the location of the next instruction to be executed
● the state of address, data and control lines when stopped

The location of the instruction just executed is called PCLAST; the location of the next instruction is PCNEXT. As mentioned in the discussion for the trace line, PCLAST, the last executed instruction and the current register contents, are acquired and displayed to the user for analysis.

PCLAST is acquired by latching the value of the address bus during each instruction fetch while the prototype program is executing. Circuitry on the emulator latches the address, which the operating system may read when it has control. The latching is disabled when the break starts, so the address acquired will be the location of the last instruction executed. The data byte is either read from the corresponding memory location or from a data latch on the emulator to be decoded as the last executed instruction.

PCNEXT is latched in the same manner, but by the first fetch that occurs after the break condition. The emulator control circuitry allows the fetch to occur, but prevents the processor from executing the instruction by placing the microprocessor in an idle or halted state. This latched address may be used to continue prototype program execution from where it was interrupted.

Break using interrupts

For those processors where fetch indication cannot be determined, an alternate approach must be used to stop the microprocessor and start the break sequence. This is done by using an interrupt input to the processor. To ensure the development system ability to gain control, the microprocessor interrupt must have a few capabilities:

● activation of the interrupt must unconditionally stop the processor from the current instruction sequence
● response to the interrupt must be to a predefined vector or location
● the interrupt acknowledge sequence of bus cycles must be determinate
● certain processor status must be stacked or saved so restarting may be done by the emulator

Most microprocessors that must use this method have a nonmaskable interrupt (NMI) input which meets these requirements. The emulator must share this input, so the user is not precluded from its use in the prototype.

Minimally, the microprocessor will save the PCNEXT information and the processor condition code register contents, when the interrupt is acknowledged. The emulator must arbitrate this interrupt to determine whether it was generated by the user externally, or the emulator started a break sequence. If it is a break condition, the emulator must provide the microprocessor with an alternate interrupt service routine so the emulator may interrogate status information and idle the microprocessor. This again involves switching in an alternate memory space containing the instructions to service the interrupt condition. The instruction and bus cycle sequence of the emulator-supplied routine are determinate, so the switching sequence of the different memory spaces controls the microprocessor actions as the operating system requires. Once the sequence is complete, the microprocessor is idled in a specific state and location.

The interrupt method does not acquire PCLAST information; instead a number of the previous bus cycles acquired by the logic analyser may be displayed for the user to determine where the break condition occurred. PCNEXT is available and displayed, but the break may have occurred on a jump or return instruction, leaving the user at the beginning of a new software module.

SVC breaks

SVCs are a special break condition, since only a pause of the microprocessor may be necessary. If there is no need for the PCNEXT or PCLAST information by the operating system when performing the service request, then the processor is waited or halted, while the operating system completes the request. Once complete, the microprocessor is unhalted and prototype program execution is continued. If the break condition status is required to complete the request, then the aforementioned sequence must be entered.

STEP 5 (REGISTER INFORMATION)

Once the microprocessor is again under the operating system's control, requests are made to emulator routines to acquire register status information – 'dumping the registers'. The emulator microprocessor executes an instruction sequence which transfers the register contents to a reserved space in the operating system's memory space. This is the same space where register values are stored for the restore register sequence. Again circuitry on the emulator must switch the microprocessor between the different address spaces so the prototype memory is not disturbed. The dump register instruction sequence has the same basic requirement as the restore register sequence; the register contents must not be altered during the transfer out of the microprocessor to the reserved memory space.

STEP 6 (STATUS INFORMATION)

The control program for the emulator reads the values from the reserved memory space and formats the information into a display of the current microprocessor status. The information is displayed for every break condition and takes form as the emulator trace line is printed on the development system terminal. The control program that formats this display translates data transferred by the emulator control routines into a mnemonic display of the last instruction executed and the current microprocessor register contents (fig. 7.7).

Additional information may be contained in this status display; there may be I/O ports present on the microprocessor, or special sense lines, whose present value may help in debugging the prototype program.

STEP 7 (ALTERING PROGRAM OR 'PATCHING')

Upon examination of current microprocessor status, the user may need to alter the prototype program. The memory for the prototype program could be mapped to both development system memory and prototype memory. There are two separate sequences necessary, depending on whether the operating system is accessing one or the other.

The access to memory in the development system is done by switching the memory space so it is accessible by the operating system. There is direct access to the address data and control lines to this memory. The emulator access to this memory is turned off while the operating system processor is reading or writing to this memory. Any memory protection set for this memory is also disabled during this sequence, since it is the operating system, not the prototype program, which is accessing the memory. The emulator regains control of this memory once restarted.

Accessing prototype memory or I/O ports is a different situation since the operating system does not have direct access to its address, data and control lines. The prototype memory may also rely on specific timing characteristics of the microprocessor to control memory accesses. The only connection to this memory is via the microprocessor probe plugged into the prototype. When the user commands the operating system to alter this memory, the software instructs the emulator to execute an instruction sequence which will read or write to the prototype memory or I/O ports. Parameters specifying the address and data are passed to this control routine by another special memory space. This instruction sequence and the control circuitry must be designed so only the specified portion of the user's program is altered. Once the desired changes are made, the user and the emulator go back to Step 1 to continue the debugging session.

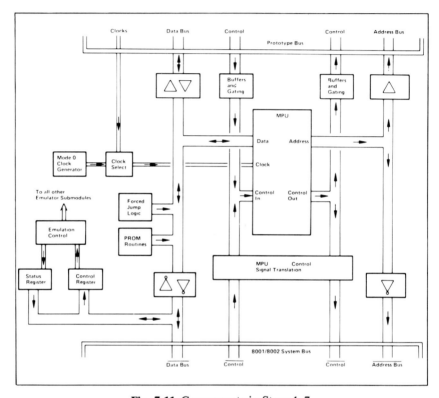

Fig. 7.11 Components in Steps 1–7

Emulator configuration

Fig. 7.11 shows the components described in the previous steps. The microprocessor is the main component of the emulator; its address, data and control lines are connected to both the prototype and the development system busses by buffers and gating. These buffers control the switching of the microprocessor between development system memory and resources and the prototype. The control signals from the microprocessor do not always match the requirements of the development system bus, so translation circuitry is sometimes necessary for those signals.

EMULATOR TIMING

There are two sources for the microprocessor clock; the clock-select block selects either the prototype clock or a clock generated on the emulator. The latter clock is used when running the emulator without a prototype. The circuitry must be designed to minimise the skew and delay between the microprocessor and the prototype circuitry. It is impossible to reduce this delay to zero, so the user of the emulator must take these delays into consideration when using the emulator with the prototype. If no margin has been included in the prototype design, the emulator may not work with the prototype under worst-case conditions. Emulator vendors usually supply a difference document indicating emulator probe timing in comparison to the specified microprocessor timing.

CONTROL TRANSFER
The forced-jump logic block is the section used to supply the jump instruction sequence to the microprocessor during transfer of control between the operating system and the prototype program execution. Control ports accessible to the operating system are programmed with the desired starting address in the prototype program.

PROM ROUTINES
The PROM routine block consists of the special memory space containing the instruction sequences for the microprocessor routines which dump processor registers, restore processor registers and read or write prototype memory and I/O ports.

EMULATOR CONTROL AND STATUS
The last block contains circuitry to control operation within the emulator and to indicate the current emulator status.

SINGLE-CHIP MICROCOMPUTER EMULATION
The discussion in this section covered the operation of emulators for microprocessors which have the same basic architecture; i.e. all have address, data and control information present at the microprocessor's pins, or socket connection. There is a special class of processors, single-chip microcomputers, with the microprocessor, memory and I/O circuitry contained in the same package. The external interface is in the form of I/O ports only, with not indication of the status of address, data and control lines available. This requires additional effort in the design of the emulator. Two approaches can be taken.

USE OF SIMILAR MICROPROCESSOR
In the first approach, there may be another microprocessor available in the family of the microcomputer with the same instruction set and address, data and control lines available externally instead of the I/O ports. In this case, circuitry is included on the emulator to duplicate the missing I/O ports and pass these connections to the microprocessor probe. The prototype sees what it thinks is the I/O ports of the microcomputer, while address, data and

control information is monitored by the emulator control circuitry and the development system bus.

With the other approach, a special emulation microprocessor is made available by the vendor. This part is usually in a larger package with additional pins to make address, data and control lines available. The emulator makes use of this additional information, while passing the I/O ports directly to the microprocessor probe.

Using an emulator

In order to use an emulator to execute a prototype program, the following components are necessary:

- an emulator and development system
- a prototype program
- a prototype
- memory for the program
- I/O facilities to control or respond to program execution

When one of the pieces is missing, save for the emulator and prototype program, the development system resources must be used as a substitute. The user selects an emulation mode to indicate which functions are to be performed by the development system, and which are to be performed by the prototype. The three possible modes are:

- Mode 0 (system mode). Mode 0 uses the clock provided by the emulator as the clock for the microprocessor. Memory requirements are also supplied by the development system. No interrupts are honoured by the microprocessor except for development system break conditions. I/O is handled through service requests, or SVCs, to the operating system. Until the prototype is available, the program can execute only in Mode 0.
- Mode 1 (partial emulation mode). Mode 1 uses the prototype clock for the microprocessor and may use SVCs for simulated I/O. The prototype's I/O facilities may also be used. Mode 1 allows the program to access memory either in the development system or in the prototype. With memory located in the development system at the same address as the prototype's memory, the PROM or ROM environment is duplicated without programming a PROM. Memory mapping circuitry on the emulator determines whether a particular memory block refers to development system, or prototype memory.
- Mode 2 (full emulation mode). Mode 2 uses the full resources of the prototype. The emulator resources are used to monitor, or transfer control back to the development system.

In all three emulation modes, the emulator takes the place of the processor that will eventually reside in the working prototype.

When starting a debugging session, integrating hardware and software, the user must define the prototype environment to the emulator and development system. Operating system commands are used to specify what memory will be in the prototype, what memory the development system will provide and, if so, what address range should be write-protected to simulate PROMs. If SVCs are used, the user must also specify where the parameter information is located in the prototype program. Flexibility in locating this parameter block is provided so it may be placed in unused memory space, which will not conflict with the prototype program memory requirements.

Once the environment is set up, including the emulation mode, the user instructs the operating system to load the program into memory. This program is the result of a compiler or assembler producing object code that represents the user's program. If everything is working properly, the user then specifies the starting address and starts program execution. There are usually problems at the outset, which must be identified and solved. Verifying proper program operation may take several options.

The user could single-step through the program, checking operation as each instruction executes, though this is unlikely other than for very short programs or sequences. Another way is to set a break condition at the end of some operation and examine the results at that point. By setting a number of steps such as this, the user can isolate problems to some small area and debugging efforts can then be concentrated on this section.

Flexibility in defining these break conditions is provided. Triggers may be defined as any combination of address, data and bus cycle status. Counters are also available to set a trigger on the nth occurrence of some event. Bus transactions such as interrupt-acknowledge cycles, address-space references and memory stack operations, in addition to normal read or write cycles, can be specified by monitoring processor control line information with the trigger circuitry.

Real-time emulation
When using the emulator, it is important to remember when real-time execution of the prototype program is taking place. Some emulators may insert delays into memory cycles to accommodate propagation delays and skews between the emulator and prototype. The best example of real-time operation would be to picture a prototype whose function is to inform the user of time of day. Software timing loops based on a particular microprocessor clock rate may be used to keep track of the time. If the emulator did not perform as the microprocessor would, say, adding on additional delays to memory accesses, then the prototype would gradually lose time in proportion to the added delays.

Real-time execution can only occur when the prototype program instructions are executing. Whenever a break condition occurs, the acquisition of processor status information and its display, interrupts the prototype program, stealing a chunk of time from the program. If a processor were available such that the status information could be acquired as the program executes, a superior emulator could be produced, one that would not require the interruption of prototype program execution for the special instruction sequences required to gain register and status information.

Successful emulation depends on the user's understanding of the capabilities and limitation of the emulator and the microprocessor used. Transparent emulation does not require the user to reserve memory, interrupts or I/O space to accommodate the emulator. The prototype may need all the processor's capabilities. The emulator's microprocessor probe should be able to replace the microprocessor without any change in the prototype or its program; operation of the prototype with the emulator or the microprocessor should show no differences in performance.

The perfect emulator is not technically possible due to cost limitations, and what the user will pay for. Vendors of emulators make available the differences in characteristics between the processor's operation and the emulator's operation.

What an emulator can do:

In general, emulators can execute prototype programs in several environments, including the environment of the prototype hardware itself. The emulator and development system provide debug capabilities to the user that can be removed from the prototype when the product design has been completed. The debug facilities could have been added to the prototype, and the final product, but would add significantly to the total cost, because of the development effort necessary for the additional capability.

The user would have little need for the included debugging tools, but the service personnel may. The emulator's operation in the prototype should be completely transparent to the user until a problem occurs, or a break condition is encountered. Then the facilities of the emulator and development system can be used to track down the problem.

What an emulator cannot do:

As was discussed previously, the display of processor-status information requires interrupting the prototype-program execution. This requires a short amount of time that may affect the proper operation of the prototype in time-critical applications. The logic analyser's capability helps overcome this deficiency. The electrical characteristics of the microprocessor probe are different from the microprocessor it replaces. Microprocessors are static sensitive MOS devices with limited drive capabilities. The emulator buffers the microprocessor lines for static protection and increased drive for the interconnecting cables between the prototype and the emulator. These buffers also introduce propagation delays and signal skewing which must be taken into consideration.

If direct memory access (DMA) capabilities are built into the prototype, the splitting of memory between the development system and the prototype may cause improper program operation, since it is impossible to DMA into the development system memory from the prototype memory. In DMA, the microprocessor is removed from the address, data and control lines, with the DMA circuitry controlling memory bus cycles. Since the only path connecting the development system to the prototype is the microprocessor socket, the emulator is disconnected during the DMA operation. One way to display the limitations, or the capabilities of an emulator, is to get another emulator, and use it to emulate the microprocessor on the other emulator.

EDITOR'S CONCLUSIONS

In the accepted concept of the MDS, the in-circuit emulator is one of the most important facilities. The choice of which could even determine the selection of the MDS itself. Of all the facilities provided on the MDS, the emulator is one which is new and truly innovative, specifically produced for debugging and testing with microprocessors.

The contribution from Intel was most interesting because of the description of all the Intel in-circuit emulators, where the evolvement of the emulator can be seen. Intel have provided some of the most advanced and powerful in-circuit emulators available.

Tektronix have given us a good insight into the complexities of producing an in-circuit emulator, especially on the subject of timing considerations for real-time emulation and the difficulties in implementing emulators for single-chip microcomputers.

An important criterion to judge the new generation of in-circuit emulators is their ease of use and the user's confidence in the system. Symbolic debugging with mnemonic display should now be the norm and restrictions to hexadecimal or binary representation should not be tolerated. In other words, we should be allowed to debug in the language we programmed in. User's confidence has to be high, as we are using these devices to test other systems, and if we cannot trust the test equipment, how can we ever be sure of the quality of any tested product?

CHAPTER 8

Development Without Development Systems

This chapter describes how microprocessor application development can be undertaken without conventional microprocessor development systems. This discussion can help to highlight important features and areas where improvements to the MDS can be made.

The contribution

Although this book centres on microprocessor development systems, the readers should not be lead into thinking that the use of the MDS is the only valid way for an application development. Here in balance is an account of microprocessor application development without development systems, with case studies of areas of applications. Many facilities do already exist in established equipment (e.g. mainframe and minicomputers, logic analysers, etc.) and by knowing the types of tools required to carry out microprocessor application development, one can provide the necessary facilities to constitute a microprocessor development system.

Our contribution for this chapter is from Liverpool University, which is one of the early pioneering establishments to take on the application and training in microtechnology in England. Professor Jim Alty is Director of the Computing Laboratory for Liverpool University, and was responsible for providing the development facilities for microprocessor work at the university as well as the policy decisions on the way development work is to be carried out.

It should be noted that an academic environment is different from the commercial. In the academic environment there is more time and resources to look for the ideal solution, whereas in the commercial environment, this approach may be uneconomical for the short term. But the findings from academic establishments are very valid and relevant – and they often lead to improvements to product lines. So there are many lessons to be gained from the approach and experiences of Liverpool University.

Note: The costs for the various applications described by Professor Alty are for convenience also given in US$ (using £1 = US$2), but it should be noted that prices in England are generally higher than the equivalent in the USA. Also the prices are pre-1980 and there have been price reductions in many components, including the Intel SKD-80 kit mentioned. Even so the costs shown are remarkably low for the types of applications under consideration. Professor Alty has included the development costs, which show that the cheapest hardware is not necessarily the most economical solution. Lack of correct development facilities can lead to much increased man time and effort.

DEVELOPMENT WITHOUT DEVELOPMENT SYSTEMS
By Professor Alty (Liverpool University)

The relevance of the approach

In previous chapters of this book the use of a microprocessor development system has been regarded as the normal way of supporting the design and development of a microprocessor based system. In fact there are a number of situations where the use of such a development aid is not essential and can sometimes be uneconomic. A development system is really a dedicated computer supporting a range of software to aid the development process. Such a system will have assemblers, editors and a filing system, as well as a number of debugging aids.

Existing computers

Much of the above software already exists on standard mainframe and minicomputers (for example, a filing system and an editor) and there is no reason why software should not be developed on an existing computer in an organisation to assist with the development of microprocessor systems. Such an approach obviates the need to buy in an additional special-purpose system solely for such requirements. Using an existing computing system however also has other advantages. It will often already be supporting a comprehensive terminal network throughout the organisation and will be accepted and familiar to a wide range of users. If a set of assemblers and compilers is added to the existing mainframe software repertoire which produce binary code for downloading into the appropriate storage chips, a development service can be provided which will offer many of the facilities of the traditional development system.

The technique of using one computer to assemble or compile binary code for another is called cross-assembly or compilation and the development of such software can often be achieved by modifying the output stages of already existing assemblers or compilers. Further software aids can be added which enable the user to simulate the actions of the microprocessor whilst at his mainframe terminal and a whole range of debugging aids and facilities can be provided to enhance the support capability.

Debugging aids

Having produced and loaded the binary code into the microprocessor system, the user is still faced with testing the produced code in situ, and a mainframe user will certainly feel the lack of the powerful in-circuit emulation facilities which a development system can provide. Whilst one can never completely get over this problem, additional hardware diagnostic aids such as logic state analysers are adequate in most cases and such hardware has the advantage of being more portable than development systems so that it can be used to test the system in its actual environment. Indeed it is quite usual for those working with development systems to have such additional aids so that their cost cannot really be said to be a penalty of the mainframe approach.

Generality

A further advantage of the in-house computer approach is generality. Often a development system is targetted at particular ranges of microprocessor systems (e.g. Intel or Motorola) whereas a mainframe or minicomputer with the appropriate range of software can support a very wide range of dissimilar systems. Additional software can be mounted at the appropriate time to support new systems as they are announced.

Software is not cheap to write or buy and the servicing of a wide range of systems will necessarily be expensive, but there are techniques for minimising the cost of such developments which will be described later. There will, of course, always remain the difficult application for which the use of a development system is essential, but our experience with the Liverpool University microprocessor unit has shown that such situations are not common in our environment.

Familiarity

The use of a standard mainframe system which is already familiar to users has obvious advantages. They will already be familiar with its job control, its filing system, its editors and with terminal usage. They will often have a terminal close to their place of work. The editing facilities and terminals will, in many cases, be superior to those of a development system (e.g. full screen editors) and there will be no need to queue for such a system. They will, of course, have to learn some new skills such as the use of some diagnostic hardware aids but we have found that this is not usually a difficult exercise particularly for equipment such as the software/hardware analyser.

Laboratory environment

While the assembly compilation and simulation of code can take place at the user terminal, the actual loading and testing of the code is best centralised in a small number of locations. In the University (which is geographically compact), we have one main microprocessor laboratory which is staffed by a small number of experts. Having developed their software on the mainframe users, they tend to work in the laboratory while testing their system, sharing both the expertise and equipment situated there. In a distributed organisation, this sort of approach would create difficulties but there is no reason why a small number of such units should not be set up. The same difficulty, of course, applies to the use of development systems.

Development systems are ideal for the expert user whose major concern is the design and development of complex microprocessor systems. Their use implies a high degree of commitment on the part of the user (often full-time) and such systems are not really shareable amongst a large number of users. The mainframe approach however provides an adequate and economic service for a wide range of users whose main activity may not be microprocessor development. It is convenient in the situation where a wide range of microprocessors need to be supported. This is why in the university environment, where a user sees microprocessor developments only as an aid to improving his research, we adopted the cross-software and simulation philosophy.

Phases of development

Use of a mainframe or minicomputer to support microprocessor developments can be conveniently divided into three main phases:

- Phase 1 – the production of the binary code on the mainframe
- Phase 2 – the execution of such code on the mainframe to test out all possible code paths (i.e. simulation)
- Phase 3 – loading of the binary code into its chip and the subsequent testing in the laboratory or in the actual environment using logic state analysers

These three phases interact and a failure in one phase results in retracing of steps in earlier phases to correct errors. The broad approach is shown in fig. 8.1.

An initial design takes place which will result in the product of a file containing the source code. This is then compiled or assembled and any errors eliminated in the usual way. The code is then run on the simulator which further tests out the code and exercises the various paths. By using the terminal its response to different input/output conditions can be determined. Further errors will normally be found which will generally result in further source code generation and a re-run of phase 1.

Once the simulation has proceeded satisfactorily, the code can then be loaded into chips and the system tested either in the laboratory or in its actual environment. In the laboratory, the input/output signals are usually simulated using pulse generators or similar devices. Once again errors will often be found which will result in a re-run of phases 1 and 2. It is possible at this stage to make minor hand patches if the changes are small. The software and hardware for these phases will be discussed in the next sections.

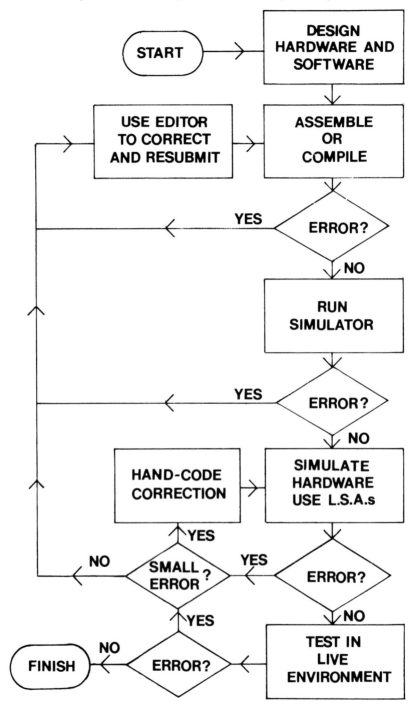

Fig. 8.1 Development phases

The software in the support computer (phases 1 and 2)

To achieve phases 1 and 2 on the support computer, the user will require assemblers, compilers, simulators and debugging facilities for the microprocessor systems of interest. A great deal of such software support is already in existence, much of it derived from adaptations of existing compilers. The language used to write such software is often FORTRAN. This enables software to be adapted fairly easily from other computer systems. Whilst users should be aware of the software effort involved, many organisations have written their own inhouse software which works reasonably well so that the effort involved is not prodigious. Nevertheless the user would be advised to consider available commercial software before producing his own. There are a number of packages now coming on the market which are well documented, reasonably robust and which support a range of microprocessors.

The MicroSim product as an example
One standard product which is widely used is the assembler/simulator package of MicroSim[1] (Cosserat, 1979). This product, originally written for DEC PDP-11 systems is now available for a range of hosts. It consists of an assembler, a simulator, an editor and a set of debugging aids. There are four variants available at the time of writing though one expects the range to increase with time. The systems supported are the Intel 8080/8085, the Motorola M6800, the RCA 1802 and the Zilog Z80. Each variant is almost identical in its use by the user. Before attempting any assembly or simulation the user must, of course, be familiar with the assembler instruction set of the appropriate system.

PROGRAM ENTRY
The MicroSim system allows the user to type in his Assembler program line-by-line. As each line is entered it is checked for validity and a diagnostic message produced on a detectable error condition. Such an error can be immediately corrected. The program can be entered as a series of separate segments which can be combined into one program at any time. Indeed when running interrelated segments the linkages are constructed as and when they are required so that the programmer need not be involved in a complicated compile, link and load procedure. Plate 8.1 shows the output using the MicroSim 8080 system. Each line is automatically numbered giving an editing facility rather like that provided by a BASIC interpreter.

EDITING ERRORS
Line 700 for example was typed with an error. This was identified and the user invited to retype the line with a prompt of the line number 700. At the completion of text entry, shown by a $ character, MicroSim checks for further inconsistencies (note the additional invalid expression in the figure) and then awaits the user's next instruction. The programmer may re-enter the segment and alter offending lines simply by typing the line number

followed by replacement text. Deletion is achieved by typing the line number only. The choosing of an editing system similar to that offered by a BASIC interpreter results in a package which is extremely easy to use in edit mode. Whole segments may be renumbered, renamed or deleted.

```
*SEG EX1
SEGMENT CREATED
    100  ; THIS PROGRAM ADDS TWO NUMBERS AND LIGHTS LAMPS
    200  ; ACCORDING TO THE RESULT.
    300  INITL:  MVI  A,0FFH    ;
    400          OUT  02        ; INITIALISE I/O PORTRS
    500          MVI  A,00FH    ;
    600          OUT  03        ;
    700          MVI  A,6B      ; SWITCH ALL LAMPS OFF PRIOR COMMENCING EXECUTION
UNACCEPTABLE DIGIT FORMAT: 6B
    800          OUT  0BFH      ;
    900  START:  LDA  NUMBA     ;
   1000          MOV  B,A       ;
   1100          LDA  NUMBB     ;
   1200          ADD  B         ;
   1300          STA  RESULT    ;
   1400          CPI  023       ;
   1500          JNC  GREATR    ; BRANCH IF RESULT > 23H
   1600          MVI  A,0BEH    ;
   1700          OUT  0BFH

LINE 1500       INVALID EXPRESSION  -  CONTAINS UNDEFINED SYMBOL

*_
```

Plate 8.1 Assembly language creation in MicroSim

RUNNING THE PROGRAM

Once a set of segments is regarded as satisfactory by the user, he simply types RUN followed by the segment name. This invokes the simulator (in this case, the 8080 simulator). The simulator executes each instruction according to the program sequence. The program will halt in one of three situations:

- it encounters a halt or break (BRK) instruction
- it is interrupted by the clock
- it encounters an error condition

Halt or break statements can be inserted in a program segment at any point. They both have the same result – a halting of the program – BRK, however, is extremely useful because it is converted into a NOP (no operation) instruction when binary code is produced so that it will not affect the binary code production at the appropriate time (apart from adding a 1 byte penalty in storage for each occurrence of BRK).

CLOCK

During simulation, the clock is incremented by the appropriate time period for each instruction executed. At termination the clock value is printed.

However, the user may assign a value to the clock such that for a positive value, the clock begins to increment at that value. For a negative value, the clock is incremented until zero is reached at which time the program is halted with a clock interrupt. A halted program may be continued by typing the CON command. Registers, machine status indicators and interrupt flags may be set before running the simulator.

DIAGNOSTIC FEATURE

During the assembly process, a special diagnostic feature – byte segregation – aids debugging at a later stage. While assembling, a byte is designated as either an instruction, an address or a data byte. Each byte is tagged so that the simulator can trap an overwrite instruction or the treating of a data value as an address. Furthermore, an address is always checked to be within the address limits of the segment.

Byte segregation tagging is not carried over into the binary code produced. The existence of byte segregation does impose some restrictions. For example in some systems (particularly for the user of a Z80 or 8080), addresses must not be manipulated as if they consisted of 2 bytes of data and an attempt to carry out an arithmetic operation on an address pair would cause a fault in the simulator. A FIX facility is provided to overcome this problem.

SIMULATOR

For a simulator to be useful it must be able to support input/output via ports. The MicroSim simulator achieves this either by special subroutines assigned to the port number, or by using the VDU or teletype as an I/O device. On the 8080 for example, a port is accessed in the assembler code via the IN (port number) statement. The command, IASN (port number), (segment name) enables a segment call to take place on execution of that command. The routine which has to be written by the user returns an 8-bit value to the accumulator as in the real situation.

If an input port has not been assigned a segment name, the teletype or VDU is assumed to be the normal input mechanism. It types PORT N? at the VDU and awaits data. The VDU or teletype is the normal default output port, though as for input, the OASN (port number), (segment name) command may be used to connect a segment with that port output. For the Motorola M6800, a MAP facility is provided to assign specific memory locations as input/output device registers.

INTERRUPTS

One drawback of the simulator (and most simulators) is that it cannot handle interrupts. It does execute interrupt enable and disable instructions which set or reset a flag and by using these in conjunction with a negative clock command, response to an external interrupt can be approximated. The only sure way however is to test the binary code in the real environment.

Individual byte contents may be viewed by use of a PRINT command and there is a character editor for carrying out complex editing functions on segments (altering or exchanging specific text strings wherever they occur for example). Editor commands can be grouped into sequences and repeated a number of times.

TRANSFER TO PROM

The program is transferred to the chip either via paper tape or direct loading. The segments are loaded in order, but a specified loading address can be given via the ORG statement. All segments of a program need not be loaded (for example, where some segments may already exist in binary form in the chip). The transfer system will link these with new code being loaded into the target system. Loading may also be staged over a number of PROMs.

The MicroSim system attempts to give the user the benefits of both the interpretive and compiling approach. An interpreter retains the program in its source form (in some internal representation) and reads each program statement in turn when executing it. This has the advantage of line-by-line error correction and enables run-time failures to be easily associated with source code. A compiler, on the other hand, converts the source code into object code, which is then executed. Errors during execution are often difficult to relate back to the source code.

Interpreters are very slow compared with executed compiled code and can be inefficient in storage space. The MicroSim system uses what is termed an interassembler. It accepts program text typed in line by line and performs a syntax analysis on each, but it assembles the code into the object code of the target microprocessor so that the program is immediately ready to run when text entry is complete. The assembly on a line-by-line basis also means that errors detected by the simulator can be related back to the source code.

System testing (Phase 3)

Once the code is in the memory chip and plugged into the system of interest, it needs to be extensively tested. To do this there are a variety of logic state analysers which can be used to verify correct operation or to troubleshoot in cases of difficulty. A wide range of analysers is available from a number of manufacturers (Hewlett-Packard, Biomation, GEC, etc.) and their use will be illustrated using examples from the Hewlett-Packard range. This does not imply that the others are in any way inferior and a user should always assess the merits of different analysers according to his particular problem area. Hewlett-Packard provide three very useful devices[2]:

- the 1611A software/hardware analyser
- the 1615A simultaneous time state and glitch analyser
- the 1610A/B synchronous real time tracer

The first two are an essential part of any microprocessor laboratory. The third is a very powerful device but may not be needed in most application areas. Each of the devices uses a screen menu to simplify front panel complexity.

The 1611A software/hardware analyser

The 1611A is personalised to a particular microprocessor by a plug-in personality module. At present such modules exist for the 6800, 8080, F8, Z80, 6502, 1802 and 8085 systems. The analyser traces program flow within the system being monitored. The memory can contain up to sixty-four lines of code (32-bit wide) and it is examined through a 16-line moveable window. The display is formulated either in absolute or mnemonic mode. In absolute mode the memory address and the machine-language operation code or data are displayed. In mnemonic mode the program address is shown together with the assembly code mnemonic and the 8- or 16-bit operand. Both displays can be in octal or hexadecimal format. An example of mnemonic mode is shown in plate 8.2 where the 16-line window shows the last sixteen addresses which were executed, their assembly operation codes and operands. For each line the state of eight external input lines can also be displayed.

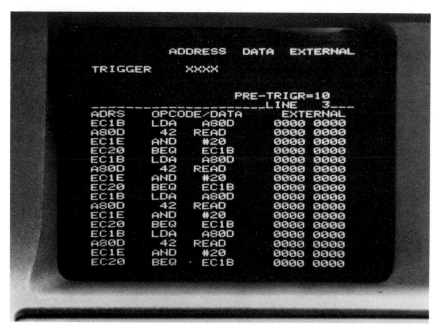

Plate 8.2 Mnemonic mode on the 1611A

TRIGGER CAPABILITY

The real power of the system derives from its trigger capability. The user can enter a trigger word of up to 24 bit in hexadecimal, octal or binary format and qualify the use of this trigger with appropriate additional information. For example, the *n*th trigger ($1 \leq n \leq 256$) can be recognised, or an address can be entered such that the trigger recognition is less than or greater than the address entered. Finally a trigger can be defined over an address range so that any activity within this range will be recognised.

The user, having defined the trigger condition can ask for activity starting up to sixty-three words before the trigger or up to 65 472 words after the trigger, so that events leading up to a trigger can be examined as well as those after it. This is illustrated in plate 8.3.

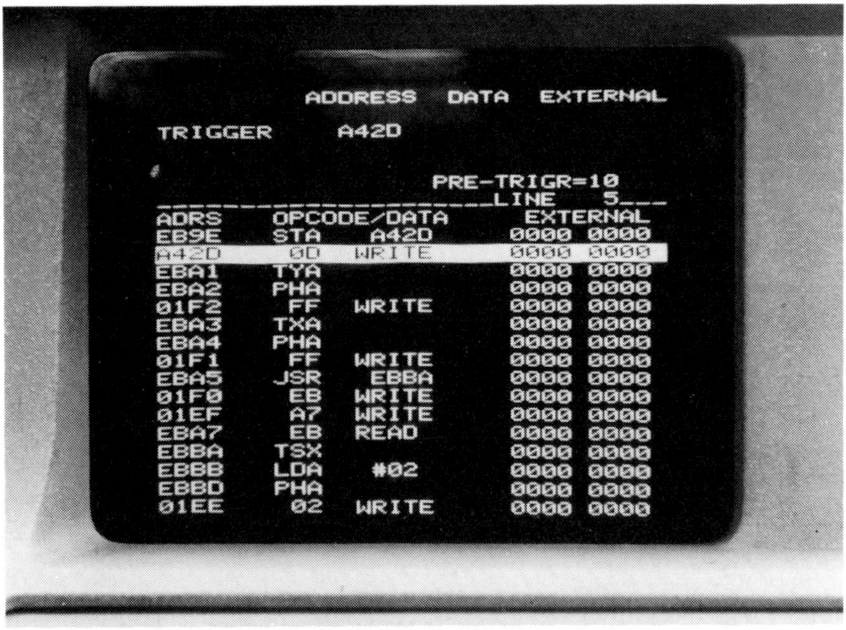

Plate 8.3 Use of the trigger on the 1611A

Finally, other measurements such as a count of the number of trigger matches within an address range, or the time between two selected points in the program can be displayed. Logic state analysers like the 1611A are very useful in debugging software at the system test phase. They are also very straightforward to understand and use.

The 1615A simultaneous time, state and glitch analyser
This analyser is a useful partner for the 1611A and is essential if a user is designing his own interfaces or is connecting nonstandard units to his microprocessor system. Whereas the 1611A examines program flow, the 1615A enables a user to study timing logic and sequential states on the address, data and control lines of a microprocessor. Signals entering or leaving the microprocessor are its main field of interest rather than actual program execution.

The analyser can be used in two ways – in synchronous or in asynchronous studies. In synchronous mode, a clock within the device being tested is used to sample the appropriate logic lines. In asynchronous mode, an internal clock in the analyser regulates the sampling. Synchronous mode is used when one is interested in the various states of the microsystem and changes to these states. Asynchronous mode enables information related to the time between state changes to be examined (e.g. an asynchronous interrupt).

Measurements can be of two types – timing analysis and state analysis and the analyser can perform either measurement, or both simultaneously. Timing analysis consists of the simultaneous measurement and display of the activity on eight logic lines. This is conveniently displayed in square wave format as shown in plate 8.4. Glitches, or very short duration (2–3 ns) changes in a logic condition, are displayed as highlighted vertical lines. The display of glitches is very useful indeed since a glitch can sometimes cause unwanted state changes such as an interrupt. Glitch identification and analysis is an important part of hardware design. The display can be expanded horizontally by a multiplicative factor to enable particular parts of the display to be examined in more detail.

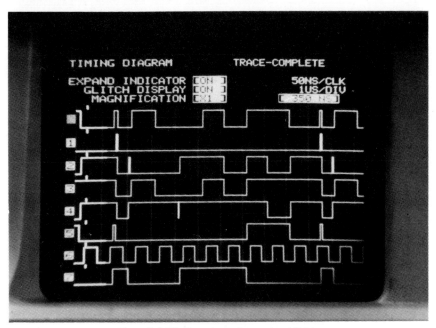

Plate 8.4 Timing analysis on the 1615A

In state analysis one can look at the simultaneous state of up to twenty-four logic lines and its progression over time. Plate 8.5 illustrates the use of the 1615A in this manner where the line number (in synchronous situation) is essentially the clock pulse and the C display shows the configuration of the 24-bits. This grouping format can be specified by the user. A state measurement is equivalent to looking at a timing diagram end-on (though twenty-four states may be examined in this way as opposed to a maximum of eight for timing measurements). Up to 256 state or time measurements can be collected for examination.

LINE NO.	C BIN
037	1111111101111101101111101
008	111111111011111101000110
009	111111111111110110110111101
010	111111111011111101000110
011	111111111111111011101111101
012	111111111011111101000110
013	111111111111111011101111101
014	111111111011111101000110
015	111111111111111011101111101
016	111111111011111101000110
017	111111111111111011101111101
018	111111111011111101000110
019	111111111111111011101111101
020	111111111011111101000110
021	111111111111111011101111101

Plate 8.5 State measurement on the 1615A

Three modes of operation are possible:

- an 8-bit timing measurement (e.g. plate 8.4)
- a 24-bit state measurement (e.g. plate 8.5)
- simultaneous timing measurement on eight lines and state measurement on sixteen lines (enabling the user to switch between both displays at will)

The user decides upon a set of logic conditions to be satisfied on the relevant logic lines as a trigger. The device will then show activity before or after the specified state. The 1615A is no harder to use than the 1611A but the user has to have an in-depth knowledge of the data he is measuring.

The 1610A/B 32-bit logic analyser
This is a very powerful device which can be used for the digital analysis of microprocessor systems, minicomputers and even mainframes. It is not normally required in a microprocessor laboratory but it is particularly useful if the user is involved in, say, the building of bit-slice devices. It can be triggered on up to seven sequential 32-bit conditions and will display up to sixty-four traced states. One extremely useful feature is the trace graph facility whereby all sixty-four states may be viewed as a time sequence, with

the value of the state plotted vertically. This is useful in tracing looping conditions. Another valuable feature is the trace capture facility in which a sequence of states can be stored from, say, a working system and this then compared with the same output from a second system highlighting differences.

Simulator difficulties and multiprocessing

Most simulators are rather weak on handling I/O conditions and interrupts. The MicroSim package, for example, requires user input at a terminal, or from a program, and interrupt handling is cumbersome. Whilst simulation of input/output for a single system has its problems, in the case of a multi-processor configuration possibly embracing a number of different manu-facturers' systems, the approach fails completely.

An approach to this difficulty using mainframe software has been described by Van der Linden[3]. This software simulation system is mounted on the Science Research Council interactive computing facility network which consists of a number of Prime and GEC systems situated at various institutions in the UK. The approach uses the ISP notation of Bell and Newell[4] and it is implemented in a language called ISPS. This language is a high-level structure ALGOL-like language which is used to describe the microprocessor of interest. It is claimed that the writing and testing of such a procedure takes about 1 man-week of effort for an 8-bit microprocessor system. This description is then compiled and run under the simulator.

Any microprocessor may be modelled in this way and, of course, there is no restriction on the type and variety of processor being modelled. Additional hardware connected to the system may also be modelled in the same way and run in parallel. This approach can be used to model a complex system of dissimilar microprocessors connected to other special-purpose hardware.

The simulator connects port registers to files. Whenever a register is accessed or written to, the value is taken from, or written to, a file. This simulates simple input/output. In the case of complex peripherals, a separate ISPS routine can be written and simulated to create the required file values. Interrupts are handled by a timer procedure in ISPS which decrements an interrupt variable tested in the instruction sequence of the microprocessor ISPS description. The advantages of the approach are obvious. Simulation of different microsystems in parallel is possible within one consistent language. Additional hardware can be simulated in parallel. In the case of multiprocessor systems additional routines need to be written to specify communication between systems.

An additional benefit of this approach is that a facility can be created for educating users. By executing simulations of microprocessors of interest, a wide range of users can improve their understanding of the comparabilities and limitations of the hardware. It could be used to assist decision making in hardware selection.

Minimising the software cost

There are two areas where techniques or languages exist to minimise costs when using a mainframe or minicomputer support system. Firstly, the production of assemblers can be simplified by using macro-processor techniques. Secondly the development time for actual software (e.g. phases 1 and 2) can be significantly reduced by using high-level language compilers such as PASCAL, PL/M, BASIC, CORAL or FORTRAN.

Writing of assemblers

Although a number of cross-assemblers are available for many of the existing microprocessor systems on the market, a user, or support unit, can be faced with the task of writing their own. Whilst such an activity is not a difficult task techniques exist which can simplify the process. One such technique is that of macroprocessing. The technique has been described by Davie[5] in its application to the production of microprocessor cross-assemblers. In its simplest form, a macroprocessor can be used to create additional commonly used sequences of instructions to simplify and speed up the programming process. The macroprocessor operates upon a set of macro definitions, i.e. uniquely labelled sequences of assembler instructions. When such a unique label is encountered during assembly, the code is replaced by the actual stored instruction sequence.

A trivial example from Davie illustrates the point. The Intel 8080 does not have a single instruction for moving data from one storage location directly to another. A user has to perform a load accumulator operation followed by a store accumulator instruction. A new instruction, say, MOVE MEM A,B can be defined which generates both these instructions (with the correct storage name variables) on the occurrence of the macro instruction label during assembly. In this way the instruction set can be considerably enhanced and laborious instruction sequences eliminated. Extending the use of a macroprocessor to create loadable code for a particular system is achieved by providing a macro definition for each instruction mnemonic of interest which will construct the correct machine code using the normal data statements available to any assembler.

There are limitations to the approach. Any conventions within the source code which the host assembler requires will, of course, apply to the cross-assembler (e.g. labels). Furthermore a loading program will usually be required to handle the binary output which will follow the output conventions of the host assembler. Davie describes particular techniques for dealing with difficulties which occur for certain types of instructions which are followed by control characters to define addressing modes, but the techniques result in non-standard assembly instructions. The more powerful the macroassembler, the more easily such difficulties are overcome.

General purpose ('universal') assembler

In theory it is possible to create an assembler which is not restricted to one microprocessor. Such a general-purpose assembler has been described by

Ferguson[6]. One such interesting product which runs on a number of main-frames is the transportable meta-assembler developed by Microtec[7]. This was designed primarily for those using bit-slice devices and the user can define his own hardware configuration and instruction set.

There are three user stages – definition, assembly and format. The definition stage allows a user to define his own instruction set and hardware configuration. He defines the associated mnemonics, constants and reserved symbolic names for any microprocessor of interest. The output of this stage is then cross-assembled resulting in object code for the micropro-cessor. The format stage allows the user to break-up the object code into organisations which are compatible with the target PROM or ROM array. Potentially a meta-assembler could provide a general purpose program for the support of any microprocessor system. Simply feed in the appropriate instruction set, mnemonics and data definitions and the problem would be solved.

At Liverpool, however, we have found that it is not really suitable for general-purpose cross-assembly generation. It does not cope with variable instruction sets. Thus instructions in the 8080 set which can be 8, 16 or 24 bits long have all to be defined as 24-bits with no operation fillers. Secondly, each mnemonic can only have one format regardless of operands. Thirdly, it cannot cope with instructions which have, say, register operands with different meanings in different instructions (e.g. INR B and INX B for the 8080. In one case B is the single register B, in the second case it refers to the register pair BC). Thus our conclusion is that meta-assemblers in their present form, while suitable for certain bit-slice applications, are not appro-priate for the established instruction sets of many common microproces-sors.

High-level languages
Using a high-level language approach for the production of microprocessor software can have two advantages. Firstly, the user is less likely to make mistakes and can realise the solution to his problem in an easily readable source language. This means that development time is considerably reduced. Secondly, by the use of appropriate techniques described below, the software effort involved in producing high level language support software on a mainframe for a variety of microprocessors can be minimised. One language which has considerable acceptance is PASCAL.

PASCAL is a structured high-level language written in blocks. A block consists of a definition part, or header, and an action part. The language has the essential constructs required of a structured language[8] – IF . . . THEN . . . ELSE . . ., CASE, FOR . . ., WHILE . . . etc. – and a PASCAL listing exhibits excellent clarity which considerably aids modifica-tion or debugging. In certain time critical situations however the code generated may be too slow particularly if an interpreter is used. At Liverpool we code the main algorithms in PASCAL but resort to assembler in time critical situations (usually I/O handling).

PASCAL and P-code

Existing PASCAL compilers can be modified to produce the required object code for a particular microprocessor. This however can result in considerable software effort if a number of different systems are to be supported. One way round this is to produce, as output, a pseudo-code or P-code which will be the same for any target microprocessor. In this way only one PASCAL compiler is required on the mainframe but a P-code interpreter is needed in each target microprocessor (a simple task). A straightforward description of the P-code approach is given by Chung and Yuen[9]. Another advantage of the approach is that a user can run one PASCAL program easily on different microprocessor systems.

The difficulty with all interpreter-like solutions is the slowness of execution resulting from this type of approach. One interesting way round this has resulted from the development of the UCSD PASCAL Microengine[10]. This is a stack-orientated 16-bit microcomputer which directly executes P-code. It is a hardware realisation of the pseudo P-machine. As a result the execution of the P-code is considerably faster than compiled PASCAL and avoids the drawbacks of the interpreter approach.

A hybrid system – MicroAde

MicroAde was developed by CAP–CCP MicroProducts to provide a means of developing software for microprocessors independent of the processor for which it was being generated. Additionally, however, it provides facilities for testing out the software as it actually executes on the target system so that it is really midway between the MicroSim approach and a development system. It currently handles 8080, 8085, 8068, Z80, 6800 and TI9900. The system is based upon a PDP-11. Interactive testing on the target system is achieved by using a serial link between the host and target device. The program actually executes on the microprocessor under test. It runs under the control of the interactive debugging system on the PDP-11 which converts all trace and state information into a microprocessor independent format.

Programs are written in the assembler language of the target microprocessor. Whilst the various cross-assemblers are produced using MACRO-11 and the code generated is obviously specific to a particular microprocessor, a general processor-independent environment is provided for defining data areas and program sections.

The RT/11 operating system, the editor, filing system, the file transfer program and the macroassembler MACRO-11 of the PDP-11 are all used. A version will shortly be available using RSX-11M to provide a multiuser configuration. A linkage editor (or cross-linker) assembles relocatable segments for loading and execution. The interactive debugging system allows the user to interact during a test run. A particular feature is the provision of a set of test management macros, which when incorporated into the program provide tracing, dumping and communication at any point. The user can trace, inspect memory locations, set break points, resume and can make modifications to the code whilst online.

This is not true in-circuit emulation but it provides a midway environment between the pure mainframe support approach and the development system. It has the advantages of multiuser support, is not dedicated to single development process and uses existing minicomputer software. In this connection for example users can create their code using SPO (a variant of PL/M) which provides a high-level-like approach to the assembly process.

Experience with the mainframe support approach at Liverpool

At Liverpool University, the Computer Centre is responsible for providing support to all user departments who wish to develop microprocessor based systems. The main interest of the users is research, and microprocessor systems are only of interest to them in connection with the furtherance of their research programme. Particular areas of interest are:

- data capture; the reading of signals from apparatus in the field or laboratory which are stored on paper tape or cassette for later analysis. The emphasis is normally on ruggedness, a low power requirement and reliability
- data reduction; similar to data capture but requiring in addition some sampling and simplification of the data
- control; input signals from hardware are received and result in control signals to the apparatus. This area may require data analysis to effect the control.
- interfacing; signals are accepted and modified, often being passed on to other systems. Typical examples would include protocol matching and buffering
- data processing; traditional computing such as statistical calculations and data retrieval

The environment lends itself ideally to the mainframe approach. There are a large number of inexperienced users (in microsystems) spread across the campus, but with access to a mainframe VDU. We have thus created a central microprocessor support unit whose responsibility is to develop cross-software on the mainframe and provide extensive laboratory facilities for later stages in development. We support the MicroSim package as well as other assemblers and simulators, we have a PASCAL P-code compiler, macroprocessors and a meta-assembler. The laboratory contains all the equipment necessary for formal testing – pulse generators, oscilloscopes and analysers. Recently we have acquired a development system but this is mainly used by laboratory staff rather than users, particularly for in-circuit emulation.

Until a user is satisfied with the simulation of the binary code he need not use the laboratory. Once this position is reached he usually works in the laboratory testing out his actual software in the target hardware. To assist this process we have developed a workstation (based upon a PASCAL Microengine) which is connected to the mainframe. On this workstation, which will shortly have multiple user ports, a user can converse with the mainframe as a normal terminal; transfer code into a PROM programmer and produce a loaded EPROM; store its binary code on disc or tape for later use; add in standard library routines to his own code; and make simple patchings to the binary code. Having loaded the EPROM, the system will then be tested using equipment in the laboratory. We have found that most users adapt very quickly to using the logic state analysers, but the staff of the laboratory are on hand to assist in cases of difficulty.

Over the past two years a large number of successful microprocessor-based projects have been completed. A few have been selected, in chronological order, to illustrate the success of the mainframe approach and to highlight some lessons learnt.

Case Study 1.   A communications controller for geophysics
The Department of Geophysics has a small minicomputer which is used to collect magnetic data from rock samples. A small number of manually operated workstations feed the data directly into the computer. A much more powerful system was needed to carry out detailed analysis of the data so that a link was required between the local minicomputer and the mainframe.

An Intel 8080 based system was developed which communicated with each system in their respective protocols and provided buffering where necessary to match the different line speeds. The system is based upon a SDK-80 board with 256 byte of RAM, 1 kbyte of EPROM, a parallel interface, power supply and case (total hardware cost £500 or US$1000).

This was the first project undertaken by the microprocessor laboratory. No mainframe software was working at the start of the project and the programming was originally done in machine code. The project progressed very slowly indeed. Machine code was input to the chip from a VDU using only the simple monitoring facilities available from the SKD-80 boards. The system was then tested in situ and debugged using a Hewlett-Packard 1611A with the 8080 instruction set option. Not only did the actual design and writing of the code take considerable time but the debugging process was error prone and time consuming. The computation of jump address and subroutine addresses (for example) is very tedious. Furthermore the designer was simultaneously working on two other projects and had to break-off repeatedly to attend to the other systems. Actually remembering where one has reached is problematic in such an environment.

For four months the system was intermittently debugged, when fortunately the mainframe cross-assembler became available, together with a disassembler. Within three weeks the system was working. Productivity improved by a factor of ten, and it was much easier to carry on the development intermittently. Since its installation this project has required virtually no maintenance and has now been transmitting and receiving data from four work stations for two years. The project illustrates the penalties of working machine code. The system development cost was over £2500 (US$5000) in man-hours, compared with a hardware cost of £500 (US$1000).

Case Study 2. A cartridge tape controller
User departments collect data offline in the field. Traditionally paper tape used to be employed in this process but most departments are now switching to magnetic cartridges. A controller was needed to connect a cartridge reader to the mainframe. The controller had to do the following:

- connect a standard VDU
- allow the VDU to communicate with the mainframe as a normal terminal
- allow files (controlled at the VDU) to be transferred to the mainframe, and in the reverse direction
- provide a series of control commands which were compatible with the mainframe operating system so that the user interface would be identical to that on the mainframe
- match the protocols of the VDU, cartridge reader and mainframe, and provide buffering to match the different line speeds

The system was based upon a SDK-80 system with 1 kbyte standard monitor, 1k of RAM, 2.5k of ROM, power supply and case(total hardware cost £900 or US$1800). The complete system was written in assembler on the mainframe and loaded into the PROM. The code was time-critical. The Hewlett-Packard 1611A was used to clear up outstanding bugs in the software. By this time we had installed a mainframe terminal in the Microprocessor Laboratory and the designer was able to work by the terminal, altering assembler code in the mainframe when necessary and down line loading into the PROM within seconds. The correction of an error, the loading of the PROM and testing in the system was able to be accomplished in less than five minutes.

The system had to communicate in the respective protocols of the mainframe and the cartridge reader. Whilst the operating manuals for these devices were available and supposedly provided the required information, there were a number of inconsistencies and the use of a communications protocol analyser from our Network Unit proved invaluable. Total software development time was 6 man-weeks (an approximate cost of £1500 or US$3000).

The system has now been in operation for 18 months. Since going into production the system has proved very popular for storing back-up copies of binary code produced by cross-software, and one reader is now connected to the microprocessor workstation. Users normally load code onto tape first directly from the mainframe, and then load it into the storage chips later.

Case Study 3.   A tensile system for metallurgy

We soon realised that many users in the University were not experienced at using assembler and would prefer to program their application in high level languages such as PASCAL. We therefore modified the Queen's University (Belfast) PASCAL compiler in order to produce down-line loaded subset of P-code. Users created their PASCAL files in the normal way on the screen editor, compiled it, and when free of compilation errors it was loaded into EPROMs. If errors were found the process was repeated.

The first research project fully to utilise the system was concerned with the design of a tensile system controller for the Department of Metallurgy. A large tensile rig is used to apply three types of stress on a specimen – torque, linear stress and pressure – and the resultant strains are measured. Any combination of these stresses may be applied at one time. A system was needed to control the application of the stresses. For example, in some experiments constant strain rates are essential and the stress has to be continuously modified to achieve this. In addition a considerable additional amount of circuitry was needed to ensure safety limits of pressure were not exceeded and to detect fluid leaks and prevent damage. The output data is collected on magnetic cartridges.

A packaged Intel 8080 system (a SBC-80-204) was used with 8k of RAM, 8k of EPROM, and ninety-six programmable I/O lines. Eight levels of vectored interrupt, sixteen A/D and six D/A channels, a power supply and case (total hardware cost £3000 or US$6000).

All the control software was written in PASCAL on the mainframe and the P-code was loaded into the microprocessor and executed using a single P-code interpreter. Critical input/output routines were written using the mainframe cross-assembler. By this time we had also implemented an 8080 simulator which was used to debug a considerable portion of the assembler routines. In the final stage these routines were checked using the Hewlett-Packard 1611A and 1615A logic state analysers.

Total software development time is difficult to estimate. The user initially had no previous knowledge of microprocessor systems and had to be taught assembler coding and use of the simulator. He already had some knowledge of PASCAL. We estimate that about four man-weeks of consultancy time of laboratory staff were required and the user spent about five months completing the project (not full time). The cost was approximately £3000 (US$6000). The user was enthusiastic about the use of PASCAL and felt that this considerably shortened his development time. Furthermore he was able to develop the project intermittently. This is usually an essential requirement in a research environment. He was also pleased with the combined use of the simulator and logic analysers for assembler debugging.

The system has now been in full operation for about one year and has not needed extensive modification. The trade-off between the slower operation of the P-code and its ease of development compared with assembler was considered to be very worthwhile. The user also emphasised that the logic state analyses had enabled him fully to understand the operation of the hardware, and he was able to pick up enough knowledge to use the devices in a matter of hours.

Case Study 4. *Tropical medicine project*

The particular project of interest involved the measurement of the activity of worms which live in the blood stream. By showing light through a glass tube containing the blood, the variations in the transmitted light give an indication of activity. This is measured using a photoresistor in a bridge circuit. Five experiments (which typically last about six hours) are run in parallel and statistical analysis is required on periods of peak activity. Different drugs are fed into the blood and their effects observed.

The equipment used was a SDK-80 board with 4k of ROM, 4k of RAM, parallel interface, V24 lines, programmable timer, sixteen A/D converters, two D/A converters, interrupt controller, power supply and case, keyboard and printer (total hardware cost £2000 or US$4000).

All the programming was done in interpretive PASCAL which was developed on the ICL 1906S mainframe. Since data rates were low there was no need for assembler routines even for input/output handling. All statistical routines were also written in PASCAL. No significant use was made of the hardware equipment in the microprocessor laboratory.

The user was familiar with PASCAL but had no knowledge of microprocessor systems. The Laboratory provided him with the SDK-80 board mounted in a standard case with power supply, keyboard and printer. He was able to design, code and test the complete system in six man-weeks, almost entirely at the terminal in the Microprocessor Laboratory or at a terminal near his department. Initial software development costs were therefore about £1500 or US$3000.

When the system was tried out in the experimental environment it failed. The problem was traced to inadequate sensing equipment connected to the experimental apparatus. This was redesigned and minor modifications made to the software, and the system has now been operating successfully for about one year. The initial failure is a common occurrence when applying microsystems to existing equipment. Once the power of a microsystem is made available, weaknesses not previously apparent are highlighted in the equipment and some redesign is often necessary. The advantages of PASCAL in this respect are obvious. This is an example of a straightforward application (and there are many of them) where the activity on the mainframe occupies most of the time spent.

Case Study 5. *Development of ALGOL-68 facilities*

A system was required rapidly to collect and analyse data from a Nuclear Magnetic Resource Spectrometer. This involved controlling the spectrometer in order to produce a linear scan and acquire the spectral data at a rate of 8000 samples in 50 seconds.

ALGOL-68 was chosen as the implementation language because of the expected short development time resulting from mode checking and the highly structured nature of the language. The ALGOL-68 compiler on the mainframe was extended to produce either binary code for an Intel 8086, or as an alternative to produce an intermediate code, called A-code, which is related to ALGOL-68 as P-code is related to PASCAL.

The hardware consisted of:

- a packaged Intel 8086 system
- an ISBC 534 communication card
- an Analyser I/O board
- a floppy disk controller
- 4k of ROM
- crate and power supply
- multibus prototype board (including a sine-wave generator, 48 bits parallel I/O, an interrupt system, and a 9513 timer)
- peripherals including four floppy disk drives, paper tape reader/punch, digital plotting system, a matrix keyboard/printer and a VDU

The total hardware cost was about £15000 or US$30000.

The two methods of output of code-binary or A-code were developed because of the needs of other users. Whilst this project required the binary code for speed of execution, other projects preferred to use the slower A-code. The use of A-code enabled wider options to be exercised late on in the systems development. Small changes can be made to the A-code without having to retrace through the compile-load sequence, but only by sacrificing processing speed.

The screen editors and macro facilities of the mainframe were used. The Simulator was not used, partly because the system became too big for rapid turnround. Logic state analysers were rarely needed. The software effort was considerable because of the development of the ALGOL-68 facilities in parallel. It is estimated that about 24 man-months were needed (approximate cost £25000 or US$50000).

The project utilising the A-code was for the Department of Geophysics. Magnetometers are used to measure the direction and intensity of magnetic fields as in rock samples. A microprocessor system was required which controlled the measuring process and calculated the intensity and direction of magnetisation of each sample. An Acorn 6809 system was used with 12 k of EPROM, 8 k of RAM, two RS232 ports, eight A/D channels, two D/A channels, parallel interface and terminal (hardware cost £1500 or US$3000).

Conclusion

In a situation where an organisation has to provide microprocessor support for a wide range of users (varying markedly in expertise and geographic locations) a development service based upon an existing mainframe or mini-computer can be very economic. If this is supported by a small group of microprocessor system experts backed by suitable hardware equipment, many successful applications can be supported and developed. Whilst the complex application will often require the use of a development system, many applications do not need such specialised support. Some typical examples have been given in this chapter.

REFERENCES

1. Cosserat, D. (1979) 'MicroSim – a new approach to program development'. *Microprocessors and Microsystems*, **3**, 95–98
2. Hewlett-Packard (1980) *Electronic Instruments and Systems.*
3. Van der Linden, F. W. (1980) 'New generation of microsystem simulators'. *Microprocessors and Microsystems*, **4**, 5–9.
4. Bell, C. G. and Newell, A. (1971) *Computer Structures: Reading and Examples.* New York: McGraw Hill.
5. Davie, H. (1977) 'Using micro-assemblers to create microprocessor cross-assemblers'. *Microsystems* **1**, 477–481.
6. Ferguson, D. (1966) 'The evolution of the meta-assembly program'. *Commun. ACM* **9**, 190–193.
7. Microtec (1979) *Meta-Assembler* California: Microtec.
8. Jensen, K. and Wirth, N. (1978) *User Manual and Report.* New York: Springer–Verlag.
9. Chung, K. M. and Yuen, H. (1979) 'A 'Tiny' PASCAL Compiler: Part 1 the P-code interpreter'. *The BYTE Book of PASCAL* 59–69.
10. *Pascal Microengine Reference Manual.* California: The Microengine Company.

EDITOR'S CONCLUSIONS

Professor Alty's discussion shows a commonsense attitude to attaining the ideal with real-life practicality. The contribution was well argued and justified. He outlines the existing tools available to aid in development of applications and their shortcomings. For example he describes the superiority of the interactive nature of MicroSim for program entry, but the shortcomings of the simulator approach for testing I/O and interrupts. This latter point is a serious drawback, since most real applications are very dependent on timing.

Readers' attentions are drawn to the section on the general-purpose (or universal) assembler (page: 184), as opposed to the normally accepted concept of assemblers dedicated to a single microprocessor. This, along with standardised high-level languages, would ensure transportability (and thus the preservation of the investment of developed software).

It is interesting to see how the university's development facilities grew and evolved from the lessons learned in each of the case studies. Particularly noteworthy was the sympathetic, non-pragmatic way in which each project was provided with development facilities. For example, in Case Study 4, Tropical medicine project, the user's familiarity with PASCAL was taken into consideration.

The case studies illustrate clearly how mistaken it is, with any microprocessor project, to economise on correct and adequate development facilities based on a realistic assessment of the ease of use of the facilities by the user of the system.

It can be seen to provide one's own development facilities is hard work and requires full understanding of the development process and the insight to user's requirements and, of course, ingenuity.

This discussion has pointed out areas for MDS enhancement, some of which is already happening, for example in the common trend toward multiuser systems, as emphasised for the university's facilities. The other areas are more powerful operating systems and editors, and the worthwhile concept of providing the same environment/interface to the user for different microprocessors.

CHAPTER 9.

Conclusions, Future Trends and Recommendations

This chapter summarises and attempts to pool together the contributions with the general principles chapters in this book. It will then discuss the possible future trends in development systems and make recommendations for improvements based on the analysis in the preceding chapters.

Summary

This book has contributions from the microprocessor manufacturers in Intel, Motorola and Texas Instruments, with the independent offerings ·represented by two very famous test instrument manufacturers, Hewlett-Packard and Tektronix. To set the balance, Liverpool University, England, have shown that for them there was a distinct advantage in working without the accepted development systems, but the collection of facilities used by them do constitute a MDS!

Without any collusion, the concert opinion of all the contributors and your editor is that software is the major task in a microprocessor application development (one should not of course belittle the task of designing and developing hardware). Thus the aim of microprocessor development systems is to provide aids and tools to help in the task of producing and testing software.

Any selection of development systems should be based on these prime objectives with the emphasis on adequate debugging facilities that allow the testing of a remote target system in real time and in situ. This aid has been identified as the in-circuit emulator. The encouragement of good practice and documentation can be helped by the provision of easy to use coding, editing and translating facilities with high-level languages suitable for the particular application.

The opening paragraphs of the contribution from Sam Lee of Hewlett-Packard in chapter 6 bring home the importance and difficulty of proper software development.

Professor Jim Alty of Liverpool University amply illustrates what can be achieved without accepted development systems and fully demonstrates the advantages of taking this different approach. That chapter shows that there is room for improvement in microprocessor development systems and that users do not have to merely accept what is offered but can adapt equipment, add or improve facilities on MDSs. It should be noted, however, that the facilities provided by Liverpool University in essence are the same essential ones which MDSs offer, with different emphasis in some parts.

This approach, with dedicated, universal and multiuser MDS, is more about the financial considerations as opposed to the technical considerations of development. Although the aspect of this financial consideration is important and attractive in cost effectiveness and longevity of the system, one should not be side-tracked from the main consideration, and that is the suitability of purpose of the tools offered.

Future trends

The current trend is toward multiuser systems, with the microprocessor manufacturers sticking to their own range of microprocessors and single-chip microcomputers, for obvious reasons, and the independents offering the universal approach. The multiuser approach does allow more people access with less contention on the MDS; this will hopefully encourage the use of the MDS as the central point for all development work, thus aiding the documentation and record-keeping of the development. But this facility does add a greater degree of complexity and may pose problems in communications and contention in shared resources; whether these are outweighed by the advantages gained can only be decided by the individual organisation's circumstances and policy to equipment purchasing.

The general trend is in the reduction of price in the components used to make up the MDS (due to the continued improvements and price reduction of microelectronic components). Thus more for the same money is likely to be the trend rather than dramatic reductions in price (note how the MDS has already evolved offering better memory capacity and the improvements to in-circuit emulation systems). The higher density components used also mean a reduction in physical size and the integration of development systems into single compact units seems likely.

Local area networking (e.g. the Ethernet concept) can show the way to attached distributed processing and resource sharing which is not limited to other MDS workstations, but connections to other computing equipment and resources would be feasible. Taking this to the ultimate conclusion MDS as such may no longer exist as the user merely uses a workstation on the network which can provide the correct facilities and resources for proper application development (e.g. the emulator could be a module which is on the network and will service requests for its use from work stations).

Recommendations

Gaps have been shown in MDS from the discussions in the book. These are in the editors of the systems, the lack of design tools and aids and the general ease of use. Therefore recommendations for the manufacturers to consider are:

EDITORS

Improvements in this area would increase throughput on the MDS, encourage good practice in returning all changes/modifications to source code level and aid documentation. As all this is textual in nature, serious consideration should be given to providing powerful but easy to use word processing facilities.

DESIGN AIDS

Although no design aids have been offered up to now, this does not mean such facilities are impossible. Design methodologies can be implemented in software (e.g. templates for state diagrams or production rules). Some high-level languages are attempts in combining design with programming, but these are still a very long way from providing aids for design. The approach should be from the other direction, by examining the objectives to be achieved in design and providing the aids in the form of (automatic or programmed) rules for the inter-relation of functions and hierarchy.

GENERAL EASE OF USE

If a system is awkward to use, people will find ways of avoiding its use. The user normally knows what he wants to do, but tends to have to remember some almost magic incantation to invoke the required function. Operating systems are all too often painfully obvious, and appear as a collection of features, instead of being transparent and servicing the user's wishes. Since virtually all input by the human user to the system is textual, the first and only interface for the user should be a word processor and with the use of an identifying character and keyword (chosen with care), the desired service can be put into action. Thus the user never has to be confronted by an operating system, the facility is merely used!

NETWORKING

Networking using an accepted standard can end the contention between the multiuser system and dedicated system, as it gives the best of both worlds in the ability to work stand-alone (with advantages of an independent system) and the ability to communicate and share resources with other systems when necessary.

Last word

Finally the reader should by now have an opinion on the subject of improvement in MDS; voice that opinion and be heard. Improvements and advances can only come about from helpful and constructive suggestions or criticisms and, in the end, it is the view of the person who has to use the system that really counts!

INDEX

Computer, electronics and electrical engineering books from Granada:

PROGRAMMING WITH FORTRAN 77
J Ashcroft, R H Eldridge,
R W Paulson and G A Wilson
0 246 11573 4

PROGRAMMING MICROCOMPUTERS WITH PASCAL
Martin D Beer
0 246 11619 6

ELECTRONIC SPEECH SYNTHESIS
Edited by Geoff Bristow
0 246 In preparation

CHOOSING AND USING ECL
P L Matthews
0 246 11877 6 In preparation

ELECTRONIC TEST EQUIPMENT
Edited by A M Rudkin
0 246 11478 9

ALPHANUMERIC DISPLAYS
G F Weston and R Bittleston
0 246 11702 8

SIXTEEN-BIT MICROPROCESSORS
I R Whitworth
0 246 11572 6 In preparation

MICROPROCESSOR DATA BOOK
S A Money
0 246 11531 9

MICROPROCESSOR DEVELOPMENT AND DEVELOPMENT SYSTEMS
Edited by Vincent Tseng
0 246 11490 8

LOGIC DESIGNERS HANDBOOK
E A Parr
0 246 11888 1 In preparation

ELECTRIC CABLES HANDBOOK
Edited by D McAllister
0 246 11467 3

HANDBOOK OF ELECTRICAL INSTALLATION PRACTICE
Edited by E A Reeves
Vol. 1 0 246 11744 3 In preparation
Vol. 2 0 246 11747 8 In preparation

ELECTROHEAT
H Barber
0 246 11739 7 In preparation

SOLID STATE POWER RECTIFIERS
R Wells
0 246 11751 6

HANDBOOK OF FIBER OPTICS
Edited by H F Wolf
0 246 11535 1

BASIC ELECTRICAL ENGINEERING
E C Bell and R W Whitehead
0 246 11477 0

ROBOT SYSTEMS
P J Drazan
0 246 11703 6 In preparation